Clean It!
Fix It!
Eat It!

Easy Ways to Solve Everyday Problems with
Brand-Name Products You've Already Got
Around the House

JOEY GREEN

Prentice
Hall Press

A member of Penguin Putnam Inc.
375 Hudson Street
New York, New York 10014

www.penguinputnam.com

Legal Disclaimer: The author has compiled the information contained herein from a variety of sources, and neither the author, publisher, manufacturers, nor distributors can assume responsibility for the effectiveness of the suggestions. Caution is urged in the use of cleaning solutions, folk medicine remedies, and pest control substances. The brand-name products do not endorse, recommend, or accept liability for any use of their products other than those uses indicated on the package label or in current company brochures. This book should not be regarded as a substitute for professional medical treatment, and neither the author, publisher, manufacturers, nor distributors can accept legal responsibility for any problem arising out of the use of or experimentation with the methods described. For a full listing of trademarks, please see page 265.

Library of Congress Cataloging-in-Publication Data

Green, Joey.
   Clean it! fix it! eat it! : easy ways to solve everyday problems with brand-name
products You've Already Got Around the House / Joey Green.
   p. cm.
   ISBN 0-7352-0295-8
   1. Home economics.   2. Brand name products—United States.   3. Cleaning.
4. Medicine, Popular. I. Title.

TX158.G6774 2001
640'.41—dc21   2001021432

Printed in the United States of America

10   9   8   7   6   5   4   3

Also by Joey Green

Hellbent on Insanity

The Unofficial Gilligan's Island Handbook

The Get Smart Handbook

The Partridge Family Album

Polish Your Furniture with Panty Hose

Hi Bob!

Selling Out

Paint Your House with Powdered Milk

Wash Your Hair with Whipped Cream

The Bubble Wrap Book

Joey Green's Encyclopedia

The Zen of Oz

The Warning Label Book

Monica Speaks

You Know You've Reached Middle Age If...

The Official Slinky Book

The Mad Scientist Handbook

Clean Your Clothes with Cheez Whiz

The Road to Success Is Paved with Failure

For

Honi, Arlene, and Michael,
David, Rob,
Barbara Ann,
Steven, and Robert

Ingredients

BUT FIRST, A WORD FROM OUR SPONSOR   vii

1 **Bathe It**   1

2 **Clean It**   10

3 **Cook It**   48

4 **Decorate It**   66

5 **Drive It**   70

6 **Fix It**   87

7 **Flush It**   104

8 **Groom It**   113

9 **Grow It**   132

10 **Heal It**   140

11 **Make It**   171

12 **Mop It**   182

13 **Organize It**   187

14 **Paint It**   191

15 **Pet It** 196

16 **Play It** 207

17 **Polish It** 210

18 **Remove It** 216

19 **Repel It** 222

20 **Rough It** 235

21 **Sew It** 241

22 **Wash It** 244

23 **Wear It** 257

ACKNOWLEDGMENTS 264

TRADEMARK INFORMATION 265

INDEX 271

ABOUT THE AUTHOR 279

But First, a Word from Our Sponsor

Every day, upstanding citizens from all walks of life visit my web site and, inspired by the hundreds of wacky uses for brand-name products posted there and in my books, send me e-mail, sharing their own innovative uses for brand-name products. I am constantly awed and amazed by the ingenuity of these suggestions.

For months, I didn't know what to do with all these marvelous letters. Most of the tips I receive are all-new uses for products I've already featured in my previous books—like Bounce, Coca-Cola, and Jif Peanut Butter. How was I supposed to go back and add these new uses to my other books? So I kept all these contributions in a box, until one day I realized I had collected hundreds of remarkable new tips that I was selfishly keeping hidden from the public.

I was keeping some astonishingly useful information to myself. Efferdent cleans stainless-steel sinks. French's Mustard relieves burns. Hellmann's Mayonnaise kills head lice. Jell-O deodorizes smelly feet. I felt horribly guilty.

And so, I decided to organize all the suggestions and share them with the world, giving credit where credit is due—to the ingenious individuals who courageously tested these wacky uses and then unselfishly submitted their findings to me. Here then are tips, hints, and suggestions from a virtual "secret laboratory" of private citizens. I hope you'll forgive me for keeping all these tips to myself for so long. Unless you think that's where they should have stayed.

Bathe It

Bathing

Make wonderful bath salts with...

- **ARM & HAMMER BAKING SODA.** "Mix one tablespoon Arm & Hammer Baking Soda, one tablespoon Epsom Salt, one tablespoon Morton Salt, and add a few drops fragrance of your choice (optional). Pour into running bath water. This can be made and stored for gifts or future use. Relieves aching muscles."

  —DEBBIE G., *Columbia, South Carolina*

Take a soothing milk bath with...

- **CARNATION NONFAT DRY MILK.** "I use a handful of Carnation Nonfat Dry Milk in the bathtub and have myself a milk bath. The lactic acid in the milk softens the skin incredibly."

  —CAROL F., *St. Paul, Minnesota*

Take a luxurious bath with...

- **JOHNSON'S BABY OIL.** "A few drops of Johnson's Baby Oil in the bathtub makes a wonderful bath oil."

  —MICHAEL T., *Owings Mills, Maryland*

- **L'EGGS SHEER ENERGY PANTY HOSE.** "I fill the foot on a clean, old pair of panty hose with herbs (rosemary, orange peel, and mint) and hang it from the faucet in the bathtub under running bath water."

  —SANDRA N., *Livingston, California*

Wash your back in the shower or bath with...

- **L'EGGS SHEER ENERGY PANTY HOSE.** "Cut off the leg of a pair of used L'eggs Panty Hose, stick a bar of soap inside at the knee, tie a knot around both ends, and use the panty hose to wash your back."

  —BRANDY M., *Loganville, Georgia*

Take a coffee bath with...

- **MAXWELL HOUSE COFFEE.** "Once a week, after I have my coffee in the morning, I take a bath with the coffee grounds. First I rub the warm grounds all over my body from the neck down while in the tub. About ten minutes later I fill the tub with hot water. *Voila!* Instant spa. They charge up to two hundred dollars for this treatment in California, and you won't believe how wonderful your skin will feel. The caffeine supposedly reduces cellulite (although I don't have that problem)."

  —BRIDGETTE L., *Temecula, California*

Bubble Bath
Make bubble bath with...

- **CLAIROL HERBAL ESSENCES SHAMPOO.** "If you want a great, inexpensive, all-natural bubble bath, simply add a capful of Herbal Essences Shampoo into the bathtub. It makes massive amounts of bubbles."

  —DEBBIE W., *Forest Hills, New York*

Conditioner
Condition hair with...

- **BUDWEISER.** "Budweiser makes a great hair rinse. It gives hair body."

  —CAROLYN S., *New Richmond, Ohio*

- **CARNATION CONDENSED MILK.** "Mix one small tin of Carnation Condensed Milk with one teaspoon of Heinz White Vinegar and one teaspoon of SueBee Honey. Apply to hair, wait two minutes, then rinse thoroughly."

  —CATHY W., *Gracemere, Australia*

- **COCA-COLA.** "Coca-Cola will make your hair shinier and more beautiful. Pour a can of Coke over your hair slowly, working it in well. Then rinse your hair or shampoo it and your hair will be shiny."

  —PHILIP A., *Goose Creek, South Carolina*

- **COPPERTONE.** "Use Coppertone sunscreen to condition your hair at the beach and also to prevent frizzies if you have dry hair."

  —BRANDE S., *Poughkeepsie, New York*

- **DOWNY.** "In a pinch for a hair conditioner? Mix one-half capful of Downy liquid fabric softener and four cups water. Pour through your hair, comb, then rinse clean. Your hair will be tangle-free, shiny, and soft."

  —CHERYL W., *Richmond, Texas*

- **HEINZ APPLE CIDER VINEGAR.** "Give freshly washed hair a high shine with Heinz Vinegar. Mix one-third Heinz Apple Cider Vinegar and two-thirds water in a spray bottle and spray hair after washing."

  —JEAN J., *Arnold, Missouri*

- **HELLMANN'S** OR **BEST REAL MAYONNAISE.** "Use Hellmann's Real Mayonnaise to help tame flyaways. Massage it through your hair like you would conditioner, put on a shower cap, wait about five minutes, and shampoo out."

  —KAT H. *Richmond, Virginia*

- **LIPTON TEA.** "Brew Lipton Tea bags in boiled water for five to ten minutes, let cool, then use the solution as a final rinse after washing your hair. The tea gives a natural shine to hair."

  —MATHANGI J., *Wisconsin Rapids, Wisconsin*

- **MIRACLE WHIP.** "I use Miracle Whip to hot oil condition my hair on occasion."

  —LISA D., *Hopkins, Michigan*

- **REDDI-WIP.** "Reddi-Wip makes great conditioner and speeds up the hair lightening process caused by Sun-In."

  —ELIZABETH O., *Keene, New Hampshire*

- **STAR OLIVE OIL.** "Rubbing a few drops of Star Olive Oil between your palms and running it through your wet hair will condition your hair and help protect it from being damaged from blow drying."

  —SHIRLEY S., *Milwaukie, Oregon*

Exfoliate Skin

Exfoliate your face with...

- **ARM & HAMMER BAKING SODA.** "Wet your face, sprinkle a little Arm & Hammer Baking Soda in your palm, and rub gently on your face. Rinse with warm water."

  —VANESSA L., *South Porcupine, Ontario*

- **JOHNSON'S BABY OIL** AND **MORTON SALT.** "Mix Johnson's Baby Oil and Morton Salt to scrub your face."

  —TAMMY S., *Alamogordo, New Mexico*

Exfoliate skin with...

- **DOMINO SUGAR.** "Sprinkle some Domino sugar on a damp cloth and rub over rough spots like knees and elbows."

  —CATHERINE F., *Baytown, Texas*

Exfoliate and moisturize your elbows with...

- **JIF PEANUT BUTTER.** "Rub on Crunchy Jif Peanut Butter, let sit for five minutes, then wash off."

  —HILDA R., *Laredo, Texas*

- **REALEMON.** "Mix ReaLemon lemon juice and Arm & Hammer Baking Soda, and apply the paste to dry elbows to make them smooth."

  —RUTH W., *Simi Valley, California*

Green Hair

Prevent chlorine from dying blond hair green with...

- **HEINZ APPLE CIDER VINEGAR.** "I was on the swim team in high school. Practicing every day caused the chlorine to turn my blond hair green. To prevent this, I applied Heinz Apple Cider Vinegar to my hair, let it set for fifteen minutes, and rinsed it out. The vinegar acts as a powerful shampoo that deep cleans your hair down to the roots to remove dirt and grime."

  —CAITLIN S., *Westland, Michigan*

■ **HEINZ KETCHUP.** "Heinz Ketchup gets rid of chlorine build-up and other hair grime that shampoo doesn't get out. Massage the ketchup through your hair, let it dry, then shampoo your hair. It will leave your hair feeling cleaner and softer."

—KAT H., *Richmond, Virginia*

■ **KOOL-AID.** "To get rid of green hair from the swimming pool, make a paste from banana-flavored Kool-Aid and water, and run it through your hair to return your hair to its natural blond color."

—JENNIFER M., *Kemp, Texas*

■ **OCEAN SPRAY CRANBERRY JUICE COCKTAIL.** "Mix two cups Ocean Spray cranberry juice and one cup lemon juice, pour through hair to instantly remove the green build-up from chlorine in your hair."

—CAITLIN B., *Ann Arbor, Michigan*

Hand Cleanser

Clean hands with...

■ **BLUE BONNET MARGARINE.** "Need an emergency hand cleaner that not only works but is also user-friendly? Open the refrigerator and grab the margarine. Works great and you smell like popcorn."

—DOUGLAS W., *Burnsville, North Carolina*

■ **HELLMANN'S** OR **BEST REAL MAYONNAISE.** "Use Hellmann's Real Mayonnaise to get the grease off of your hands after working on your car."

—DON S., *Campbell, New York*

■ **MORTON SALT.** "After working on my car or cooking greasy foods, I always use salt sprinkled on my soapy hands to help break up the grease. It always works, sometimes even better than the soaps sold for that purpose. Salt breaks down many greases and the grit helps scrub."

—CHRIS Y., *Tallahassee, Florida*

■ **STAR OLIVE OIL** AND **DOMINO SUGAR.** "I use small amounts of Star Olive Oil mixed with Domino Sugar for a wonderful hand scrub. Simply pour a tiny amount of the olive oil then a tiny amount of sugar into the palm of your hand and gently rub together for a couple of minutes. Rinse off thoroughly and dry. You won't believe how soft your hands will be."

—PAMELA H., *East Greenbush, New York*

- **WD-40.** "When you work on your car and get your hands all black and greasy, just spray WD-40 on your hands, wipe clean with paper towel, then wash your hands with soap and water."

—TED N., *Gilroy, California*

- **WESSON CORN OIL** AND **IVORY.** "I use Wesson Corn Oil and Ivory liquid dish soap as a hand cleaner after working on my old truck. Just place a dollop of Wesson Corn Oil in your palm, work it in thoroughly all over your hands, use the same amount of liquid soap, then rinse with water. It leaves my hands moist, clean under the nails, and clean deep down in the pores."

—RICHARD S., *San Antonio, Texas*

Clean grease from hands with...

- **PAM NO STICK COOKING SPRAY.** "If your hands get sticky, clean your hands with Pam No Stick Cooking Spray. It really works"

—TRACY G., *Lakewood, Ohio*

Wash the smell of garlic from hands with...

- **MAXWELL HOUSE COFFEE.** "Wash your hands with a teaspoon of Maxwell House Coffee grounds and a small amount of water to remove garlic odor after handling raw garlic."

—RON P., *Merrillville, Indiana*

Eliminate the odor of fish from your hands with...

- **DOMINO SUGAR.** "Wash your hands with soap and water, then wash your hands with two tablespoons of Domino Sugar and water, just as you would using a bar of soap. Rinse again with soap and water, and the odor is totally gone."

—ROBERT G., *Oshawa, Ontario*

- **DOWNY.** "Wash your hands as usual, then place a teaspoon of Downy on your hands, rub in well, and rinse. Odors will be almost nil."

—CHARLES G., *Warminster, Ontario*

- **FEBREZE.** "My father cleans a lot of fish. He cleans the smell from his hands with Febreze. It works really well."

  —CONNIE J., *Frenchmans Bayou, Arizona*

- **JIF PEANUT BUTTER.** "Use Jif Peanut Butter to remove fish and onion or garlic smells from your hands."

  —SALLY J., *Toledo, Ohio*

Ink

Clean ink from skin with...

- **HUGGIES BABY WIPES.** "When your child decides to use the markers or ink pens on himself, use Huggies Baby Wipes to remove the ink from skin."

  —EDWINA P., *Manchester, Tennessee*

- **PURELL.** "I use Purell hand sanitizer to remove ballpoint pen ink from my children's arms and hands."

  —MELISSA T., *Crest Hill, Illinois*

Kids

Get kids to take a bath with...

- **BARBASOL SHAVING CREAM.** "Use shaving cream to entertain your children in the bathtub. They can draw on the walls with it, and it will wash right off with water."

  —SUE D., *Gilbert, Arizona*

Clean kids' dirty faces with...

- **HUGGIES BABY WIPES.** "I provide day care and have found that Huggies Baby Wipes also work great for yucky noses and are tender on the kids' faces."

  —MEGAN M., *Trenton, New Jersey*

Oil

Wash oil from hair with...

- **JIF PEANUT BUTTER.** "If you are working on a car and get motor oil in your hair, rub Jif Peanut Butter into your hair before you use shampoo and conditioner. It works. I have long hair and I've tried it."

  —JIM L., *Jesmond, Australia*

Sand

Remove sand from skin with...

▪ **KINGSFORD'S CORN STARCH.** "Corn starch is the best way to get sand out of tiny crevices in a baby's diaper area. It makes the sand sheet up and slide away, no matter how sticky it is. I discovered this on my own in a moment of desperation. I have never seen this tip in any parenting book, of which I own hundreds."

—LAUREL P., *Acworth, Georgia*

Shampoo

Shampoo your hair with...

▪ **ARM & HAMMER BAKING SODA.** "To clean hairspray residue from your hair, make a thick paste from Arm & Hammer Baking Soda and water. Put it on your hair, let sit for five minutes, then rinse well, shampoo and condition as usual."

—REBECCA R., *Millsboro, Delaware*

▪ **COMET.** "Strip all the build-up from gel and hairspray out of your hair by dissolving a tablespoon of Comet (without bleach) in a tall glass of water. Pour through your hair and let set for three minutes. Shampoo and condition as usual. You will notice your shampoo lathers extra well and your hair will be extra clean."

—JOYCE T., *Six Mile, South Carolina*

▪ **DAWN.** "Dawn dishwashing liquid makes excellent shampoo. I ran out of shampoo one day and started to panic, until my six-year-old daughter brought the Dawn to me. At first I laughed, then realized it was my only choice. The Dawn worked so well that now it's all I use. It cuts through the grease and film in my hair."

—BILLI W., *Maple Ridge, British Columbia*

▪ **HEINZ APPLE CIDER VINEGAR.** "Add one tablespoon of Heinz Apple Cider Vinegar to your regular eight-ounce bottle of shampoo. Shake well. The vinegar emulsifies the shampoo, making it thicker, so you use less. This not only makes the shampoo more economical to use, but it also helps rinse styling-product build-up from your hair and makes your shampoo rinse cleaner. Don't fret about the smell of the vinegar. Once you rinse, the smell is gone."

—CHRIS M., *Revere, Massachusetts*

■ **SMIRNOFF VODKA.** "Add one jigger of Smirnoff Vodka to your twelve-ounce bottle of shampoo. The alcohol will keep your scalp clean, remove all the pollutants from your hair, and stimulate your hair to grow faster and healthier."

—KIM N., *Silverdale, Washington*

■ **SUNLIGHT.** "Every couple of months, wash your hair with Sunlight dishwashing liquid. It removes build-up and leaves your hair nice and shiny."

—SHELLY G., *Marmora, Ontario*

■ **WOOLITE.** "Every few months I wash my hair with Woolite and then condition it with my normal conditioner. The Woolite is gentle on hair, gets rid of the hairspray and shampoo build-up, and leaves my hair feeling soft and clean."

—TAMMY N., *Menominee, Michigan*

Skunk

Wash away the smell of skunk with...

■ **COCA-COLA.** "Pour four two-liter bottles of Coke into a bucket, sponge yourself down in the shower, and rinse clean."

—KEN D., *Mississauga, Ontario*

Clean It

2

Air Freshener

Freshen the air in your home with...

- **ARM & HAMMER BAKING SODA.** "Dissolve one teaspoon of baking soda in one cup of water in a spray bottle, and spray the air of a room that reeks from the smell of paint or any other odor you wish to banish."

  —AGNES A., *Great Bend, Kansas*

- **BOUNCE.** "To get rid of a nasty odor (cat litter, smoke, the stench of a man who just got back from fishing), tape a sheet of Bounce to the front of a fan (or air conditioning vent) and turn it on."

  —CHRISTINA B., *Chicago, Illinois*

- **CAR-FRESHENER PINE TREES.** "I hang my favorite scented Car Freshener Pine Tree in the house on the blinds. When the air conditioner or furnace kicks in, it gives the house a nice smell."

  —BRENDA S., *Eagle Grove, Iowa*

- **DOWNY.** "Mix one tablespoon Downy with water in a spray bottle and use as an air freshener."

  —BRANDI S., *Troy, Alabama*

- **MAXWELL HOUSE COFFEE.** "I use a freshly opened can of Maxwell House Coffee as a room deodorizer and air freshener."

  —MELISSA S., *Conway, South Carolina*

- **MENNEN SPEED STICK.** "Simply take off the lid and place a Speed Stick in the drawer where you keep clothes or under the seat of your car. You can even cut up chunks and place in different places."

  —DENIS B., *Gloucester, Ontario*

Eliminate smoke odor with...

■ **HEINZ VINEGAR.** "If you want to eliminate the odor of cigarette smoke from a room, simply pour four ounces of Heinz Vinegar in a cup or decorative container and leave it in the room."

—DENNIS B., *Pittsburgh, Pennsylvania*

Barbecues

Clean a barbecue grill with...

■ **CASCADE, GLAD TRASH BAGS, AND PARSONS' AMMONIA.** "To clean your outdoor barbecue grill (just the cooking surface), place the grill in a Glad Trash Bag, add one cup Parsons' Ammonia, one cup Cascade, and two gallons hot water. Secure the bag closed. Let this sit for about forty-five minutes, then hose down the grill and wipe clean."

—J.J., *Page, Arizona*

■ **EASY-OFF OVEN CLEANER.** "Place the grill in a plastic trash bag. Spray the racks well with Easy-Off Oven Cleaner, close the bag, and secure with a twist tie. Let set for at least three or four hours. Rinse with a garden hose. This works even faster if left out in the sun."

—DARRELL B., *Toledo, Ohio*

■ **WD-40.** "I made my old, used barbecue grill look like new by spraying on WD-40 and scrubbing. It did a great job."

—FRAN N., *Cincinnati, Ohio*

Bicycles

Clean bicycles with...

■ **DOW BATHROOM CLEANER.** "Dow Bathroom Cleaner works wonders for cleaning bicycle wheels, spokes, and drive trains without having to hand wipe difficult areas."

—JIM L., *Maplewood, Missouri*

Bird Droppings

Clean bird droppings easily with...

■ **HEINZ VINEGAR.** "I have four cockatiels, one canary, and one lovebird. Needless to say, dried bird poop is difficult to clean off—

but not with Heinz Apple Cider Vinegar. Spray on the spot or apply with a rag. In no time, the droppings wipe right off."

—SALLY E., *Perrysburg, Ohio*

Books

Clean books with...

■ **HUGGIES BABY WIPES.** "If one of my children gets fingerprint marks or spills on a book, I clean it up with a Huggies Baby Wipe."

—JANICE V., *Wallaceburg, Ontario*

Eliminate musty smells from old books with...

■ **BOUNCE.** "Place several sheets of Bounce throughout the pages of an old book, enclose in a large Ziploc bag, and wait several weeks."

—STACY G., *Birmingham, Alabama*

Bowling Ball

Clean a bowling ball with...

■ **HUGGIES BABY WIPES.** "Huggies Baby Wipes are great for cleaning your bowling ball during a match or tournament."

—COLIN J., *Merseyside, England*

Brass

Clean tarnish from brass with...

■ **BOUNCE.** "Polish brass lamps and other brass household items with used Bounce dryer sheets. It works great."

—JENNIFER B., *Delhi, California*

■ **HEINZ KETCHUP.** "Ketchup works wonders to polish brass. Cover the brass with Heinz Ketchup, let sit for ten minutes, then rinse clean."

—DONNA B., *Altus, Oklahoma*

■ **KOOL-AID.** "Mix Kool-Aid and soak your brass or silver in it. Cherry seems to work best. (Don't drink it after cleaning.)"

—MIKE L., *Des Moines, Iowa*

Broken Glass

Pick up broken glass with...

- ▪ **WONDER BREAD.** "Just ball up the Wonder Bread until it gets sticky, then roll it over the broken glass."

  —CARMEN S., *Panama City, Florida*

Cabinets

Clean dried grease from wooden kitchen cabinets with...

- ▪ **EASY-OFF OVEN CLEANER.** "Spray with Easy-Off, let it set for a few minutes, then wipe clean. It works wonderfully."

  —DIANNA R., *Maynard, Arkansas*

Cards

Clean a deck of cards with...

- ▪ **JOHNSON'S BABY POWDER.** "Johnson's Baby Powder works well for keeping an old deck of cards from sticking together."

  —DAWN D., *Milwaukee, Wisconsin*

Carpet

Clean lipstick stains from carpet with...

- ▪ **LESTOIL.** "Just apply a little bit of Lestoil to a rag and dab the lipstick stain until it comes clean."

  —CARRIE K., *Livonia, Michigan*

Clean stains from carpet with...

- ▪ **BARBASOL SHAVING CREAM.** "I use Barbasol Shaving Cream to remove stains from carpet. Just spray on some foam, scrub with a wet scrub brush, and then rinse with a wet cloth to blot up the extra foam. I have never missed a carpet stain with this stuff."

  —CONNIE M., *China, Michigan*

- ▪ **CANADA DRY CLUB SODA.** "Pour a small amount of Canada Dry Club Soda onto the stain, rub gently with a sponge, then blot up with paper towels."

  —SHARON M., *Venice, Florida*

■ **GUNK BRAKE CLEANER.** "After a friend changed an oil pressure regulator under the engine cover inside my van and forgot to put the new one on, the light tan interior of my vehicle was saturated with dirty black oil. I sprayed the entire area thoroughly with brake pad cleaner, rubbed it in, and vacuumed. The brake cleaner dries, removing all moisture, and any remaining powder can be vacuumed easily."

—RAND L., *Phoenix, Arizona*

■ **HUGGIES BABY WIPES.** "For lifting stains from carpet, rub with a Huggies Baby Wipe. It lifts the stain right off the carpet."

—JEANNE S., *Philadelphia, Pennsylvania*

■ **PAMPERS.** "Blot up spills from carpet with Pampers. The chemical in Pampers disposable diapers is very absorbent and picks up messy spills fast."

—LORIE B., *Tucson, Arizona*

■ **SHOUT.** "Spray Shout on the stain, then wipe clean with a wet rag. The Shout leaves a nice smell and sets the stage for great results when you finally have the carpet steam-cleaned."

—KIM S., *Bartlesville, Oklahoma*

■ **SMIRNOFF VODKA.** "Smirnoff Vodka is fantastic for cleaning spots out of carpets. Just spray Smirnoff Vodka on the stain, scrub with a brush, then blot up with a clean towel or napkin."

—PAMELA M., *Modesto, California*

■ **STP CARB SPRAY CLEANER.** "Use STP carburetor cleaner on your carpet to get tar, paint, or almost anything out of your carpet. You don't even have to leave it on long. It really works. I use it all the time."

—JAMES M., *Venus, Texas*

■ **TIDE.** "Mix one cup Tide with two cups Heinz White Vinegar. Scrub the stain with this solution. Rinse with cool water, blot up, and let air dry. I took tar out of my pink carpet with this solution, and Tide is color safe."

—JULIE N., *Steilacoom, Washington*

■ **WD-40.** "You can use WD-40 to take stains out of your carpet. Just put a small amount on a rag and scrub the spot."

—DREW R., *Jasper, Alabama*

■ **WINDEX.** "I use Windex for all my cleaning needs. I spilled cherry Kool-Aid on my white rug and I used Windex to clean it right out, without leaving a stain."

—LILA W., *San Diego, California*

■ **WONDER BREAD.** "If you have an oil or grease stain on your carpet, take a slice of Wonder Bread and rub it all over the spot until the stain is gone, then vacuum up the crumbs. I have done this a few times and each time the bread cleans the stain right up."

—ROBERTA S., *Newtonfalls, Ohio*

Clean melted crayons, Silly Putty, or chewing gum from carpets with...

■ **WD-40.** "Spray WD-40 on a cloth and rub the area until the gunk comes out, then shampoo with dishwashing liquid mixed with a very small amount of water. My kids left a box of crayons in my new car, and they melted all over my velour seats. The WD-40 really worked."

—BRIAN D., *Jackson, Mississippi*

Clean wine stains from carpet with...

■ **MORTON SALT.** "Pour Morton Salt to cover the stain, then watch the salt suck up the wine. The wine will completely disappear from the carpet."

—HARRIET B., *Clearwater, Florida*

Deodorize carpet and remove dust easily with...

■ **DOWNY.** "Want your carpeting to look great and be more dust resistant? Add one part Downy Fabric Softener to six parts water in a spray bottle, and spray your carpet before vacuuming. The carpet stays cleaner, smells great, and feels soft on the tootsies. I use fleecy vanilla scented fabric softener."

—SHELLEY P., *Delta, British Columbia*

Cast-Iron

Clean a cast-iron skillet with...

- **CANADA DRY CLUB SODA.** "Pour Canada Dry Club Soda over your skillet while it is hot. The club soda cleans off the baked-on food left over from grilling. This trick is used in restaurants."

  —CINDY W., *Palmerton, Pennsylvania*

- **MORTON SALT.** "Sprinkle Morton Salt in the cast-iron skillet, and wipe clean with a wet cloth, then rinse clean. Repeat if necessary."

  —CINDY S., *Kelowna, British Columbia*

Cast-Iron Frying Pans

Rejuvenate cast-iron pans with...

- **MORTON SALT** AND **WESSON CORN OIL.** "To get my cast-iron frying pan to look like new, I boil water in the frying pan for five minutes, empty out the water, and coat the bottom of the pan with salt. Then I take a plastic scrubbing pad and scrape the bottom and sides of the pan. Rinse and apply vegetable oil with a paper towel."

  —LINDA O., *West Fargo, North Dakota*

Ceiling Tiles

Clean ceiling tiles with...

- **DOW BATHROOM CLEANER.** "Spraying Dow Bathroom Cleaner with foaming bubbles on old ceiling tiles (the kind that have a thin layer of plastic) removes all the crud, then rinse well. Just don't get the insulation part wet."

  —KIMBERLY S., *Cambridge, Ohio*

Chrome

Shine chrome with...

- **COLGATE TOOTHPASTE.** "Colgate Toothpaste cleans and polishes chrome."

  —JIM L., *Lufkin, Texas*

- **REYNOLDS WRAP.** "Rub Reynolds Wrap over rust spots on the chrome to remove them."
  —SHELLY G., *Marmora, Ontario*

- **SMIRNOFF VODKA.** "Simply put some Smirnoff Vodka on a paper towel and apply directly to your faucets or other chrome. It removes soap scum, calcium, and lime deposits."
  —TINA K., *Gainesville, Florida*

Copper Pots

Clean tarnish from copper pots with...

- **REALEMON.** "Make a paste from ReaLemon lemon juice and salt. Rub onto copper pots to remove tarnish and restore the shine."
  —JILDA T., *Englewood, New Jersey*

Cobwebs

Clean dust and cobwebs from vaulted ceilings, walls, and hard-to-reach corners with...

- **BOUNCE.** "Take a length of PVC pipe long enough to reach the farthest point. Put an old sock on one end of the pipe, put several layers of used Bounce sheets over the sock and fasten in place with a rubber band. Wipe corners and ceilings until all the dust is gone. Replace Bounce sheets as needed."
  —NANCY M., *Temecula, California*

Coffee Cups

Remove stains from coffee cups with...

- **CASCADE.** "Use Cascade to clean coffee or tea stains from cups. Fill the sink with hot water, add one tablespoon Cascade, mix well, set the cups in the water, and let soak for twenty minutes. The cups will rinse clean like new."
  —TRACY P., *Brick, New Jersey*

- **EFFERDENT.** "To remove coffee stains, drop one Efferdent tablet into the cup or mug and fill with warm water. Let it sit overnight. Do the same thing with glasses, bowls, and basins stained by well-water deposits."
  —CAROL J., *Hermosa Beach, California*

Coffeemakers

Clean a coffeemaker with...

- **ALKA-SELTZER.** "Commercial cleansers for coffeemakers contain ascorbic acid, which can be found in Alka-Seltzer. Once a month, I fill the water chamber of my drip coffeemaker with water, drop in four Alka-Seltzer tablets, and let 'er rip. Then I flush the system clean with three cycles of clean water."

—DIANNE S., *South Bend, Indiana*

Real-Life Story

COCA-COLA HITS THE SPOT

"When I was a young girl, my family had a cat. On our vacation one year, the cat got on the countertop in the kitchen and knocked over my Mom's jar of bacon grease onto the linoleum floor. Since no one was there to clean it up, the grease soaked into the linoleum. Mom tried every kind of soap and detergent to get rid of the stain, but none worked. Years later, during my brother's birthday party, someone spilled a Coca-Cola on the floor, right over the stain, and it got left there until the party was over. When that mess got mopped up, the ugly grease stain had disappeared!"

—ANNA H., *Petaluma, California*

Coffeepots

Clean a glass coffeepot with...

- **COCA-COLA.** "If you fill your coffeepot with Coke and let it stand overnight, the pot will be clean in the morning."

—BETH D., *Mikado, Michigan*

- **EFFERDENT.** "Fill the coffeepot with water, drop in two Efferdent tablets, let sit for twenty minutes, then wash clean."

—ANDRA S., *Richmond, California*

■ **MORTON SALT.** "Fill the bottom of the glass coffeepot with Morton Salt, fill the pot with ice cubes, and then swivel the pot for several minutes so the ice cubes and salt swirl around the pot, cleaning it."
—LINDA T., *Mount Sinai, New York*

Coins

Clean coins with...

■ **ARM & HAMMER BAKING SODA** AND **HEINZ WHITE VINEGAR.** "Fill a clean, used mayonnaise jar with Heinz White vinegar, then add one teaspoon Arm and Hammer Baking Soda. Stir well, then drop the coins into the jar, and let soak overnight. In the morning, rinse the coins clean with water."
—JEREMY E., *Alta Loma, California*

■ **COCA-COLA.** "For coin collectors or others who like clean money, fill a glass with Coke and drop in tarnished pennies. Let sit for one hour, then wipe clean with a cloth."
—ANDY L., *Orlando, Florida*

■ **MORTON SALT** AND **REALEMON.** "To make dirty pennies shine again, mix ReaLemon lemon juice with Morton Salt in a small Tupperware container. Add several dirty pennies. Shake well for two minutes, let sit for five minutes, then remove the pennies, rinse under warm water, and dry."
—SARAH G., *Carteret, New Jersey*

■ **TABASCO PEPPER SAUCE.** "Wipe pennies with Tabasco Pepper Sauce and they come clean."
—MERLIN O., *Fenwick, Michigan*

Compact Disks

Clean compact disks with...

■ **JIF PEANUT BUTTER.** "To clean compact disks and sometimes fix scratches, just rub creamy Jif Peanut Butter on the CD with a soft cloth, then swirl it around and wipe it off. Unbelievable, but it works."
—MELANIE P., *Pflugerville, Texas*

■ **MR. COFFEE FILTERS.** "When searching for a disk cleaner for compact disks, I tried using a Mr. Coffee Filter and it worked great."

—MARIETTA S., *Ft. Myers, Florida*

■ **PLEDGE.** "If you have a compact disk that skips, spray a small amount of lemon Pledge on it, wipe with a soft cloth starting from center and working out to the edge until clean. Your disk will play properly again."

—MARTY W., *East Haven, Connecticut*

■ **PURELL.** "Purell, the soapless, antibacterial hand sanitizer, cleans CDs."

—FRAN G., *Calabasas, California*

Computers

Clean computers with...

■ **BOUNCE.** "If you wipe your computer screen with a used sheet of Bounce, the dust will come off and the anti-static elements in the dryer sheet prevent dust from resettling as quickly."

—NAOMI B., *East Liberty, Ohio*

■ **DOW BATHROOM CLEANER.** "Computer components—the monitor case, motherboard, speakers, and mouse—are easy to clean with Dow Bathroom Cleaner. Spray the foam on a clean rag and scrub away. Wacky as it seems, getting this product out of the bathroom now and then is a really good idea."

—JANET H., *Conway, New Hampshire*

■ **HUGGIES BABY WIPES.** "As a typing teacher, I have my students clean their computer, screen, keyboard, mouse, mouse pad, and their hands with Huggies Baby Wipes. This keeps the machines much cleaner and hopefully cuts down on germs."

—JANICE G., *Lubbock, Texas*

■ **LISTERINE.** "Listerine is the best cleaner for computer monitor screens I have found. It cuts through the residue better than any glass cleaner."

—CHARLES B., *Pottsboro, Texas*

■ **STRIDEX MEDICATED PADS.** "Use Stridex pads to clean the oils from your keyboard keys."

—BRANDI S., *Troy, Alabama*

Contact Lenses

Clean hard contact lenses with...

■ **CLOSE-UP CLASSIC RED GEL TOOTHPASTE.** "Close-Up Toothpaste has no grit and works better than most hard lens cleaners. Be sure to rinse thoroughly. I've been using it for years."

—Lois W., *Federal Way, Washington*

Cookware

Clean baked-on food from pots and pans with...

■ **ARM & HAMMER BAKING SODA.** "Fill the pot or pan with enough water to cover the food baked inside, add one tablespoon Arm & Hammer Baking Soda, place on the stove, and bring to a boil for five minutes. Let cool and the baked-on food will wash off easily."

—Catherine V., *Paris, Ontario*

■ **BOUNCE.** "Fill the pot, pan, or casserole dish with water, put a sheet of Bounce in the cookware, and let sit overnight. Washes clean easily the next morning."

—Gail Y., *Twentynine Palms, California*

■ **CASCADE.** "Pour some Cascade in the pot or pan, fill with hot water, and wait about thirty minutes. The pot or pan will easily wash clean."

—Trish H., *Abilene, Texas*

■ **COCA-COLA.** "You know that pan that you let burn so badly on the stove? Boil some Coca-Cola in the pan and the crud will come off."

—Mary S., *Colorado Springs, Colorado*

■ **DOWNY.** "I use Downy Liquid to soak baking dishes, pots, or pans that have baked-on food."

—Deb D., *Tulsa, Oklahoma*

■ **EFFERDENT.** "Place melamine crockery or china in the sink, fill the sink with hot water, and drop in three to four Efferdent denture cleansing tablets. Let sit overnight."

—Patty G., *Atlanta, Georgia*

■ **HEINZ WHITE VINEGAR.** "Pour a small amount of vinegar in the pot or pan, then wipe with a sponge. This works best if the utensil is still warm. Prevents any need to scrub (and damage) non-stick surfaces."

—GORDON J., *Titusville, Florida*

■ **L'EGGS SHEER ENERGY PANTY HOSE.** "Place a used pair of L'eggs Panty Hose in a webbed onion bag from the grocery store to make a great pot scrubber."

—ELLA G., *Lodi, New Jersey*

■ **MAXWELL HOUSE COFFEE.** "Use a cup or two of Maxwell House Coffee to deglaze a pan in which you've browned beef, and make gravy with the resulting mixture."

—LISA H., *Mystic Island, New Jersey*

"Use used Maxwell House Coffee grounds to scrub pots and pans that have a build-up of food and stains. Rinse well."

—MARY G., *Grand Bay, Alabama*

Real-Life Story

HELLO JELL-O

"Quite by accident, we discovered that Jell-O Instant Chocolate Pudding is very good at cleaning brass. After dinner, I gave our cat a bite to eat on a brass coaster. He ate some, but left a hefty dollop, and when I washed it off, I found really clean and shiny brass underneath!"

—ROSE H., *Birmingham, Alabama*

■ **MCCORMICK** OR **SCHILLING CREAM OF TARTAR.** "Sprinkle Cream of Tartar on stubborn burned-on food in pots and pans, then scrub. It works great."

—KATHY G., *Fremont, Ohio*

■ **MORTON SALT.** "Use Morton Salt to scrub calcium deposits from glassware or baked-on food from pots and pans."

—ELIZABETH F., *Chicago, Illinois*

- **REYNOLDS WRAP.** "Use Reynolds Wrap aluminum foil for a pot scrubber. Wad up a piece of foil and use it to clean baked-on food from a pot. The foil is soft and does not scratch the pot."

  —DOROTHY Y., *Rialto, California*

Copper
Clean tarnish from copper with...

- **HEINZ KETCHUP.** "Pour a thick coat of Heinz Ketchup over the bottom of Revere copper-bottom pots, let sit for an hour, then wash off. The acids from the tomatoes and vinegar in the ketchup clean the tarnish so the copper shines like new."

  —WILMA G., *North Miami Beach, Florida*

- **HEINZ VINEGAR** AND **REALEMON.** "Mix equal parts Heinz Vinegar and ReaLemon juice. Wet a clean cloth with the mixture, then dip the wet cloth into salt and rub the copper gently until it sparkles."

  —GEORGINA W., *Salt Lake City, Utah*

- **TABASCO PEPPER SAUCE.** "Tabasco Pepper Sauce cleans copper."

  —KATHY H., *Owensboro, Kentucky*

Countertops
Clean countertops with...

- **HUGGIES BABY WIPES.** "I use Huggies Baby Wipes all the time. I keep them in almost every room in my house. They are great for quick clean-ups around the toilet and sink in the bathroom. They are also great for wiping up sticky messes on the floor after the kids eat."

  —JULIE D., *Yankton, South Dakota*

- **SOFTSOAP INSTANT ANTIBACTERIAL HAND GEL.** "Squirt Softsoap on a paper towel and shine a Formica countertop. The countertop will look spotless and feel extra smooth. Rub your hand over the surface and you'll definitely feel the difference."

  —SHERYL L., *Clearlake, California*

Crayon

Clean crayon marks off walls with...

- **CASCADE.** "Make a paste from a teaspoon of Cascade and a teaspoon of water, smear the paste over the crayon marks, wait ten minutes, then wipe clean with a damp cloth. It works every time without any scrubbing."
  —MICHELLE C., *Cedar Park, Texas*

- **COLGATE TOOTHPASTE.** "If your toddler decides the wall makes a nice canvas for crayons, just put a little Colgate Toothpaste on the marks and scrub. The crayon will come right off."
  —KATE Y., *Bath, New York*

- **CONAIR PRO STYLE 1600.** "To get crayon marks off walls, use a hair blower. It melts the wax and the crayon wipes off easily with a paper towel, leaving the wall clean."
  —JENNIFER F., *Gulfport, Mississippi*

- **EASY-OFF OVEN CLEANER.** "Easy-Off takes crayon off wood without any damage."
  —PATI T., *Eugene, Oregon*

- **HUGGIES BABY WIPES.** "I use Huggies Baby Wipes to clean crayon marks off the walls and floors."
  —TAMMY R., *Missoula, Montana*

- **WD-40.** "I have removed crayon from painted walls with WD-40. Just spray it on and wipe it off with a paper towel. If any residue is left on the wall from the WD-40, just wipe it off with some soapy water. It works like magic."
  —DANIEL J., *Aurora, Illinois*

Curling Irons

Clean a curling iron with...

- **S.O.S STEEL WOOL SOAP PADS.** "Use S.O.S pads to scrub a curling iron coated with baked-on hair spray. Just make sure the curling iron is unplugged first."
  —JANA C., *Crawfordsville, Indiana*

Cutting Boards

Disinfect cutting boards with...

- **CLOROX BLEACH.** "I put Clorox Bleach in a spray bottle for use in the kitchen. I use it to disinfect my cutting boards."

  —BARB B., *Lorain, Ohio*

Desktops

Clean desktops with...

- **BARBASOL SHAVING CREAM.** "My mom uses shaving cream to have her first-grade students clean their own desks. They love to play and practice writing in the shaving cream—while cleaning their desks at the same time. Barbasol removes glue, pencil marks, and other markings from desktops and tabletops."

  —AMY S., *Nixa, Missouri*

Diaper Pails

Freshen a diaper pail with...

- **BOUNCE.** "Place a sheet of Bounce in the lid of your diaper pail to deodorize the pail."

  —DEA G., *Enterprise, Alabama*

Dishes

Scrape food from dishes with...

- **MASTERCARD.** "My grandmother saves the free, unrequested credit cards she gets in the mail and keeps them near her kitchen sink to scrape tough build-up from her dishes when she washes them. Credit cards are the perfect size for scraping food from dishes."

  —JENNIFER T., *Westland, Michigan*

Wash dishes with...

- **TIDE.** "If some of your dishes just won't come clean, use Tide to get your dishes clean and smelling fresh."

  —ELIZABETH S., *Early, Texas*

Dishwashers

Clean soap scum from the tubes and pipes of a dishwasher with...

- **HEINZ VINEGAR.** "Pour a cup of Heinz White Vinegar down the spout located in the middle of the floor of the machine."

  —KATHY G., *El Centro, California*

- **TANG.** "Simply fill the detergent cups with Tang powder and run the dishwasher through its regular cycle. The citric acid in Tang cleans the soap scum and mineral and iron stains. I use it once a month."

  —SHARON H., *Klamath Falls, Oregon*

Eliminate excessive soap suds in the dishwasher with...

- **BOUNCE.** "If you use the wrong detergent or too much detergent in the dishwasher and it starts to overflow with suds, open the door and put in a sheet of Bounce. It will absorb the extra suds."

  —BETTY R., *Ft. Pierce, Florida*

Drain Boards

Clean hard-water stains from a drain board with...

- **HEINZ VINEGAR.** "I use Heinz White Vinegar on my drain board to help eliminate hard-water stains. Let it soak, wipe off, and hard-water stains are gone."

  —LINDA H., *Samson, Alabama*

Drains

Flush your kitchen sink drain with...

- **MAXWELL HOUSE COFFEE.** "I keep my kitchen drain clean by flushing it with Maxwell House Coffee grounds and hot water."

  —BETTY A., *DuQuoin, Illinois*

Dusting

Dust with...

- **BOUNCE.** "Use a used Bounce fabric softener sheet for dusting. The antistatic elements prevent dust from resettling as quickly."

  —SANDY S., *Dallas, Texas*

- **HUGGIES BABY WIPES.** "We have always used Huggies Baby Wipes to dust our entertainment center. One swipe with a Huggies Baby Wipe and it's all clean."

  —TRACY B., *Brunswick, Georgia*

Egg

Clean a broken egg from the floor with...

- **MORTON SALT.** "Pour Morton Salt over the broken egg. Let the salt blend with the egg and let sit for one minute. You can then easily wipe up the mess with a paper towel."

  —JUDY S., *Middletown, Ohio*

Eraser

Erase pencil marks from paper with...

- **WONDER BREAD.** "Simply rub the white part of the bread to erase the clean and natural way."

  —EUEE R., *Auckland, New Zealand*

Eyeglasses

Clean eyeglasses with...

- **BOUNCE.** "I use used sheets of Bounce to clean my glasses. They don't scratch the lenses, and they do a great job of cleaning. Also, they can be folded up and kept in a pocket of my purse easily."

  —JANICE V., *Wallaceburg, Ontario*

- **CREST TOOTHPASTE.** "Put a small dab of Crest Toothpaste on your eyeglass lens and wipe clean. Crest also removes small scratches from the lens."
  —CYNTHIA W., *St. Louis, Missouri*

- **HUGGIES BABY WIPES.** "I wear glasses with plastic lens, and I use Huggies Baby Wipes to clean my glasses. They clean quickly and also repel dirt during the day."
  —SANDY M., *Beaverton, Oregon*

- **PLEDGE.** "Lemon Pledge will clean eyeglasses. I got this tip from my eyeglasses repair man."
  —TIM W., *Clearwater, Florida*

- **PURELL.** "Purell Hand Sanitizer is great for cleaning eyeglasses. Put a dab on a tissue and polish the lens."
  —PATTY K., *Houston, Texas*

- **SMIRNOFF VODKA.** "I used to work in a bar and I hate talking to a person with dirty eyeglasses. I would ask the person for their glasses, put a drop of Smirnoff Vodka on each lens, and wipe with a clean bar towel. The glasses would come out very clean so I could see the other person's eyes."
  —JESSICA R., *Fairplay, Missouri*

Defog eyeglasses with...

- **COLGATE TOOTHPASTE.** "Coat eyeglasses with Colgate Toothpaste, then rinse off on hot summer days to avoid the fog associated with going from cool air conditioning to the hot outdoors."
  —PHYLLIS C., *Sunnyvale, California*

Fireplace
Clean a brick fireplace with...

- **EASY-OFF OVEN CLEANER.** "I use Easy-Off Oven Cleaner to clean the light-colored brick in our fireplace. Just follow the directions: spray, wait fifteen minutes, and wash off. The brick looks like new when I'm finished."
  —BONNIE G., *Ashtabula, Ohio*

Freezer
Make defrosting a freezer a breeze with...

- **PAM NO STICK COOKING SPRAY.** "For many years now I have sprayed a thin coat of Pam No Stick Cooking Spray on the inside of my freezer after defrosting it. This helps tremendously the next time it needs to be cleaned. When I turn the freezer off to defrost it, the ice falls off the sides within minutes. I have passed this hint along to many, many of my friends. At first they laugh, but after trying it they thank me."
  —ELDA F., *Latrobe, Pennsylvania*

Garbage Disposals
Freshen a garbage disposal with...

- **REALEMON.** "Pour a quarter-cup of ReaLemon lemon juice down the drain into your garbage disposal and let sit for fifteen minutes."
  —CHERI R., *Greeneville, Tennessee*

Grease
Remove grease and goo with...

- **GOJO HAND CLEANER.** "When you move your oven and there is an old greasy mess, spread on Gojo, wait a while and then wipe with a wet rag. It comes right off."
  —JUDIE B., *Johnstown, Pennsylvania*

- **JIF PEANUT BUTTER.** "Jif Peanut Butter is a better goo remover than Goo Gone. Just smear some peanut butter on dried grease or glue on a stove or refrigerator, let set a few minutes, then wipe off."
  —BARBARA G., *Kingsland, Texas*

Hockey Helmets
Clean a hockey helmet with...

- **EASY-OFF OVEN CLEANER.** "Easy-Off removes puck marks from a helmet visor."
  —BRANDON N., *Peace River, Northwest Territory*

Ink

Clean indelible marker ink with...

- **ALBERTO VO5 HAIR SPRAY OR LYSOL.** "I am a fourth-grade teacher. To keep costs down, I like to reuse my charts each year. I laminate them and write on them with washable overhead markers. Once I accidentally wrote on one of my charts with a permanent marker. I discovered that hair spray takes permanent marker off of a laminated surface. I also accidentally discovered (when I grabbed the wrong bottle) that Lysol spray also works."

  —SUSAN S., *Morehead City, North Carolina*

- **ARM & HAMMER BAKING SODA.** "Just sprinkle Arm & Hammer Baking Soda over the indelible ink mark on wood or plastic surfaces and wipe with a damp cloth or paper towel."

  —MARY S., *Cherokee, Iowa*

- **MURPHY'S OIL SOAP.** "I have used Murphy's Oil Soap to remove permanent marker from a varnished wood door. I have also used it at the school where I teach to remove permanent marker from desks and tables."

  —KATHERINE R., *Atkinson, Nebraska*

- **POND'S COLD CREAM.** "I used Pond's Cold Cream to remove permanent marker from the skin of a two-year-old. Just smear on the cold cream and wipe off the ink."

  —MARY S., *Cherokee, Iowa*

- **SMIRNOFF VODKA.** "You know those Sharpie permanent markers? Smirnoff Vodka takes the marks right out."

  —JOFF R., *Clarksburg, West Virginia*

Clean ink from children's toys with...

- **CRISCO ALL-VEGETABLE SHORTENING.** "I found a Cabbage Patch doll head at a junk sale. It had ink all over the face. I tried everything to remove it, but nothing worked—until I tried Crisco All-Vegetable Shortening. I just rubbed a little on the ink marks, set it in the sun for a short time, then wiped. It took two applications, but all the ink came off. I sewed a body for the doll, and my granddaughter never knew it was an old head."

  —LOIS L., *Gainesville, Florida*

- **JIF PEANUT BUTTER.** "Jif Peanut Butter can remove pen scribblings from children's toys. Just smear on, let sit a few minutes, and wipe off."

  —LORI V., *Boston, Massachusetts*

Clean indelible marker off a dry-erase board with...

- **COFFEE-MATE.** "At the office, someone used an indelible marker rather than a dry-erase marker on the white board. The whiteboard cleaning spray would not remove the ink. I was pouring a cup of coffee and noticed the Coffee-Mate. Would Coffee-Mate clean the white board? It did. Unbelievable. No scratches either."

  —HENRY B., *Edson, Alberta*

Weird Fact

DEADLY SMELLS

"Embalmers and pathologists smear Vaseline petroleum jelly on their upper lips during autopsies to avoid smelling the stench of decaying human flesh."

—D. WHEELER, *Franklin Square, New York*

Jewelry

Clean jewelry with...

- **ARM & HAMMER BAKING SODA.** "Instead of buying jewelry cleaner, I use a paste of baking soda and water to clean my jewelry."

  —DEBBIE M., *Mt. Hope, West Virginia*

- **COLGATE TOOTHPASTE.** "I use Colgate Toothpaste to clean my earrings, then I simply rinse them off."

  —AMANDA P., *Pilot Grove, Missouri*

- **DOW BATHROOM CLEANER.** "I use Dow Bathroom Cleaner to clean my diamond engagement ring. I spray the Dow into a small cup, drop in the ring at night, and rinse with hot water in the morning."

  —MELISSA S., *Conway, South Carolina*

- **EFFERDENT.** "Use Efferdent denture cleansing tablets to clean your jewelry. It makes diamonds sparkle like new. Drop two Efferdent tablets in a glass of water, soak the jewelry until the water turns clear, then take a soft toothbrush and scrub gently."

  —CHARLOTTE B., *Northford, Connecticut*

- **MENTADENT TOOTHPASTE.** "Use Mentadent Toothpaste to clean rhinestone jewelry. The whitening formula works the best. You can make stones that are yellow with age shine brighter than diamonds."

  —VICTORIA H., *Veguita, New Mexico*

- **PARSONS' AMMONIA.** "Mix one part Parsons' Ammonia with two parts warm water and soak jewelry (diamonds and gold) for five minutes. Take it out and brush it with a clean, used soft toothbrush and rinse. Watch it sparkle."

  —SANDY K., *Camp Verde, Arizona*

- **PURELL.** "Purell, the soapless, antibacterial hand sanitizer, polishes gemstones and metal jewelry (but don't use Purell on pearls)."

  —FRAN G., *Calabasas, California*

- **SIMPLE GREEN.** "Place gold and silver jewelry in a plastic film canister, fill with Simple Green (from the trigger-spray bottle), swirl the jewelry a few times, and let stand for two hours. Rinse jewelry thoroughly in running water, dry, and watch it shine. You can reuse the cleaner ten to fifteen times before discarding."

  —GARRY M., *Arcadia, California*

- **SMIRNOFF VODKA.** "Soak the jewelry in Smirnoff Vodka."

  —ELISE L., *Richmond, Virginia*

Knick-knacks

Clean wooden knick-knacks with...

- **PAM NO STICK COOKING SPRAY.** "Use Pam No Stick Cooking Spray to clean oil and dirt from all kinds of wood. It's great for polishing outdoor furniture that has a natural wood finish."

  —RUSSELL W., *Spanaway, Washington*

Leather

Clean leather with...

- **HUGGIES BABY WIPES.** "To clean any leather item (boots, hand-bags, and coat) nothing beats Huggies Baby Wipes. They clean the leather and moisturize it at the same time."

  —JONATHAN K., *Plattsburgh, New York*

- **JIF PEANUT BUTTER.** "Clean your leather or vinyl purse or shoes with Jif Peanut Butter. Just smear on a thin coat of peanut butter, wait a minute, then wipe off. Polish with a soft cloth."

  —LIA I., *Brampton, Ontario*

Lost Items

Retrieve small items from crevices with...

- **SILLY PUTTY.** "Use Silly Putty to pick up small, dropped items like beads, or get them out of crevices."

  —PHYLLIS P., *Bellwood, Pennsylvania*

Mattresses

Freshen mattresses with...

- **BOUNCE.** "Place a Bounce sheet between the mattress and the box spring."

  —ROGER P., *Pomona, New York*

Microwave Oven

Clean a microwave oven with...

- **ARM & HAMMER BAKING SODA.** "I use Arm & Hammer Baking Soda to clean my microwave oven. Just put a couple of tablespoons of baking soda in a cup of water. Boil in the microwave for five minutes, then wipe clean."

  —DENISE V., *Cleveland, Ohio*

- **BOUNCE.** "Once you've used a Bounce sheet in the dryer, you can reuse it in the microwave. Dampen it with water and use it to wipe clean your microwave. It's a great nonabrasive scrubber and helps get rid of strong odors."

—SHERRY S., *Richardson, Texas*

Mirrors

Clean mirrors with...

- **BOUNCE.** "When you're done using your Bounce sheets in the dryer, use them to shine up your bathroom mirrors."

  —CLEDA S., *Algoma, Wisconsin*

- **COLGATE TOOTHPASTE.** "Use toothpaste to clean mirror tarnish."

  —KAILASH M., *Carlisle, Pennsylvania*

- **GLADE AIR FRESHENER.** "Air freshener does a great job cleaning glass and, better still, leaves a lovely smell to the shine."

  —ABBY Q., *Manchester, Iowa*

- **MOTT'S APPLESAUCE.** "You can clean your mirrors with applesauce. It does a remarkable job."

  —COLLEEN G., *Round Rock, Texas*

- **MR. COFFEE FILTERS.** "The tight weave of Mr. Coffee Filter paper leaves no lint."

  —LINDA S., *Cedar City, Utah*

Oven

Clean an oven with...

- **KOOL-AID.** "Mix up a batch of Kool-Aid (without adding any sugar) and use it like cleanser. The citric acid cuts through the gunk in the oven."

  —KATE Y., *Bath, New York*

Oven Racks

Clean oven racks with...

- **EASY-OFF OVEN CLEANER.** "Place the racks in a plastic trash bag. Spray the racks well with Easy-Off Oven Cleaner, close the bag, and secure with a twist tie. Let set for at least three or four hours.

Rinse with a garden hose. Hey, they look like new! This works even faster if you leave the bag in the sun."

—DARRELL B., *Toledo, Ohio*

▪ **PARSONS' AMMONIA.** "Put oven shelves and boiler pans in a plastic garbage bag, add one cup of Parsons' Ammonia, tie shut, and let set overnight. The fumes from the ammonia weaken the bond of the baked-on food and grease. Moderate build-up will clean off quite easily."

—DANA G., *Brookfield, Vermont*

▪ **TIDE.** "Pour one cup of liquid Tide into a clean, empty, plastic garbage can and then fill the garbage can halfway with water. Place the oven racks in the garbage pail. Let sit for one hour, then rinse clean."

—HARRIET Z., *Hubbard Lake, Michigan*

Paintings or Photographs

Clean a painting or photograph with...

▪ **WONDER BREAD.** "Rub a slice of Wonder Bread over the picture, then wipe off the crumbs. The bread cleans the dirt, grime, and mildew from oil paintings and your picture will look like new."

—PHYLISS M., *Glens Falls, New York*

Patent Leather

Clean patent leather with...

▪ **WONDER BREAD.** "The best thing I've found for cleaning patent leather is a slice of Wonder Bread. Just take the slice and rub it over the item."

—BEVAN C., *Plantation, Florida*

Pencil

Clean pencil marks with...

▪ **HUGGIES BABY WIPES.** "Huggies Baby Wipes are great for removing pencil marks from white painted walls."

—ROXANNE C., *Detroit, Michigan*

Pet Hair

Clean pet hair from furniture with...

▪ **HUGGIES BABY WIPES.** "My dog sheds badly. The couch was full of hair, and our vacuum cleaner was broken. In desperation, I grabbed my son's Huggies Baby Wipes. They worked great. I will be using them from now on to wipe hair from couches."

—CARRIE P., *New Hartford, New York*

Piano Keys

Clean piano keys with...

▪ **CREST TOOTHPASTE.** "Regular Crest Toothpaste does a wonderful job polishing antique piano keys (the ivory, not the plastic types). Brush as you would your own teeth."

—JAMES P., *Abigdon, Virginia*

▪ **HELLMANN'S OR BEST REAL MAYONNAISE.** "You can use Hellmann's Real Mayonnaise to clean the ivory keys to your piano."

—VALERIE L., *Richmond, California*

Plasticware

Clean tomato sauce stains from Tupperware and Rubbermaid containers with...

▪ **CLOROX BLEACH.** "Mix one-eighth cup Clorox with one-quarter cup water, and soak plastic containers in the solution for ten minutes to clean stains."

—JANE D., *Mississauga, Ontario*

▪ **EFFERDENT.** "Fill your Tupperware or Rubbermaid bowls and containers with very hot water, drop in two Efferdent tablets, and let them sit overnight. Then wash as usual with detergent."

—CHARLA D., *Ashtabula, Ohio*

▪ **REALEMON.** "Rub discolored plastic storage items with ReaLemon and let sit in the sun for a day or so. Works like a charm."

—SUSANNAH B., *Gulfport, Florida*

Clean Rubbermaid and Tupperware containers with...

- **PURELL.** "If you add a squirt of Purell hand sanitizer to your Rubbermaid or Tupperware container when washing, you will have a squeaky clean container."

—Lynn C., *Boynton Beach, Florida*

Pool Balls

Clean pool balls with...

- **MIRACLE WHIP.** "Use Miracle Whip to clean discolored pool balls. Just use it straight from the jar. I have no idea why it works, but it does."

—David L., *Houston, Texas*

Refrigerators

Clean mold from refrigerator drains with...

- **CLOROX BLEACH.** "Mix three-quarters cup Clorox to a gallon of water, and use a turkey baster to shoot the solution into refrigerator drains."

—Louise G., *Arlington, Texas*

Freshen the air in a refrigerator with...

- **MCCORMICK** OR **SCHILLING VANILLA EXTRACT.** "If, after cleaning your refrigerator, you're still plagued by that bad smell, wipe down the inside of your fridge with vanilla extract and you will have a fresh vanilla smell."

—Jill F., *Gansevoort, New York*

- **USA TODAY.** "Filling an empty, unplugged refrigerator with crumpled up balls of newspaper will absorb unpleasant odors."

—Joel K., *Kempner, Texas*

Silver

Clean tarnished silver with...

- **ARM & HAMMER BAKING SODA** AND **REYNOLDS WRAP.** "Dissolve two tablespoons of baking soda in a stainless steel pan filled with water. Place a sheet of Reynolds Wrap aluminum foil in the pan, and place the silver item(s) on top of the foil. Heat the pan on the stove on low heat (without boiling) and watch the tarnish disappear."

—DAN J., *Pasadena, California*

■ **BIZ.** "Several years ago I noticed that my stainless steel silverware was looking very old. I had been soaking my dish drainer in a Biz solution and decided to try it on my stainless steel. It works great on both. Be sure to use Biz with the little green crystals in it."

—CAROL L., *Largo, Florida*

■ **COLGATE TOOTHPASTE.** "I use Colgate Toothpaste to polish silver, including my jewelry and flute."

—MARY B., *Slidell, Louisiana*

■ **HEINZ KETCHUP.** "The acid from the tomatoes removes that black gunk from silver jewelry. Squirt a little ketchup on a paper towel or clean cloth, rub gently into the tarnish, and *voila*. If the tarnish is heavy, soak the item in the ketchup for about fifteen minutes, then rub it, and rinse. Do not soak in ketchup too long; ketchup is so acidic it can ruin the finish on some silver."

—MONICA L., *Laguna Hills, California*

■ **MCCORMICK** OR **SCHILLING CREAM OF TARTAR.** "Use a paste made from Cream of Tartar and water to clean silver."

—SHARON H., *Hemet, California*

■ **MORTON SALT** AND **REALEMON.** "Mix two tablespoons of Morton Salt to one tablespoon ReaLemon lemon juice. Carefully rub the paste on the tarnished silver item, then wipe clean with a dry cloth. Repeat if necessary."

—BECKY H., *Bakersville, California*

■ **SOFTSOAP INSTANT ANTIBACTERIAL HAND GEL.** "Squirt a little Softsoap on a clean cloth and rub the silver. Oxidized silver sparkles like new."

—VERNON M., *Morgan Hill, California*

■ **WINDEX.** "Windex removes light tarnish from silver. Spray and polish clean."

—CATHERINE B., *Athens, Georgia*

Sliding Doors

Clean sliding door tracks with...

■ **WD-40.** "Spray WD-40 into the grooves and wipe with Q-Tips Cotton Swabs or paper towels. This not only cleans the tracks, but makes the doors easier to slide."

—PATTI W., *Thornton, Colorado*

Sponges

Wipe down the kitchen counter with...

■ **WONDER BREAD.** "Lost the sponge you use to wipe down the kitchen counter? Just use a piece of Wonder Bread."

—FRANK H., *Stamford, Connecticut*

Sports Bottles

Clean sports bottles with...

■ **EFFERDENT.** "Fill the sports bottle with warm water, add two Efferdent tablets, let sit for five minutes, then rinse well."

—HENRY T., *Munster, Ontario*

Static Electricity

Eliminate static electricity from your television screen or venetian blinds with...

■ **BOUNCE.** "Wipe the screen or blinds with a sheet of Bounce to keep dust from resetting."

—ANGIE L., *Norman, Oklahoma*

Steam Rooms

Deodorize a musty steam room with...

■ **MCCORMICK** OR **SCHILLING VANILLA EXTRACT.** "Are you tired of that stale, musty smell in the steam room at your local health spa? Just pour a few drops of McCormick or Schilling Vanilla Extract where the steam comes out for a wonderful smelling room."

—TOM H., *Clarksburg, West Virginia*

Stoves

Clean stove drip pans with...

- **CASCADE.** "I use Cascade to clean my stove top burner drip pans. I just put very hot water in my sink, add one-half cup Cascade, let the pans soak for a few minutes, and—presto—they're clean and shiny."

  —JERI D., *Wichita Falls, Texas*

Clean stove pit rings with...

- **ARM & HAMMER BAKING SODA.** "Fill a large pot with water, add two tablespoons Arm & Hammer Baking Soda, drop in the stove pit rings, place on the stove, and bring to a boil. Let cool and the baked-on food will wash off easily. There's no need to scrub and scour."

  —CATHERINE V., *Paris, Ontario*

Clean a stove with...

- **COLGATE TOOTHPASTE.** "I've used Colgate Toothpaste to remove cooking oil from the stovetop after I finish cooking. I place a dollop of toothpaste on a clean cloth and wipe. The toothpaste helps clean off the oil without leaving any slickness behind. Afterwards, I wipe the stove top clean with a damp cloth. It's great for countertops as well."

  —NICOLE P., *Bronx, New York*

- **HEINZ WHITE VINEGAR.** "I use Heinz Vinegar to clean my stove. It leaves my stove clean, shining like glass, and smelling fresh."

  —TOLIDA D., *Richlands, North Carolina*

- **LIPTON TEA.** "I brew a triple-strength cup of Lipton Tea which I use to clean the stovetop after cooking greasy hamburgers."

  —PAT M., *Brooklyn, New York*

- **MORTON SALT.** "Sprinkle Morton Salt on a spill on the stove. It acts as a cleanser and scouring agent, less abrasive than regular scouring agents."

  —CHRISTINE G., *Renfrew, Pennsylvania*

- **SHOUT.** "I spray Shout stain remover on baked-on grease on my stove top. I let it set for a little bit and then just wipe clean."

  —JO A., *Princeton, Kentucky*

Swimming Pools

Clean body oils from a swimming pool with a...

- **WILSON TENNIS BALL.** "Keep a tennis ball floating in your swimming pool. It absorbs oil."

  —CRYSTAL N., *Honolulu, Hawaii*

Real-Life Story

GOOD TILL THE LAST DROP

"**Warning: I once poured Maxwell House Coffee grounds into our central air registers in the hopes of deodorizing the whole house at once. When my husband turned on the heat, coffee grounds went flying all over the house.**"

—MELISSA S., *Conway, South Carolina*

Table-Saw Blades

Clean table-saw blades with...

- **EASY-OFF OVEN CLEANER.** "As a woodworker, I use Easy-Off Oven Cleaner to clean my table-saw blades. They get gummed up from sap and slow down the cutting action. Spray with the oven cleaner, let soak for a few minutes. Wearing rubber gloves and eye protection, use an old toothbrush to scrub around the teeth. Rinse with water. It works much better than the commercial stuff."

  —ALFRED K., *Simpsonville, South Carolina*

Tea Kettles

Clean hard-water stains and calcium build-up from a tea kettle with...

- **COCA-COLA.** "If you have lime scale in your kettle, it can be cleaned off by using Coca-Cola."

  —BEN P., *Hereford, England*

- **EFFERDENT.** "Fill the teapot with water, drop in two Efferdent tablets, let sit overnight, then scrub with a bottle brush and rinse with hot water."

  —ANNETTE D., *Colorado Springs, Colorado*

- **HEINZ WHITE VINEGAR.** "Pour three cups of Heinz White Vinegar into your tea kettle, fill the rest with water, and let sit overnight to remove stains or calcium build-up."

  —LINDA D., *Consecon, Ontario*

Telephones
Disinfect a telephone with...

- **SOFTSOAP INSTANT ANTIBACTERIAL HAND GEL.** "Simply take a paper towel, fold it in quarters, pump one squirt of Softsoap Instant Antibacterial Hand Gel onto the paper towel, and rub on the phone."

  —SHERYL L., *Clearlake, California*

Televisions
Clean a television screen with...

- **ARMOR ALL.** "You can use Armor All to polish just about anything. It gives things a really nice shine. On TV screens, it helps to keep the dust from being attracted to it."

  —BELINDA M., *Richland, Washington*

- **HUGGIES BABY WIPES.** "Huggies Baby Wipes are great for a quick way to wipe fingerprints off a television screen."

  —OLENA F., *Lake Villa, Illinois*

Tempera Paint
Clean tempera paint from walls, floors, and tables with...

- **HUGGIES BABY WIPES.** "Just wipe off the tempera paint with Huggies Baby Wipes."

  —STEPHANIE G., *Overland Park, Kansas*

Thermos Bottles

Clean Thermos bottles and decanters with...

- ■ **ARM & HAMMER BAKING SODA.** "Mix two tablespoons of Arm & Hammer Baking soda in two cups hot water and let it soak away coffee stains in Thermos bottles and decanters."

  —CARYN F., *Tucson, Arizona*

- ■ **EFFERDENT.** "Fill a Thermos with water, drop in two Efferdent tablets, and let sit overnight. The Thermos comes out clean and smelling fresh."

  —ANDRA S., *Richmond, California*

Toasters

Shine a toaster with...

- ■ **COLGATE TOOTHPASTE.** "Use toothpaste to shine up your toaster."

  —JENETTE G., *Wyoming, Michigan*

Toys

Clean toys with...

- ■ **HUGGIES BABY WIPES.** "I also use Huggies Baby Wipes to wipe down toys that look dirty."

  —DAVID N., *Ashland, Oregon*

Varnished Wood

Rejuvenate varnished wood with...

- ■ **ARMOR ALL.** "I had an old door with a varnish over cherry stain. I could not find any way to renew the milky finish nor could I find cherry stain. One day, in desperation, I used Armor All on it. It made the varnish look like new for about two months. Eventually I found a varnish, but I kind of missed the old treatment. It was a lot less work."

  —JIM L., *Laramie, Wyoming*

Vases

Clean vases with...

■ **EFFERDENT.** "Just fill the vase with water, add two Efferdent tablets, wait ten minutes, then rinse. The denture cleanser gets in all the nooks and crannies without a brush, and leaves everything sparkly. (And it's nontoxic)."

—MARLA T., *Centralia, Illinois*

Venetian Blinds

Clean venetian blinds with...

■ **BOUNCE.** "I use Bounce to dust my blinds."

—LORI A., *Medford, Oregon*

■ **CASCADE.** "Just sprinkle one-half to one cup Cascade into warm water in a bathtub. Place your venetian blinds in the tub and let soak for five to ten minutes. Use a sponge or cloth to rub over each blind. Rinse clean with a hand-held shower nozzle, or take the blinds outside, hang them on a clothes line, and rinse with a hose."

—BETTY B., *Portland, Oregon*

■ **DOW BATHROOM CLEANER.** "I own a Bed and Breakfast and dirty blinds used to be a hassle to clean. Now I simply take down greasy mini-blinds, spray them with Dow in the bathtub, and let sit for ten minutes to let the Scrubbing Bubbles work. Then I rinse them clean with hot water. A miracle!"

—KARA ANNE K., *Austin, Texas*

Vinyl Siding

Clean vinyl siding with...

■ **THOMPSON'S DECK WASH.** "Use Thompson's Deck Wash to clean the vinyl siding on your house or trailer."

—CLYDE K., *Tuscola, Illinois*

Walls

Clean walls with...

- **HUGGIES BABY WIPES.** "Baby wipes remove food splatters from walls without scrubbing or harming the wall in any way."

  —LYNDA H., *Lansing, Michigan*

- **LYSOL.** "To clean almost anything off painted walls, use Lysol Antibacterial Kitchen cleaner. It works well and leaves a good smell, too."

  —HEATHER A., *New Haven, Missouri*

Washing Machines

Clean soap scum from a washing machine with...

- **ARM & HAMMER BAKING SODA.** "Every once in a while, I do a load of laundry using just Arm & Hammer Baking Soda. There is enough soap built up inside the washer to clean the clothes, and the baking soda gets rid of the rest. The washer is free from soap build-up once the load is finished."

  —KELLI H., *Winthrop, Massachusetts*

Whirlpool Baths

Clean pipes in a whirlpool bath with...

- **CASCADE.** "I use Cascade to clean out the pipes in whirlpool bathtubs. Fill the bathtub with enough warm water to run the whirlpool. Add two cups Cascade and run the system for fifteen minutes, then drain the water, refill with fresh water and run the system for one minute to rinse it out. Doing this once a month keeps the system clean."

  —DAN K., *Albany, Georgia*

Window Sills

Clean window sills with...

- **HUGGIES BABY WIPES.** "I take Huggies Baby Wipes outside and use them to clean the aluminum window sills. They clean them up great."

  —DAVID N., *Ashland, Oregon*

Window Screens

Clean window screens with...

- **CASCADE.** "Dissolve one-quarter cup Cascade in one gallon of very hot water. Scrub window screens with a large scrub brush. Rinse with a hose."

  —Harriet Z., *Hubbard Lake, Michigan*

Windows

Clean windows with...

- **CANADA DRY CLUB SODA.** "Use club soda to clean windows. It's great."

  —Mary Kay C., *Ft. Lauderdale, Florida*

- **CASCADE.** "Mix two tablespoons Cascade in a gallon of water in a bucket. Use a clean mop and wash the windows outside. Rinse with water from a hose. The windows will dry without streaks or spots and won't need to be finished with a glass cleaner."

  —Nancy P., *Tracy City, Tennessee*

- **HEINZ WHITE VINEGAR.** "You don't have to spend money on paper towels or expensive glass cleaner. In an empty spray bottle, mix one-quarter cup Heinz White Vinegar to one quart water. Now find yesterday's newspaper. Spray glass and wipe with crumpled newspaper."

  —Marcie M., *Kempton, Pennsylvania*

- **KINGSFORD'S CORN STARCH** AND **DAWN.** Mix one teaspoon Kingsford's Corn Starch and one teaspoon Dawn dishwashing liquid in a gallon of water to make an amazing window cleaner. Just clean the windows with a clean cloth soaked in the foamy liquid. Dry with a clean cloth. No streaks."

  —Laura B., *Cochrane, Alberta*

- **MCCORMICK** OR **SCHILLING CREAM OF TARTAR.** "Mix a teaspoon of Cream of Tartar with water in a sixteen-ounce trigger-spray bottle to make a great window cleaner."

  —Shirley H., *Cairnbrook, Pennsylvania*

- **MR. COFFEE FILTERS.** "Clean windows with Mr. Coffee Filters. They're 100-percent virgin paper and don't leave behind any lint."

    —JEANETTE F., *Fenton, Missouri*

- **PLEDGE.** "Using Pledge on the outsides of windows keeps them shiny and clean for a long time. When cleaning time comes around again, they clean up much faster and easier. You may not need to reapply wax for several years. I've had Pledge on my windows for about five to six years."

    —MARLENE H., *Wilmore, Kentucky*

- **RAIN-X.** "Rain-X window treatment product added to automobile windshield washer product (antifreeze or regular) washes house windows better than commercial products. Nothing sticks to the windows anymore."

    —KAREN E., *Cleveland, Ohio*

- **SMIRNOFF VODKA AND DAWN.** "Fill a spray bottle with one part Smirnoff Vodka to one part water and add a couple drops of Dawn dishwashing liquid, and shake well to make an excellent cleanser for glass and windows."

    —MARIDEL A., *Sacramento, California*

- **USA TODAY.** "I use old newspaper (rather than paper towels) and glass cleaner to clean windows, glass table tops, and mirrors. Using newspaper does not leave streaks, while paper towels do."

    —DEANNA W., *Birmingham, Alabama*

Wood Paneling

Clean wood paneling with...

- **BARBASOL SHAVING CREAM.** "We use Barbasol Shaving Cream to clean and polish our wood-paneled walls. It not only removes dust, grime, and finger prints, but it also leaves the walls shiny and looking like new."

    —DONNA E., *Griffin, Georgia*

Cook It

3

Apple Pie

Enhance an apple pie with...

- **JELL-O.** "Before putting the top crust on a two-crust apple pie, sprinkle one-quarter cup Jell-O powder (raspberry, strawberry, or whatever flavor you please) over the apples. Cover with crust and bake. The Jell-O adds a wonderful flavor and color to the pie."

  —LYDIA W., *Dover, New Hampshire*

Baked Beans

Lessen the potency of baked beans with...

- **COCA-COLA.** "Add one-half can of Coca-Cola in cooking beans to prevent flatulence from eating the beans. My mom has used this trick for years and it really works."

  —MARLENE L., *Pasadena, Texas*

Barbecue

Light a charcoal grill with...

- **CONAIR PRO STYLE 1600.** "Simply run an extension cord from the house to where your grill is and set the Conair hand-held hair dryer on high. It beats blowing."

  —MATTHEW R., *Maple Glen, Pennsylvania*

- **WD-40.** "Did you know that you can use WD-40 as a substitute charcoal lighter fluid?" [Warning: Always be careful when using any flammable liquid around a fire. Do not spray WD-40 directly onto an open flame or burning embers.]

  —BILL H., *Hackettstown, New Jersey*

Barbecue Sauce

Make barbecue sauce with...

- **COCA-COLA** AND **HEINZ KETCHUP.** "Coca-Cola mixed with Heinz Ketchup makes an excellent barbecue sauce."

  —GLENDA T., *Oakland City, Indiana*

- **MAXWELL HOUSE COFFEE.** "Add a tablespoon or two of dissolved instant Maxwell House Coffee to your favorite store-bought barbecue sauce for an authentic Cajun bite."

  —STEVEN B., *Redmond, Washington*

Beef

Marinade beef with...

- **COCA-COLA.** "Place steak in a Ziploc storage bag, pour Coca-Cola into the bag, and marinate for two to three hours. Grill the steak as usual over open fire or grill. The steak will melt in your mouth."

  —BRENDA D., *Poultney, Vermont*

Bratwurst

Grill bratwurst over a barbecue or campfire in a...

- **MAXWELL HOUSE COFFEE CAN.** "Maxwell House Coffee cans make excellent pots on the grill so you don't have to ruin a good pot. We use it to grill bratwurst in beer."

  —ESTON B., *Shreveport, Louisiana*

Bread

Bake pumpkin bread in a...

- **MAXWELL HOUSE COFFEE CAN.** "Mix the bread ingredients, stuff into a clean, empty Maxwell House coffee can as a mold, and put in the oven."

  —JEFFREY S., *Indianapolis, Indiana*

Brown Sugar

Soften brown sugar with...

■ **WONDER BREAD.** "Hardened brown sugar can be softened by placing it in an air-tight container and adding a slice of Wonder Bread. Let sit overnight."

—MOLLY S., *Phelan, California*

Make brown sugar with...

■ **GRANDMA'S MOLASSES.** "Mix one teaspoon Grandma's Molasses (unsulfured mild) with one-quarter cup granulated sugar. For larger quantities, mix one-quarter cup molasses to one cup sugar. This is basically how brown sugar is made at refineries."

—VINCE A., *Aberdeen, New Jersey*

Brownies

Bake moist brownies with...

■ **COCA-COLA.** "Substitute Coca-Cola for water in brownie recipes. The brownies come out yummy and so moist."

—JULIE P., *Newton, Massachusetts*

Separate brownies with...

■ **MR. COFFEE FILTERS.** "Place Mr. Coffee Filters between layers of brownies or cookies when serving on a plate to keep the layers from sticking to each other."

—SALLY F., *Knox, Indiana*

Cake

Mix cake batter with...

■ **ZIPLOC STORAGE BAGS.** "Fill a gallon-size Ziploc Storage Bag with cake batter ingredients, then squeeze the bag to mix."

—SUE T., *Tillamook, Oregon*

Substitute for cooking oil with...

■ **MIRACLE WHIP.** "You can use Miracle Whip as cooking oil in baking a cake. If you run out of Crisco or the like, just add the same amount of Miracle Whip. It contains a lot of oil and doesn't affect the taste."

—ROBERT H., *New Brighton, Minnesota*

Candles

Avoid scorching your fingertips when lighting candles with...

- **CREAMETTES SPAGHETTI.** "Take an uncooked piece of Creamettes Spaghetti, light the end, and let it serve as one long match."

  —LESLIE S., *Dayton, Ohio*

Celery

Prolong the shelf life of celery with...

- **REYNOLDS WRAP.** "Wrap celery in Reynolds Wrap when storing it in the refrigerator. It will keep for weeks."

  —GRAHAM B., *West Richland, Washington*

Cheese

Strain cheese with...

- **L'EGGS SHEER ENERGY PANTY HOSE.** "Boil L'eggs Panty Hose in water, let cool, and use to strain cheese before pressing."

  —SHIRLEY W., *Blairsden, California*

Prolong the life of cheese with...

- **HEINZ VINEGAR.** "Soak a paper towel in vinegar, wring it out, and place the towel and cheese together in an airtight container."

  —MICHELLE M., *Dana, North Carolina*

Cheese Graters

Prevent cheese from sticking to graters with...

- **PAM NO STICK COOKING SPRAY.** "Spray Pam No Stick Cooking Spray on graters before grating cheese. The cheese grates better, and clean up is much easier."

  —LIZ Y., *El Centro, California*

Chicken Stock

Strain chicken stock with...

- **MR. COFFEE FILTERS.** "When making chicken stock, I drain the stock through a Mr. Coffee Filter to help remove fat."

—LINDA C., *Sarasota, Florida*

Coffee

Lighten coffee with...

- **NESTLÉ HOT CHOCOLATE MIX.** "If you're all out of coffee creamer, add a teaspoon of Nestle Hot Chocolate mix to your coffee to lighten it."

—CARLIE J., *Phoenix, Arizona*

Coffee Filters

Substitute for coffee filters with...

- **BOUNTY.** "Run out of coffee filters? Tear off enough Bounty paper towel to fit in the coffee basket. Put in fresh ground coffee and proceed as usual."

—LORRAINE C., *Reno, Nevada*

Corn on the Cob

Flavor corn on the cob with...

- **CARNATION NONFAT DRY MILK.** "You can use Carnation Nonfat Dry Milk when you boil corn on the cob, instead of sugar or salt. Just sprinkle a little powdered milk in the water and it makes the corn very tasty."

—TERRI B., *Aurora, Colorado*

Corned Beef

Prevent corned beef from shrinking with...

- **HEINZ VINEGAR.** "Add two tablespoons of Heinz Vinegar to the water when boiling corned beef and it will not shrink."

—INGE B., *Hudson, Florida*

THE FIRST LITE BEER

"The Miller Brewing Co. has in the past credited itself as the first to develop and bottle 'Lite' beer. Actually, Miller acquired the 'Lite' name and the right to brew that beer by purchasing Meister Brau Brewing Co. of Chicago around 1971, after Meister Brau filed for bankruptcy. Miller's superior marketing prowess and deep advertising pockets propelled Miller Lite beer into a great selling product.

"'Lite' beer was first concocted and trademarked by Meister Brau in Chicago in the late 1960s. The first few commercially available Lite beers were brewed at The Buckeye Brewery of Toledo, Ohio, a small, one-kettle company, purchased by Meister Brau around 1965. At the time of its closing in 1972, Buckeye was the second-oldest continually operated business in Toledo, surpassed only by our local newspaper, *The Toledo Blade*. Buckeye was established in 1837, and *The Blade* was founded in 1835."

—DALE B., *Toledo, Ohio*

Deodorize

Deodorize hands that smell from onions and fish with...

■ **MAXWELL HOUSE COFFEE.** "Fill your palm with Maxwell House Coffee grounds (used or unused), add water if using fresh grounds, rub your hands together for one minute, then rinse with running water. The strong smell will be gone."

—JUDY S., *Middletown, Ohio*

■ **REALEMON.** "Rubbing your hands with ReaLemon removes the smell of onions, fish, and the like. I just pour a little lemon juice into my palm and rub my hands together. It always works."

—MADELEINE K. *Lancaster, Pennsylvania*

Deviled Eggs

Fill deviled eggs with a...

- **ZIPLOC STORAGE BAG.** "Put the ingredients for deviled eggs in a Ziploc bag, cut a corner off the bag, and squeeze to fill the eggs without making a mess."

  —SANDRA W., *Richlands, Virginia*

Dressing

Bake Thanksgiving dressing with...

- **MAXWELL HOUSE COFFEE.** "We bake our Thanksgiving dressing in large and small Maxwell House Coffee cans. You spoon the dressing into the cans and cover with aluminum foil and bake for two hours at 350 degrees Fahrenheit. Store any leftover dressing in the cans by sealing the cans with the original plastic lids."

  —FRAN C., *Pittsburgh, Pennsylvania*

Eggs

Poach eggs with...

- **HEINZ VINEGAR.** "A couple of splashes of Heinz Vinegar in the water when poaching eggs keeps the eggs in a tight, more presentable form. Don't add salt. Salting the water will cause the eggs to 'shatter.'"

  —CARMEN T., *Cheektowaga, New York*

Shell hard-boiled eggs easily with...

- **WESSON CORN OIL.** "Adding two tablespoons of Wesson Corn Oil in the water will make your hard-boiled eggs easier to peel."

  —ELAINE N., *Seattle, Washington*

Electric Mixer

Prevent an electric mixer from making a mess with...

- **PAM NO STICK COOKING SPRAY.** "I spray the beaters to my mixer with Pam No Stick Cooking Spray before I mix up batter. It keeps the batter in the bowl."

  —MARLENE M., *Denver, Colorado*

Fish

Deodorize fish with...

- **HEINZ WHITE VINEGAR.** "Soaking fish in a mixture of equal parts Heinz White Vinegar and water for a few minutes gets rid of the fishy odor and doesn't affect the fish flavor."

    —MARY W., *Gloucester, Virginia*

Frosting

Put frosting on a cake with...

- **ZIPLOC STORAGE BAGS.** "Place the frosting in a Ziploc storage bag, seal, cut a corner, and squeeze."

    —LINDA W., *North Castle, Pennsylvania*

Decorate cookies and cakes with melted chocolate by using a...

- **ZIPLOC STORAGE BAG.** "Fill a Ziploc storage bag with chocolate chips, seal the bag shut, and place in a pot of boiling water to melt the chocolate. Snip one corner and you have the perfect decorating tool."

    —CARRIE P., *Coalhurst, Alberta*

Fruits and Vegetables

Clean pesticides and insects from fruits and vegetables with...

- **ARM & HAMMER BAKING SODA.** "Wet fruits and vegetables, then sprinkle with a little Arm & Hammer Baking Soda. Rinse well before eating."

    —DAVID K., *Bethlehem, Georgia*

- **CLOROX BLEACH.** "Adding one-half cup Clorox in enough water to cover fruit and veggies will do away with any lingering bugs and also extend the storage lifetime. Rinse well before eating."

    —AL S., *Albuquerque, New Mexico*

- **HEINZ VINEGAR.** "To wash sprays and chemicals from your store-bought veggies, simply fill your kitchen sink with cold water and add one-half to three-quarter cups of Heinz Vinegar. Soak the fruits and vegetables in the water for a few minutes, using a paper towel to loosen any residue. Then rinse clean with cold water."

—LINDA S., *Charlotte, North Carolina*

Ginger

Preserve diced, fresh ginger in your refrigerator with...

■ **SMIRNOFF VODKA.** "Peel and chop fresh ginger, put in a jar, and top off with Smirnoff Vodka. The ginger will last one year in your refrigerator and is very convenient to have on hand."

—KARIMA P., *Pittsburgh, Pennsylvania*

Gloves

Improvise plastic gloves with...

■ **ZIPLOC STORAGE BAGS** AND **PAM NO STICK COOKING SPRAY.** "When spreading sticky foods, put each hand inside its own Ziploc storage bag, coat the outside of the bag with Pam No Stick Cooking Spray, and spread the messy ingredients (like flattening Rice Krispy Squares in the pan before cooling)."

—JEAN H., *Bentonville, Arkansas*

Goose

Reduce the gamey taste of wild goose with...

■ **7-UP.** "Pouring a can of 7-Up over a wild goose helps to cut the gamey taste."

—JOANNE A., *Alexandria, Virginia*

Gravy

Make red-eye gravy with...

■ **MAXWELL HOUSE COFFEE.** "In the South we make red-eye gravy by frying ham and adding water to the drippings. This is usually too weak to look like red-eye gravy. Adding a teaspoon of instant Maxwell House Coffee makes the gravy look and taste like the real thing."

—MARJORIE S., *Savannah, Georgia*

Rescue burnt gravy with...

- **JIF PEANUT BUTTER.** "Guests knocking at the door and you just burned your holiday gravy? You can use a tablespoon of Jif Peanut Butter (creamy) to salvage the mess. Just remove any burnt pieces from the gravy while still in the saucepan and stir in peanut butter on very low heat. It will eliminate that horrible burnt taste."

—MADCAKES, *Trenton, New Jersey*

Grilled Cheese Sandwiches

Make a grilled cheese sandwich with a...

- **PROCTER-SILEX ULTRA-EASE IRON** AND **REYNOLDS WRAP.** "Wrap a cheese sandwich in Reynolds Wrap aluminum foil and iron each side until golden brown."

—BEV T., *Revere, Massachusetts*

Ham

Bake a moist ham with...

- **COCA-COLA.** "While baking a ham in aluminum foil in a pan, baste it with one can of Coca-Cola. For the last half hour of cooking, remove the aluminum foil and allow the ham to bake directly in the soda. It makes a delicious gravy."

—NAOMI M., *Oshawa, Ontario*

Hot Chocolate

Sweeten hot chocolate with...

- **JIF PEANUT BUTTER.** "Add a tablespoon of Jif Peanut Butter to a cup of hot chocolate and stir well for a real taste treat."

—TOM H., *Clarksburg, West Virginia*

Hot Dog Buns

Substitute for a hot dog bun with...

- **EGGO WAFFLES.** "Use Eggo Waffles as hot dog buns. Adding a little Log Cabin Maple Syrup for flavor really brings the two tastes together for a real treat."

—MEGAN F., *Kailua, Hawaii*

Ice Cream

Make ice cream with a...

■ **MAXWELL HOUSE COFFEE CAN.** "Mix up a batch of pudding to fill about two-thirds of a small, empty Maxwell House Coffee can. Tape the plastic lid on to make the can watertight. Place the small can into a large, empty Maxwell House Coffee can. Pack the large can with ice and rock salt. Tape the plastic lid on so the larger can is also watertight. Give it to the kids and tell them to take it outside and roll it back and forth to each other for a half-hour and then bring it back. When they do, bring out ice cream cones and scoop it in."

—ANNE Y., *Scranton, North Carolina*

Ice Cream Cones

Prevent ice cream cone drips with...

■ **JET-PUFFED MARSHMALLOWS.** "Stuff a Jet-Puffed Marshmallow in the bottom of a sugar cone to prevent ice cream drips."

—GRAHAM B., *West Richland, Washington*

Jars

Open jars with ease with...

■ **PLAYTEX LIVING GLOVES.** "If you have a problem opening a jar, put on a pair of Playtex Living Gloves. They give you a non-slip grip that makes opening jars easy."

—GRAHAM B., *West Richland, Washington*

Jelly

Strain homemade jelly with...

■ **MR. COFFEE FILTERS.** "Try using a Mr. Coffee Filter to strain the impurities from homemade jelly. We no longer have any more hazy jelly around this house."

—J.P., *Blanket, Texas*

Lamb

Reduce the mutton taste from lamb with...

- **CANADA DRY GINGER ALE.** "Roasting and basting lamb in Canada Dry Ginger Ale removes the mutton taste. It's amazing. It really improves lamb bought in the supermarket."

  —MARY S., *Colorado Springs, Colorado*

Lettuce

Prolong the life of salad mix with...

- **BOUNTY.** "A sheet of Bounty paper towel placed in an open bag of salad mix will prevent the lettuce from turning brown. The paper towel absorbs moisture."

  —SALLY P., *Liverpool, New York*

Liver

Sweeten the taste of liver with...

- **CARNATION CONDENSED MILK.** "Soaking liver in milk for at least four hours gets rid of that strong taste and actually makes it edible. I learned this trick from a Swedish friend many years ago."

  —PHYLLIS S., *Exton, Pennsylvania*

Meat

Marinate meats with...

- **HEINZ VINEGAR.** "I have always soaked my meat in Heinz White Vinegar. It's more tasty and it's purified."

  —HENRIETTA N., *Exeter, Pennsylvania*

- **LIPTON TEA.** "Add two Lipton Tea bags when cooking pot roast. The tannic acid in the tea makes the meat tender and juicy. Instant tea also works well. A few tablespoons will do the trick."

  —KATHY S., *Lock Haven, Pennsylvania*

- **7-UP OR SPRITE.** "Sprite or 7-Up can be used for marinating meat to make it tender and tasty."

  —MARIDEL A., *Sacramento, California*

- **WISH-BONE ITALIAN DRESSING.** "Wish-Bone Italian Dressing is a fabulous marinade for venison, chicken, rabbit, and duck. Simply cover meat with dressing overnight, refrigerate, drain, and cook as desired."
  —MARY LOU G., *Marine City, Michigan*

- **ZIPLOC STORAGE BAGS.** "Use Ziploc Storage Bags to marinate food. The bags allow the marinade to really cover the food, and you only have to turn the bag over (as opposed to stirring the marinade in a bowl)."
  —LINDA W., *North Castle, Pennsylvania*

Napkins

Subsitute for napkins with...

- **MR. COFFEE FILTERS.** "In a pinch, you can use a Mr. Coffee Filter as a napkin or paper towel at those coffee stations that have run out of both."
  —JOHN M., *St. Louis Park, Missouri*

Onions

Store onions with...

- **L'EGGS SHEER ENERGY PANTY HOSE.** "Cut off the legs from a used, clean pair of L'eggs Panty Hose, insert one onion down to the bottom, tie a knot after it, and repeat until you either run out of onions or panty hose leg. Then hang the onions wherever you want. They stay good for a long time."
  —JANET B., *Eustis, Florida*

Prolong the life of onions with...

- **REYNOLDS WRAP.** "Wrap green onions in Reynolds Wrap aluminum foil. They keep fresh for a long time."
  —LYNN S., *Dubuque, Iowa*

Pie

Bake pies with...

- **GLAD FLEXIBLE STRAWS.** "Cut a Glad Flexible Straw into three-inch lengths and insert vertically into the pie crust, leaving one end exposed. Bake the pie as directed. The straws allow the steam to escape, preventing the pie from boiling over and making a mess."

—JODI T., *Thunder Bay, Ontario*

MACHINE CUISINE

"Machine cuisine is brightening the lives of the culinary-challenged," according to an article by Eileen Daspin in *The Wall Street Journal.* "People steam salmon in the dishwasher, dry spinach and shrimp in the dryer, and roast a chicken on the car engine during a long drive."

—CHRIS M., *Albuquerque, New Mexico*

Plasticware

Prevent tomato sauce from staining Tupperware or Rubbermaid containers with...

■ **PAM NO STICK COOKING SPRAY.** "Spray your Tupperware with Pam No Stick Cooking Spray before pouring in tomato-based sauces, and you won't get any more stains."

—GRAHAM B., *West Richland, Washington*

Pork Chops

Tenderize pork chops with...

■ **COCA-COLA.** "Before cooking, place the pork chops in a bowl filled with one can of Coca-Cola for at least two hours for very tender chops."

—JANET P., *Columbus, Ohio*

Potato Chips

Seal open potato chip bags with...

■ **SCOTCH PACKAGING TAPE.** "Scotch Packaging Tape sticks and re-sticks."

—AMY S., *Orlando, Florida*

Ribs

Marinate ribs with...

- **COCA-COLA.** "Another use for Coca-Cola is to marinate ribs. It makes the meat truly fall off the bone."

—JESSICA K., *Hudson, Florida*

Roasted Chicken

Roast a chicken with...

- **BUDWEISER.** "Prepare a whole chicken or game hen, place an open can of Budweiser upright inside the chicken. Sit the chicken on the grilling surface so the can stands up. You may have to adjust the drumsticks to balance the bird. The beer steam cooks the inner bird with an exceptional flavor. When finished discard the beer can and serve the chicken."

—CHRIS P., *Milledgeville, Georgia*

Rock Candy

Make colorful rock candy with...

- **KOOL-AID.** "Fill a clean, empty mayonnaise jar with 1/4 cup boiling hot water and slowly add 2 cups Domino sugar and one packet of Kool-Aid (whatever flavor you like). Stir well. Attach a nail to one end of a string and a pencil to the other end of the string. Place the pencil on the mouth of the jar so the nail hangs down into the thick sugar water without touching the bottom of the jar. Place the jar in a warm place and let it stand for a few days. The water evaporates and colorful rocky sugar crystals form on the string."

—RENEE W., *Bakersfield, California*

Salad

Toss a salad with...

- **ZIPLOC STORAGE BAGS.** "Simply put all of your ingredients in a one-gallon Ziploc Storage Bag, add the dressing, and seal the bag. Shake the bag until the salad is tossed and coated with dressing. It's simple and fool-proof."

—TRACY M., *Anaheim, California*

Salt

Prevent salt from sticking together with...

▪ **MINUTE RICE.** "Are you tired of having your salt stick together in the salt shaker after a week of rain and humidity? Tired of having to tap your salt shaker on the table to loosen up the salt? Simply add about twenty grains of Minute Rice inside the salt shaker. The rice absorbs the moisture, keeping your salt pouring freely."

—KENNY S., *Columbus, Mississippi*

Satay Sauce

Make satay sauce with...

▪ **JIF PEANUT BUTTER** AND **TABASCO PEPPER SAUCE.** "To make an excellent base for satay sauce, use one jar of peanut butter. Add sambal to taste, Tabasco Pepper Sauce for strength, and milk for fluidity."

—MAARTEN B., *Trondheim, Norway*

Sausages

Remove the grease from cooked sausage with...

▪ **MAXWELL HOUSE COFFEE.** "Just before the sausage is done in the pan, mix instant Maxwell House Coffee in hot water until it dissolves, then add it to the cooking sausage. The coffee absorbs all the grease, and the sausage tastes great."

—CYNDI Y., *Albuquerque, New Mexico*

Prevent large sausages from splitting with...

▪ **TROJAN NON-SCENTED CONDOMS.** "You can use Trojan non-scented condoms to prevent large sausages from splitting open when cooking. Just make sure the pot does not boil dry."

—GERALD H., *Enderby, British Columbia*

Snow Cones

Make tangy snow cones with...

▪ **TANG.** "Sprinkle Tang on a bowl full of snow and eat with a spoon. I've done this since childhood and my children do it now."

—DEBBIE C., *Webster, Indiana*

Sour Cream

Make sour cream with...

- **REDDI-WIP** AND **REALEMON.** "Add four drops of ReaLemon to a cup of Reddi-wip whipped cream, let sit for a half hour, and you've got a great sour cream substitute."

  —LEONA H., *Hamlin, Texas*

Substitute for sour cream with...

- **WISH-BONE RANCH DRESSING.** "Use Wish-Bone Ranch Dressing in place of sour cream or butter on your potato."

  —CARLIE J., *Phoenix, Arizona*

Spoons

Prevent food from sticking to a serving spoon with...

- **PAM NO STICK COOKING SPRAY.** "Spray Pam No Stick Cooking Spray on the serving spoon before dishing out sticky foods."

  —LIZ Y., *El Centro, California*

Strainers

Strain food with...

- **L'EGGS SHEER ENERGY PANTY HOSE.** "If you don't have a food strainer, use a clean pair of L'eggs Panty Hose."

  —KARA L., *San Antonio, Texas*

Strawberries

Remove strawberry stems with a...

- **GLAD FLEXIBLE STRAW.** "To remove stems from strawberries without cutting the entire top off, simply push the straight end of a Glad Flexible Straw through the center bottom of the straw-berry. The entire stem should poke through the top in one piece."

  —MICHAEL P., *Evansville, Indiana*

Thai Noodles

Make an exotic dish of Thai noodles with...

- **COCA-COLA.** "The chef at a Thai restaurant in Chiang Mai recommends tofu in a mixture of water, fish sauce, Coca-Cola, and star anise. Then add cooked noodles, bean sprouts, and chili powder."

—JULIE K., *Tamshui Town, Taiwan*

Turkey

Cook a turkey with...

- **COCA-COLA.** "Wash the turkey, place it in a plastic oven bag, pour one-half can of Coke over the turkey, and close the bag as directed. Before the last half hour, split the bag open to give the turkey a nice caramel brown. The Coke provides the salt, so there's no need to add any."

—MARLENE P., *Lubbock, Texas*

Wine

Chill wine quickly with...

- **ZIPLOC STORAGE BAGS.** "Pour the wine into a one-gallon Ziploc bag and swirl around in a sink filled with ice water. It chills the wine much faster than putting the bottle on ice."

—JIM K., *Lanesborough, Massachusetts*

Decorate It

Blacklight Paint

Paint blacklight designs with...

- **ERA.** "Use liquid Era to paint designs on the walls of your room, let dry, then turn on a blacklight for a glowing party atmosphere. Great for Halloween parties."

  —CATE H., *Glendale Heights, Illinois*

- **LIQUID TIDE.** "If you use liquid Tide to paint designs on your wall, they will dry clear and only show up under blacklight."

  —LAURA N., *Metairie, Louisiana*

Write in blacklight paint with...

- **MURINE TEARS.** "Write on skin or paper with Murine eye drops and it glows under blacklight as fluorescent yellow. This is an old trick from my college days in the early seventies."

  —FRAN G., *Calabasas, California*

Christmas

Keep cats away from the Christmas tree with...

- **BOUNCE.** "I discovered that encircling my Christmas tree with Bounce sheets keeps my cats away from my tree at night or whenever we have to leave the house for long periods during the day. I put the Bounce sheets down every night and pick them up every morning, but I hope this tip makes the holidays easier for all those cat lovers out there."

  —JOANNE A., *Granite City, Illinois*

Store Christmas lights in...

- ▣ **ZIPLOC STORAGE BAGS.** "Roll up each individual strand of Christmas lights and store in its own Ziploc Storeage Bag. The next year, you can easily test each individually packed strand of lights."

  —MICHELLE W., *Seattle, Washington*

Clean a wreath with...

- ▣ **ALBERTO VO5 HAIR SPRAY.** "Spraying a wreath with hair spray will make it look new again."

  —DEBORAH M., *Boguechitto, Mississippi*

- ▣ **CASCADE.** "Many years ago my grandmother gave me a home-made lace Christmas wreath. After she had passed away, it became one of my most cherished possessions. Over the years the wreath got dirty, but I could not clean it in the washing machine. So I put it in the dishwasher with some Cascade. When the cycle finished, the wreath was as white and clean as the day it was made. Once again I can display it with love and pride, rekindling fond memories of my grandmother."

  —KAREN W., *Albuquerque, New Mexico*

Prolong the life of a Christmas tree with...

- ▣ **HUGGIES DIAPERS.** "Remove all of the outer material from the core of a Huggies diaper. Place the crystals and cotton in a four-quart bowl. Pour two cups of filtered water over the diaper crystals. Wait twenty minutes. Add more water, a little at a time, and wait a few minutes between each addition until contents of bowl swells to the brim. Put water-filled crystals in a Christmas tree stand after tree is in place. The tree soaks up water from crystals. Water doesn't evaporate or splash. The tree will not require watering very often during holidays. Check reservoir now and then and carefully add a little more water if necessary."

  —DIXE HOPPER, *Madison, Tennessee*

Make snowflakes with...

- **MR. COFFEE FILTERS.** "Fold a Mr. Coffee Filter many times and cut tiny holes. When opened, it will look like a snowflake."

—JAN O., *Albany, Texas*

Keep angel hair in place with...

- **ALBERTO VO5 HAIR SPRAY.** "To decorate for Christmas, I place my nativity set on angel hair. Unfortunately, angel hair tends to drift around, refusing to stay put. I simply spray the angel hair with Alberto VO5 Hair Spray (just as I would hair), ending the problem with fly-aways. You may have to spray the angel hair several times, and be sure to keep the angel hair away from open flames."

—KAREN W., *Albuquerque, New Mexico*

Dried Flowers

Brighten dried flower arrangements or grapevine wreaths with...

- **ALBERTO VO5 HAIR SPRAY.** "Spray the flower arrangements or wreaths with Alberto VO5 Hair Spray. The dust won't be noticeable and the arrangement will have a slight shine as well."

—LORI B., *Baytown, Texas*

Halloween

Remove Halloween makeup with...

- **MIRACLE WHIP.** "Generously coat face or other makeup area with Miracle Whip, leave on for two minutes, then wash off."

—JENNY E., *Washington, Illinois*

Make Halloween makeup with...

- **MCCORMICK** OR **SCHILLING FOOD COLORING** AND **ELMER'S GLUE-ALL.** "Mix red food coloring and Elmer's White School Glue to imitate fake burned skin at Halloween for a trick-or-treater."

—MICHELE B., *Southaven, Mississippi*

Holiday Lanterns

Make decorative holiday lanterns with...

- **MAXWELL HOUSE COFFEE CANS.** "Spraypaint clean, empty Maxwell House Coffee cans with appropriate colors for the holiday, punch holes in the side of the can (a heart design on a red can for Valentine's Day, for instance), fill the can halfway with sand, and place a lit candle inside to make attractive sidewalk decorations."

  —JANET E., *Falmouth, Virginia*

Mashed Potatoes

Make colorful mashed potatoes with...

- **MCCORMICK** OR **SCHILLING FOOD COLORING.** "Add a few drops of food coloring to mashed potatoes to make festive holiday food."

  —LYNN H., *Port Charlotte, Florida*

Party Favors

Make party favors with...

- **MR. COFFEE FILTERS.** "Place candy in the middle of a Mr. Coffee Filter and tie the sides together with a ribbon."

  —PAT C., *Norwich, Connecticut*

Drive It 5

Battery Cable

Prevent a detached battery cable from touching metal with a...

- **WILSON TENNIS BALL.** "When you have to disconnect the car's negative battery cable to work on the car, you must prevent it from contacting the car frame or other metal. Simply cut a slit in a Wilson Tennis Ball and insert the negative battery connector into the rubber ball. The rubber tennis ball will not conduct electricity, so you can place it down without worrying about making contact with metal."

  —JEFF S., *Austin, Texas*

Battery Corrosion

Clean corrosion from automobile battery terminals with...

- **ARM & HAMMER BAKING SODA.** "Add a few teaspoons of Arm & Hammer Baking Soda to a cup of water, pour over the battery cable connections, and let it do its job. Then carefully wash off with water."

  —CHARLES G., *Boerne, Texas*

- **CANADA DRY CLUB SODA.** "Pour club soda over the battery corrosion to neutralize battery acid and dissolve acid deposits when changing a car battery."

  —BASIL A., *San Francisco, California*

- **COCA-COLA.** "Pouring Coca-Cola over battery terminals takes away the corrosion. Then coat with Vaseline to avoid future problems."

  —LEON C., *Fort Meyers, Florida*

Prevent corrosion on car battery terminals with...

■ **VASELINE PETROLEUM JELLY.** "Apply Vaseline to car battery terminals to keep them from corroding."

—MANDA M., *West Chester, Ohio*

Boats

Clean salt-water deposits from boat parts with...

■ **KOOL-AID.** "Mix six packs of unsweetened, cherry Kool-Aid with one-half gallon water in a bucket. Use to clean boat parts that have hard-to-reach areas encrusted with salt water."

—TARA M., *Oak Hall, Virginia*

Repel mice and raccoons from a covered boat with...

■ **BOUNCE.** "Place several sheets of Bounce on the floor of your boat before covering it for the winter to prevent mice and raccoons from setting up camp for the winter and destroying your interior."

—FRED H., *Wasaga Beach, Ontario*

Brakes

Clean brake dust from car wheels with...

■ **DAWN.** "Use Dawn dish detergent to wash brake dust from automobile wheels. It cuts through grease."

—JANET B., *Grapevine, Texas*

Prevent brake dust from sticking to car rims with...

■ **PAM NO STICK COOKING SPRAY.** "Spraying Pam No Stick Cooking Spray on the rims of your car prevents brake dust from sticking."

—JOANN B., *North Augusta, South Carolina*

Quiet squeaky brakes with...

■ **BON AMI.** "Throw a handful of Bon Ami cleanser at the brake pads. They'll quiet down for good."

—KIM B., *Fresno, California*

Bumpers

Remove rust stains from car bumpers with...

- **VEGEMITE.** "Smear on Vegemite and wipe off with a clean cloth."

—BOB D., *Nashville, Texas*

Bumper Stickers

Remove bumper stickers with...

- **MIRACLE WHIP.** "To remove bumper stickers, rub Miracle Whip over the entire bumper sticker. Let sit for a while. The bumper sticker will absorb the Miracle Whip which will dissolve the glue for easy removal."

—JOHN M., *Jupiter, Florida*

Car Sickness

Be prepared for car sickness with a...

- **KLEENEX TISSUE BOX.** "I always keep an empty box of Kleenex Tissues in any vehicle I am driving, including a wheelchair van. I open the top up and give it to passengers who experience car sickness. It's surprising how much the empty box will hold, and the box is easy to throw away. Believe me, it comes in handy. The box is easy to hold in your lap, and so far there haven't been any leaks."

—SUE H., *Wolfeboro, New Hampshire*

C.B. Antenna

Make a C.B. antenna more stationary with a...

- **WILSON TENNIS BALL.** "Cut a small slit in a Wilson Tennis Ball and place the ball over your C.B. antenna to prevent it from whipping around while driving."

—GREG R., *Lake City, Florida*

Chrome

Polish chrome with...

- **ARM & HAMMER BAKING SODA.** "Semi-truck drivers use baking soda and ultra fine steel wool (000) to polish chrome. Just dampen the steel wool, dip it in the baking soda to make a paste, scrub small areas at a time, and rinse. It works great."

—SONJA P., *Fernley, Nevada*

■ **CUTEX NAIL POLISH REMOVER.** "I use Cutex Nail Polish Remover to polish all the chrome trim on my husband's hotrod."

—MELISSA S., *Conway, South Carolina*

Classic Cars
Repel mice from a classic car with...

■ **BOUNCE.** "Many classic car owners (myself included) use Bounce fabric sheets to keep mice out of our cars. Don't forget to put a sheet in the tailpipe. Just be sure to remove it before driving."

—JOHN L., *Onamia, Minnesota*

Club-Locking Device
Lubricate a club-locking device with...

■ **PAM NO STICK COOKING SPRAY.** "Our club for the car was getting sticky to open, so my husband sprayed it with Pam No Stick Cooking Spray."

—WILMA G., *North Miami Beach, Florida*

Dead Insects
Clean dead insects from cars with...

■ **ARM & HAMMER BAKING SODA.** "Use Arm & Hammer Baking Soda to remove bugs from the front of your automobile, including the windshield. Use a damp cloth sprinkled with baking soda."

—RICHARD W., *Clearwater, Florida*

■ **BOUNCE.** "Here in Louisiana we have insects called lovebugs because they fly while mating. We have trillions of them in the air at a time. When they splatter on your hood and windshield, they are almost impossible to get off. Unless you remove them immediately, they pit the paint and chrome. However, if you wet down your car and then rub the dead insects with a wet sheet of Bounce, the lovebugs come off."

—HAROLD C., *Houma, Louisiana*

■ **JIF PEANUT BUTTER.** "Use Jif Peanut Butter to soften dried dead bugs from your car. Apply, let sit, then wash as usual."

—MARY M., *Scarborough, Ontario*

■ **PAM NO STICK COOKING SPRAY.** "Spraying a thin coat of Pam No Stick Cooking Spray on the hood and grill before taking a trip prevents dead insects from permanently sticking to the car and makes the car easy to wash."

—JON F., *Dauphin Island, Alabama*

Deodorize

Deodorize the inside of a car with...

■ **ARM & HAMMER BAKING SODA.** "Sprinkle Arm & Hammer Baking Soda throughout the interior of your car (avoid electronic equipment). Take a soft-bristled hand-broom and brush the baking soda in well. Leave for an hour, then vacuum. Your car will smell fresh and clean."

—ROBIN T., *Archer, Florida*

Real-Life Story

NO-STICK NASCAR

"NASCAR racing teams use Pam No Stick Cooking Spray as a nonstick additive to the inner-side of their tires at races. Applying Pam to the inner-side of the tire and rim prevents the buildup of brake dust during short races where brakes are used constantly, thereby allowing the tire to run cooler. Brake dust tends to accumulate, causing the tire to run warmer than normal. The cooking spray produces the same result on mag or chrome-spoke wheels for street use. Just a shot around the inner-side of the tire and rim, and brake dust will come right off with a shot of high-pressure water at your local carwash."

—RONNIE M., *Union, New Jersey*

■ **MAXWELL HOUSE COFFEE.** "Put one cup of fresh Maxwell House Coffee grounds in a small container or box without a lid or cover. The coffee absorbs odors. It's great for the car or van."

—WENDY C., *Luttrell, Tennessee*

Doors

Lubricate a squeaky car door or rusty tool with...

■ **PAM NO STICK COOKING SPRAY.** "Spray Pam No Stick Cooking Spray to fix a squeaking car door or hard-to-turn can opener. Wipe off the excess oil with a dry cloth."

—JOHNNIE N., *Orange, Texas*

Driveways

Clean oil spots from a driveway or garage floor with...

■ **COCA-COLA.** "Just pour a can of Coca-Cola on the oil stain, let sit overnight, and hose clean."

—ROSEANN S., *Davenport, California*

■ **TIDE.** "Cover the grease stain with powdered Tide, scrub with a wet scrub brush, then hose down the driveway. Tide cuts through grease stains—even stubborn stains on your driveway."

—SHERRY M., *Cincinnati, Ohio*

■ **TIDY CAT.** "If your car drips oil on your garage cement floor or driveway, just spread Tidy Cat over the area, let sit a day, and sweep it up. You'll be amazed at the results."

—GEORGE D., *Santa Monica, California*

■ **WD-40.** "To remove oil stains from your garage floor, spray WD-40 on the oil spot and rub with paper towel. It really works."

—ANDREA C., *Palm City, Florida*

Engine Parts

Clean car engine parts with...

■ **COCA-COLA.** "Soak the engine parts in Coca-Cola, then rinse clean."

—LISA W., *Stillwater, Minnesota*

- **EASY-OFF OVEN CLEANER.** "Easy-Off removes all the grime and grease from engine parts like valve covers and cast iron cylinder heads (but not aluminum parts like aluminum cylinder heads and pistons). Just spray it on and then hose it off."

—ROB H., *Asheville, North Carolina*

Fan Belts

Lubricate fan belts with...

- **VASELINE PETROLEUM JELLY.** "Vaseline Petroleum Jelly is an excellent lubricant for dry fan belts on automobile engines. Simply put a small dab on the inside edges of the belt, start the car, and let the engine idle for a couple of minutes. The Vaseline renews the life of the belt, grips the pulleys better than the spray-on lubricants, and eliminates squeals and slippage."

—THOMAS P., *Spokane, Washington*

Temporarily replace a fan belt with...

- **L'EGGS SHEER ENERGY PANTY HOSE.** "The fan belt broke on our car while en route to Albuquerque, New Mexico. My husband used a pair of L'eggs Panty Hose to substitute as a fan belt. It worked. We arrived in Albuquerque and purchased a new fan belt. We always keep a pair of panty hose in the trunk for an emergency."

—CATHY B., *Penasco, New Mexico*

Hubcaps

Remove a stubborn hubcap with...

- **COCA-COLA.** "My uncle owned a garage, and one day a man brought in his car with a flat tire. He could not remove the hubcap. My uncle asked his son to help. My cousin bought a bottle of Coca-Cola from the soda machine, uncapped it, shook it up (keeping his thumb on the open bottle), and then sprayed the Coca-Cola around the hubcap. After a few minutes, he removed the hubcap with hardly any effort."

—SHIRLEY K., *Avon, Connecticut*

Remove corrosion from aluminum hubcaps with...

■ **EASY-OFF OVEN CLEANER.** "Spray Easy-Off on the corroded aluminum hubcaps, let stand for one minute, then rinse well with a garden hose. The oven cleaner removes brake dust, dirt, grime, and corrosion. Not for painted wheels."

—TONY P., *St. Paul, Minnesota*

Interiors

Clean the inside of a car with...

■ **HUGGIES BABY WIPES.** "I keep a tub of Huggies Baby Wipes in my car to wipe down the cup holder, dashboard, and steering wheel when they get sticky from soda and fast food eaten in the car."

—KRIS M., *Dittmer, Missouri*

Clean automobile upholstery, door panels, and carpeting with...

■ **DOW BATHROOM CLEANER.** "Spray on Dow Bathroom Cleaner, rub in with a brush, and wipe with a clean damp cloth. It lifts the dirt and grease out like magic. It also cleans the steering wheel and interior without drying them out."

—TERRY S., *Mims, Florida*

Shine a dashboard with...

■ **JOHNSON'S BABY OIL.** "Use Johnson's Baby Oil to shine the dash of a car. The shine lasts much longer than it does with Armor All, plus it's much cheaper."

—GINA S., *Niagara Falls, Ontario*

Motorcycles

Prevent leather motorcycle pants from sticking to the motorcycle seat with...

■ **JOHNSON'S BABY POWDER.** "Before racing, motorcyclists sprinkle Johnson's Baby Powder on the seat of the motorcycle so their leather suits can slide from side to side faster and easier."

—RUDI H., *Hobe Sound, Florida*

Substitute for ear plugs with...

- **SILLY PUTTY.** "While motorcycling in states that do not require helmets, I used Silly Putty as ear plugs to prevent earaches from the wind."

  —RANDY C., *Swan Hills, Alberta*

Paint

Deoxidize dull paint on a car with...

- **COMET.** "A friend of mine used Comet on an old Dodge he bought for $600. The moment he finished washing the car with Comet, a guy drove up and offered him twice what he'd paid for it. He doubled his money in less than two hours. I've used Comet on a few cars of my own that were oxidized and it worked great. But only use Comet on oxidized paint. Do not use it regularly or you will wear through the paint. Rub lightly while washing the car and rinse well. Wax the car after washing."

  —LEE V., *West Covina, California*

Touch up dings on a white car with...

- **LIQUID PAPER.** "Liquid Paper makes great touch-up paint for white cars, especially flat finished molding and bumpers."

  —KEN E., *Narberth, Pennsylvania*

Remove paint from a car or truck with...

- **EASY-OFF OVEN CLEANER.** "Easy-Off Oven Cleaner removes sign painting from the side door of a truck."

  —ROBERT J., *Willingboro, New Jersey*

Repair a nick in car paint with... \

- **MAYBELLINE NAIL POLISH.** "Use a non-sheer Maybelline Nail Polish to fix a nick in your car's paint. Just match the color and paint until the nick is covered."

  —BERLINNETTA M., *Boulder Creek, California*

Polishing

Polish scratches out of a car's finish with...

■ **COLGATE TOOTHPASTE.** "Squeeze a dollop of toothpaste on a clean cloth, rub over the scratch marks, then buff."

—KAREN K., *Cairns, Australia*

Polish a car with...

■ **L'EGGS SHEER ENERGY PANTY HOSE.** "My husband swears that polishing a car with panty hose is the only way to go. There's no need for rags or sponges, and panty hose won't scratch the finish. And using sudsy warm water and a pair of panty hose cleans those dead bugs right off the hood."

—GAIL C., *Clarksville, Ohio*

■ **PLEDGE.** "I use Pledge furniture polish to get a quick, long-lasting wax job on my car. The Pledge goes on and comes off very easily and leaves a great protective shine. The carnauba wax in the Pledge is the same wax used in high quality auto waxes."

—ABE S., *Howell, New Jersey*

■ **SKIN-SO-SOFT.** "Waxing your clean car with Skin-So-Soft causes water and dirt to sheet off."

—SHELLIE D., *Gillette, Wyoming*

Radiator

Fix a leaky radiator with...

■ **McCORMICK OR SCHILLING BLACK.** "Put a pinch of black pepper in the radiator, fill with water, and drive."

—MARLA T., *Centralia, Illinois*

Repair a radiator hose with...

■ **WRIGLEY'S SPEARMINT GUM** AND **BAND-AID BANDAGES.** "Use a piece of chewed Wrigley's Spearmint Gum and a Band-Aid to temporarily repair a small hole in a radiator hose on a car."

—MICHELE B., *Southaven, Mississippi*

Roofs

Clean a car roof with...

■ **BOUNCE.** "My husband used dampened Bounce sheets to remove green scum from the roof of his Volkswagen camper. It worked great and required very little elbow grease."

—SUSAN W., *Shoreacres, Texas*

Sparkplugs

Revive sparkplugs with...

■ **WD-40.** "If your car engine dies during a rainy or humid day, spray WD-40 on the sparkplug wires. The WD-40 displaces water, keeping moisture away from your sparkplugs so they'll restart and work properly."

—ROGER B., *Jonquiere, Quebec*

Real-Life Story

PLAY-DOH

"I once used Play-Doh to stop up a leaking tire. I just squashed it in the obvious hole and drove on. Being a hot summer day, the heat from the pavement and friction baked the Play-Doh into the hole, sealing it. This enabled us to keep going until we reached a place where we could repair the tire, rather than having to change a flat on the side of the road."

—KATE W., *Piggott, Arkansas*

Spraypaint

Remove spraypaint from a car with...

■ **ENDUST.** "My BMW got spraypainted by some vandals during the night. When I got to work the next day, a co-worker told me to spray Endust on the paint to get it off. If you get to the paint within twenty-four hours (the time it takes for the polymers in the paint to set), Endust will gently and safely remove the paint. It does require some elbow grease, and your car will need to be washed immediately."

—STEVEN P., *Norman, Oklahoma*

Static Electricity

Eliminate static electricity from inside a car with...

- **DOWNY.** "Mix two teaspoons of Downy and one quart of water in a spray bottle. Spray fabric and carpeting inside your car to put an end to those shocks from the static electricity."

—FRANK H., *Stamford, Connecticut*

Striping

Shine striping with...

- **JOHNSON'S BABY OIL.** "I have wide silver striping along the bottom of each side of my car. After washing, it always looks dull. I use a paper towel to rub on Johnson's Baby Oil for an instant shine."

—LINDA B., *Fort Smith, Arkansas*

Tar

Remove tar and bugs from a car with...

- **COCA-COLA.** "My grandfather always used Coke to get rid of tar or asphalt spots on his car from newly paved roads. Simply pour the Coca-Cola on a clean cloth and rub the spot."

—DAVE S., *Chilliwack, British Columbia*

- **SHOUT.** "Tar from the freshly paved roads stuck all over your new paint job? Spray Shout on the tar and it will wipe clean immediately."

—TAMMY L., *Amherstburg, Ontario*

- **SKIN-SO-SOFT.** "Put Avon Skin-So-Soft over the tar, let stand for a few minutes, then rub off the tar with a soft cloth."

—DEANNA L., *Howard, Ohio*

- **WD-40.** "Just spray on WD-40 and then wipe the tar off."

—MICHAEL G., *Pembroke Pines, Florida*

Tires

Repair a flat tire with...

- **KRAZY GLUE.** "I used Krazy Glue to patch a flat tire."

—CARRIE C., *Arlington, Texas*

Traction

Create traction for a car or truck stuck on ice with...

■ **CLOROX BLEACH.** "Simply pour a small amount of Clorox Bleach straight from the jug over the tire that has lost its grip, wait a moment, and then try to move the car. The bleach chemically reacts with the ice and the rubber tire, softening both and raising their adhesive capabilities."

—TOM F., *Oil City, Pennsylvania*

Tractor

Free a rusted tractor engine with...

■ **COCA-COLA.** "When we parked a tractor outdoors over winter and forgot to put a can over the exhaust stack, water got into the engine and rusted it up. So we poured a can of Coke in each cylinder and usually this would free up the engine. Of course, we would also clean and oil the cylinders."

—LEO G., *Canby, Oregon*

Trailer Hitch

Protect a chrome trailer hitch with a...

■ **WILSON TENNIS BALL.** "Cut a hole in a Wilson Tennis Ball and put it over a trailer hitch to protect it from rain."

—TOM L., *Montrose, Colorado*

Tree Sap

Clean pine sap from a car with...

■ **HELLMANN'S OR BEST REAL MAYONNAISE.** "Hellmann's Real Mayonnaise can be used to remove pine sap from a car finish. The sap has to be fresh (not caked on for weeks). Just rub some mayonnaise on the sap, use elbow grease if necessary, then wash the car. Sap comes off rather well without stripping the car finish."

—DEBORAH H., *Huntington, Vermont*

■ **PURELL.** "I have been looking for something to remove pine pitch from my truck for a long time. I camp during the summer, and pine pitch is a huge problem among campers and others who park their cars under pine trees. Just this last weekend, I got a big drip of pitch on my windshield. I tried to scrape it off, but my hands got all sticky. I grabbed my bottle of Purell Hand Sanitizer, which instantly cleaned the pine pitch from my hands. I had to know if it would work on my truck. It immediately removed the pitch from the windshield and the hood without any effects on the paint. It's wonderful."

—NANCY M., *Wisconsin Rapids, Wisconsin*

Weird Fact

THE ABCS OF STP

"STP engine oil. What do the letters stand for? Most mechanics don't have a clue. STP stands for Scientifically Tested Petroleum."

—STEVE H., *Phenix City, Alabama*

Washing
Wash a car with...

- **DOWNY.** "Use one-third cup Downy fabric softener to one gallon of water to make the best car wash cleaner during a water shortage or when you can't use a hose. We are part-time RV-ers and use many parks where we can't wash our RV using their water. Just put this mixture in a spray bottle, spray a two- to three-foot section at a time, let set for five to ten seconds, then dry with paper towels or a leather chamois cloth until completely dry. This works for windows on your home as well."

  —SHARON H., *Klamath Falls, Oregon*

- **MURPHY'S OIL SOAP.** "Murphy's Oil Soap cleans and leaves a shine like wax. Water even beads on it. Plus, there's no need to actually wax."

  —DIANE P., *Kerrville, Texas*

- **WHITE RAIN HAIR CONDITIONER.** "Washing your car with White Rain Hair Conditioner makes the car look freshly waxed, as if you just put Rain-X on the entire car. Rain runs right off the car, possibly because there is lanolin in the conditioner."

  —RON S., *Hamilton, Ohio*

Wax

Remove car wax from trim with...

■ **JIF PEANUT BUTTER.** "When you wax a car and accidentally get white wax on the black rubber trim and moldings, wipe peanut butter on the porous molding to return the rubber to its black color again."

—KEVIN B., *Cincinnati, Ohio*

Wax a car with...

■ **ARMOR ALL.** "When we were living in Hawaii, the salt air oxidized our car badly. I bought rubbing compound and an electric buffer and I set aside an entire day to wax the car back to its original glory. After finishing one door panel, I decided to take a break by spraying the trim with Armor All. I accidentally got some Armor All on the paint. I wiped it off with a rag—only to discover that the Armor All left the paint shiny like new. So I did the entire car with Armor All. The job went faster than using the buffer. The car turned out wonderfully and never oxidized again. From that day on, I never used wax again—just Armor All—and my cars always look brand new. It takes about half the time because you don't have to use elbow grease to get a shine."

—JUANITA R., *Princeton, West Virginia*

Whitewalls

Clean whitewalls on tires with...

■ **EASY-OFF OVEN CLEANER.** "Spray Easy-Off Oven Cleaner on the whitewalls, leave it on for about two minutes, and then rinse off with a high-pressure hose. They look like new."

—ALEX O., *Calgary, Alberta*

■ **SKIN-SO-SOFT.** "Skin-So-Soft Body Oil is great for cleaning your car's tires."

—KELLI R., *Kansas City, Missouri*

■ **TIDE.** "Mix one-quarter cup liquid Tide in one gallon water, and use a scrub brush to clean automobile white wall tires."

—JAMES F., *San Jose, California*

■ **WD-40.** "To brighten whitewalls, spray with WD-40, wait a few seconds, and wipe with paper towels."

—W. R. R., *Bartlesville, Oklahoma*

Windows

Clean car windows with...

■ **HUGGIES BABY WIPES.** "I am a driving school instructor and always on the road. Just before a student gets into my car to take a road test, I clean the windows with Huggies Baby Wipes. It's easy, convenient, and cleans much faster than Windex."

—KERMIT B., *Waianae, Hawaii*

Windshield

Prevent car windshields from fogging up with...

■ **BARBASOL SHAVING CREAM.** "Rub a dab of Barbasol Shaving Cream inside your car windshield and wipe off with a clean cloth."

—JASON A., *Mississauga, Ontario*

Clean road film from a car windshield with...

■ **COCA-COLA.** "Coca-Cola was the emergency road grease remover for windshields in the 'old' South, especially in areas that had gone without rain for many weeks. When it finally did rain, car windshields would be streaked with gunk that could not be removed with straight ammonia. The trick? Stop at the filling station, buy a bottle of Coca-Cola, and pour the foaming Coke on the nasty gunk. *Voila!* It's gone in a flash." (Be careful not to let the Coca-Cola come in contact with the paint.)

—J. C., *Brandon, Florida*

■ **MCCORMICK OR SCHILLING CREAM OF TARTAR.** "Sprinkle Cream of Tartar on the windshield and wash to cut road grime and oil, especially in the winter."

—CANDY H., *Auburn, Washington*

Scrape ice from a car windshield with a...

- **DANNON YOGURT CUP.** "A clean, empty Dannon Yogurt cup has just the right sharp top edge and degree of firmness to remove ice from a windshield when used as a scraper."

  —JOHN P., *Albuquerque, New Mexico*

Clean the inside of car windshields with...

- **LISTERINE.** "Listerine is great for cleaning the inside of a car windshield."

  —CHARLES B., *Pottsboro, Texas*

- **STAYFREE MAXI PADS.** "Stayfree Maxi Pads make great windshield cleaners when you run out of windshield wiper fluid. They work in a pinch, stick to your hand, and, boy, does your windshield shine. Just remember to keep the sticky side away from the glass."

  —SUSAN G., *Albany, New York*

Windshield Wiper Fluid

Make windshield wiper fluid with...

- **SMIRNOFF VODKA.** "Mix three cups Smirnoff Vodka, four cups water, and two teaspoons liquid detergent."

  —DEBBIE G., *Columbia, South Carolina*

Windshield Wipers

Prolong the life of automobile wiper blades with...

- **HEINZ VINEGAR.** "Clean the wiper blades with Heinz White Vinegar."

  —DREW Y., *Reno, Nevada*

Wires

Reattach a loose wire with...

- **WRIGLEY'S SPEARMINT GUM.** "My friend's Volkswagen stopped and would not restart. Two wires would not stay plugged into each other. I was chewing Wrigley's Spearmint Gum. I took a piece of the chewed gum, put it on the connections, then wrapped a piece of the chewing gum foil around the gum. He drove the car for two more years and the patch never came undone."

  —PATRICIA B., *Ogden, Utah*

Fix It

Bicycles

Lubricate a bicycle chain with...

- **WESSON CORN OIL.** "My son uses Wesson Corn Oil to lubricate the chain on his bicycle."

  —Denise P., *Saginaw, Michigan*

Fix a flat tire with...

- **KRAZY GLUE.** "Remove the inner-tube from the tire, locate the puncture, stick the tip of Krazy Glue applicator into the hole, and squeeze out a small amount of glue. Remove the applicator and squeeze the rubber together for a minute or two. Replace the inner-tube in the tire and inflate."

  —Paul P., *Lake Elsinore, California*

Body Braces

Lubricate body braces with...

- **WD-40.** "My daughter's leg braces kept squeaking, so she soaked them in WD-40 overnight. She smelled like a garage for a few days but her braces never squeaked again."

  —Laura E., *Biloxi, Mississippi*

Cabinets

Secure cabinet doors closed with...

- **VELCRO.** "Several of my kitchen cabinet doors have broken hinges. To keep the doors closed, I placed adhesive-backed Velcro tabs on the inside corner of each door and the corresponding frame. I guess the wacky part of this fact is that my husband owns a cabinet shop. You know the old adage about the cobbler's children having no shoes."

  —Debbie T., *Kansas City, Missouri*

Cassette Tapes

Repair a broken cassette or video tape with...

- **MAYBELLINE CRYSTAL CLEAR NAIL POLISH.** "Just paint the ends of the tape with Maybelline Crystal Clear Nail Polish, then overlap slightly, and let dry."

    —TERRIE P., *Bellwood, Pennsylvania*

Ceiling Tiles

Cover marks on white ceiling tiles with...

- **LIQUID PAPER.** "Paint the spots with Liquid Paper."

    —VIRGINIA T., *Wilkes-Barre, Pennsylvania*

Chairs

Prevent chair legs from screeching across the floor with...

- **WILSON TENNIS BALLS.** "I'm a teacher and at school we put a small slit in tennis balls, then secure them on the bottom of the legs of all our chairs. That way, when the kids slide their chairs, there is no noise."

    —MAY R., *Tallahassee, Florida*

Closets

Make hangers glide over clothes rods with...

- **ENDUST.** "I always have far too many clothes hanging in the closet, and consequently, it just takes way too much energy to shove all those clothes over, just to pull out one item. Would I get rid of some of my clothes to make room? No way! Instead, to make those hangers glide easier, I took all my clothes out of the closet and totally saturated the wooden pole with Endust. Then I rubbed off the excess with a rag, and repeated this as many times as it took until the pole felt waxy. Then I hung my clothes back up, and it felt like I had more room in the closet, because now the hangers glided over the pole."

    —PHYLLIS R., *Burbank, California*

Compact Disks

Fix scratches on compact disks with...

- **CHAPSTICK.** "Buff scratched compact disks with ChapStick. It often helps keep them from skipping."
  —RENEE B., *Danville, Iowa*

- **COLGATE TOOTHPASTE.** "Just rub a thin layer of Colgate Toothpaste over the scratch on the compact disk, then wipe clean."
  —SARAH C., *Palmdale, California*

- **TURTLE WAX.** "Apply Turtle Wax to the compact disk, let dry, and wipe clean to cure skips."
  —DAVE A., *Bradenton, Florida*

Computer Printers

Prevent a laser printer from jamming with...

- **BOUNCE.** "At one of my former jobs, we used to put a sheet of Bounce in the front of the paper trays on the printers. This helped feed the paper through more easily by eliminating the static cling that was causing the printer to grab two or more sheets at a time. This was particularly helpful during the dry winter months."
  —DONNA R., *Lincoln, Nebraska*

Clean the rollers in a laser printer with...

- **MR. COFFEE FILTERS.** "When I called Hewlett Packard about a streaking problem in my printer, they suggested using a Mr. Coffee Filter and denatured (not isopropyl) alcohol to clean the rollers and passage ways. They said the filters leave no lint and won't tear when using."
  —MICHAEL S., *St. Petersburg, Florida*

Costume Jewelry

Prevent the stones in costume jewelry from falling out with...

- **MAYBELLINE CRYSTAL CLEAR NAIL POLISH.** "Paint clear nail polish over stones in costume jewelry to prevent them from falling out. Repeat when necessary."
  —JANE S., *Lehighton, Pennsylvania*

Dance Floors

Fix a slippery dance floor with...

- **COCA-COLA.** "Ballet dancers often discover that someone thought wax would help the stage. Mopping the floor with Coke puts down a thin coating which dries quickly and leaves just enough stickiness to keep us from sliding."

  —M. HART, *New York, New York*

Dings

Cover up dings or chips on white sinks and appliances with...

- **LIQUID PAPER.** "Touch up the spot with Liquid Paper."

  —VICKIE M., *Clover, South Carolina*

Dishes

Temporarily conceal cracks in white dishes with...

- **LIQUID PAPER.** "Dab the crack or chip on the dish with Liquid Paper."

  —ISABEL T., *Brantford, Ontario*

Dishwashers

Lubricate the racks in a dishwasher with...

- **PAM NO STICK COOKING SPRAY.** "The racks in our dishwasher were difficult to pull out and push in. I sprayed the rollers with Pam No Stick Cooking Spray and they rolled smoothly and easily—better than new."

  —DORESA D., *Sandy, Oregon*

Door Stops

Prop open doors with...

- **MAXWELL HOUSE COFFEE.** "I use a can of Maxwell House Coffee as a door stop. I replace it with a new can every time we buy a new coffee supply."

  —ANGELA T., *Mabelvale, Arkansas*

Door Hinges

Lubricate squeaky doors and wheels with...

■ **PAM NO STICK COOKING SPRAY.** "Spray Pam No Stick Cooking Spray on door hinges and wagon wheels or anything else that squeaks. I usually have Pam in the house, but I have go to the garage for the WD-40."

—HOLLY T., *Calgary, Alberta*

Drains

Unclog a drain with...

■ **ALKA-SELTZER** AND **HEINZ WHITE VINEGAR.** "Drop two Alka-Seltzer tablets down the drain, add one cup of Heinz White Vinegar, wait a few minutes, then turn on the hot water."

—RICHARD L., *Saddle Brook, New Jersey*

■ **ARM & HAMMER BAKING SODA** AND **HEINZ WHITE VINE-GAR.** "Just pour Arm & Hammer Baking Soda down the drain and quickly follow with Heinz White Vinegar. The bubbling action will unclog your drain."

—TRACEY P., *Point of Bay, Newfoundland*

■ **CASCADE GEL.** "Draining all of the water from my clogged sink that I could, I poured Cascade Gel dishwasher detergent into the drain and allowed hot water to flow slowly down behind it. In less than ten minutes, the drain was free-flowing once more. This worked just as fast as the last time I used Liquid-Plumr, and the Cascade Gel is less expensive to boot."

—DAVID C., *Salem, Oregon*

■ **DAWN.** "Boil three to four tablespoons of Dawn dishwashing liquid in a pan full of water. Most kitchen sink clogs are caused by grease, and the Dawn and boiling water, when poured straight from the stove into the drain, will power right through the clog and wash it away."

—ROBERT P., *San Bernardino, California*

■ **JELL-O** AND **HEINZ WHITE VINEGAR.** "Vinegar dissolves mineral deposits, but if you pour it down a clogged drain, it won't stick around long enough to do the job. Here's the solution. Dissolve one small package of Jell-O in one cup boiling water. Let cool. In a measuring cup, mix 1.5 ounces of Heinz White Vinegar with 6.5 ounces of water. Add the vinegar mixture to the Jell-O mixture. Let gel in refrigerator until almost set, but liquid enough to flow slowly. Pour down drains with mineral deposits. Close off the room where you are doing this and open the windows to avoid the nasty smell. Yes, I've actually done it. It was fun."

—CHRISTY A., *South Ogden, Utah*

■ **MORTON SALT** AND **HEINZ WHITE VINEGAR.** "Tub drain running slow? Dump in one-half cup Morton Salt followed by two cups Heinz White Vinegar, heated to the boiling point."

—JANET H., *Co, New Hampshire*

Real-Life Story

SUPER SOAKER

"My oldest son Daniel used a Super-Soaker 2000 to unclog a bathroom drain that was clogged with food debris after the whole family had experienced a round of stomach flu. That thing really packs a jet spray!"

—BRUCE F., *Washington, D.C.*

Remove hair clogged in bathtub, shower, and sink drains with...

■ **NAIR.** "Just squeeze as much Nair as you think necessary into the drain after you notice the shower running slow and let sit for a while. It works great. It's got to be safer than some of those plumber's helper products."

—DAVE T., *Madison, Wisconsin*

Prevent drains from clogging with...

■ **CLOROX BLEACH.** "Just pour a half gallon of Clorox down the drain once a month. Let sit for fifteen minutes, then run the water for three minutes. I've never had a clogged drain since I started doing this regularly."

—TIMOTHY V., *Gainesville, Florida*

▪ **COCA-COLA.** "In the 1930s, my grandmother began pouring a bottle of Coca-Cola down the drain in the kitchen sink every week. She never had a clogged drain. Neither did my mother, me, or my daughter, who is now twenty-eight. It does work, and there is never a grease build-up."

—TOM C., *Indianapolis, Indiana*

Drawers
Lubricate the runners on drawers with...

▪ **PAM NO STICK COOKING SPRAY.** "To prevent dresser drawers from squeaking, I spray the metal track generously with Pam No Stick Cooking Spray."

—HEIDI K., *Las Vegas, Nevada*

Drill Press
Lubricate a drill press base with...

▪ **JOHNSON'S BABY POWDER.** "The metal base of a drill press is almost always bare metal. Sprinkling this area with Johnson's Baby Powder fills in the metal's pores, keeps it shiny, prevents rust, and helps the work glide better."

—RICK B., *Brockton, Massachusetts*

Erasers
Rejuvenate dried-out pencil erasers with...

▪ **HEINZ WHITE VINEGAR.** "Bring old erasers back to life by soaking them in Heinz White Vinegar overnight."

—JEFF B., *Savannah, Georgia*

Eyeglasses
Prevent eyeglass screws from coming loose with...

▪ **MAYBELLINE CRYSTAL CLEAR NAIL POLISH.** "Paint clear nail polish over the screws on your eyeglasses to prevent screws from coming loose. This is essentially the same technique used by your optometrist."

—CHARLENE R., *Spokane, Washington*

Fire Extinguisher

Put out a fire with...

- **ARM & HAMMER BAKING SODA.** "Sprinkling baking soda on a grease fire extinguishes the fire."

  —CHUCK P., *West Palm Beach, Florida*

Gas Tools

Start gas tools with...

- **WD-40.** "WD-40 works as starting fluid for diesel engines on lawn mowers and chain saws."

  —PETER P., *Nelson, British Columbia*

Glassware

Separate stuck glassware with...

- **WD-40.** "Sometimes when one drinking glass is set into another, it gets stuck—and is seemingly impossible to remove without breaking one or both. The solution? Squirt WD-40 between the two, wait a few seconds, and pull them apart effortlessly. Be sure to clean well before using."

  —GORDON P., *Boise, Idaho*

Glue

Thin glue with...

- **HEINZ VINEGAR.** "A couple of drops of Heinz White Vinegar added to glue that has thickened will thin it out again."

  —GLORIA P., *Richton Park, Illinois*

Grout

Grout tile with...

- **ZIPLOC STORAGE BAGS.** "Mix the grout in a Ziploc Storage Bag, seal, cut a corner, and squeeze."

  —LINDA W., *North Castle, Pennsylvania*

Jewelry

Prevent inexpensive jewelry from turning your skin green with...

- **MAYBELLINE CRYSTAL CLEAR NAIL POLISH.** "Paint the inside of the ring or the back of the bracelet with the Maybelline Crystal Clear Nail Polish to create a protective barrier."

—MICHELLE W., *Seattle, Washington*

Real-Life Story

AND THE WINNER IS . . .

"Do you know how the beautiful ladies wearing those very revealing dresses at the Academy Awards keep their dresses from showing censored areas? A small dot of Elmer's Glue-All is applied to their skin and dress. That is definitely a glue to trust."

—SANDRA B., *Hillsdale, New Jersey*

Lawnmower

Start your lawnmower with...

- **WD-40.** "Spray WD-40 in the carburetor/air cleaner, and give the mower a pull."

—GRANT M., *Sterling, Colorado*

Improvise a filter for a lawnmower with...

- **L'EGGS SHEER ENERGY PANTY HOSE.** "In a pinch, fold the nylon into four layers and attach to the carburetor intake horn with electrical tape or duct tape."

—DENENE V., *Mosinee, Wisconsin*

Leaks

Fix a leak with...

■ **WRIGLEY'S SPEARMINT GUM.** "When you get a small leak in your hot water tank, just chew a piece of Wrigley's Spearmint Gum and seal it over the hole until you can get it fixed properly."

—JERILYN W., *Cleona, Pennsylvania*

Light Bulbs

Lubricate the threads of light bulbs with...

■ **VASELINE PETROLEUM JELLY.** "For years the automotive industry has recommended applying a lubricant to brass-based light bulbs before inserting them. Vaseline Petroleum Jelly keeps the threads free from corrosion, helps the threads conduct electricity, and makes the bulbs much easier to remove later."

—CHARLES M., *Tulsa, Oklahoma*

Locks

Lubricate locks with...

■ **PAM NO STICK COOKING SPRAY.** "I ran out of WD-40, so I used Pam to loosen a lock."

—ANN D., *Braintree, Massachusetts*

■ **VASELINE PETROLEUM JELLY.** "Rub a little Vaseline Petroleum Jelly on your key before inserting it into the lock."

—SHARON B., *Henrietta, New York*

Musical Instruments

Lubricate the slides on brass instruments with...

■ **VASELINE PETROLEUM JELLY.** "Vaseline can be used to make the slides on brass musical instruments move more easily for tuning when they seem too tight."

—CHARLES B., *Greenville, Mississippi*

Pipes

Unscrew rusted pipes with...

■ **COCA-COLA.** "To loosen two pipes rusted together, pour Coca-Cola over the threaded joint. Let it sit for a while and the pipes usually come free easily."

—THOMAS N., *Tillamook, Oregon*

Prevent sweating pipes with...

■ **BOUNCE.** "Tie used Bounce sheets on water pipes in your cellar. The sheets will absorb the 'sweat' from the pipes, eliminating puddles on your basement floor."

—RACHEL T., *Rochester, New York*

Plexiglass

Hide scratches in clear plexiglass with...

■ **COLGATE TOOTHPASTE.** "The aircraft industry uses toothpaste to polish airplane windows. I have also used Colgate Toothpaste to polish old lenses of goggles for my dirt bike."

—CAM C., *Little Rock, Arkansas*

Porcelain

Repair broken porcelain with...

■ **CARNATION CONDENSED MILK.** "If you break a porcelain piece, simply glue it back together with Carnation Condensed Milk. The condensed milk works like strong glue to hold the piece together and hide the break."

—FRANCOISE G., *Yellowknife, New Territory*

Refrigerators

Prolong the life of refrigerator gaskets with...

■ **VASELINE PETROLEUM JELLY.** "Vaseline can be used to prevent the seals on refrigerator doors from cracking. When I worked in an appliance repair shop, we put a thin coat on the seals of used and new refrigerators before delivering them."

—RACHAEL B., *St. Petersburg, Florida*

Rust

Free rusted nuts and bolts with...

- **COCA-COLA.** "You can loosen anything rusted together with Coca-Cola."

  —PETER W., *Brooklyn Park, South Africa*

- **PAM NO STICK COOKING SPRAY.** "When parts are rusted together, spray with Pam to break them free."

  —BRIAN B., *El Cajon, California*

Screws

Tighten screws with...

- **MAYBELLINE CRYSTAL CLEAR NAIL POLISH.** "Simply brush some polish on the screw threads and thread the screw into the hole or nut. The nail polish makes the screw lock tight and prevents it from vibrating loose."

  —RICK B., *Portland, Oregon*

Shower Curtains

Make your shower curtain glide over the rod with...

- **PLEDGE.** "Wipe furniture polish on your shower curtain rod so your shower curtain will slide easily."

  —JOANN B., *Manhattan, Illinois*

Showerheads

Fix a leaky showerhead with...

- **CHAPSTICK.** "We had a leaky bolt in our showerhead so we bought ChapStick, removed the bolt, applied the ChapStick, and put the showerhead back together. The showerhead hasn't leaked since."

  —CHRISTY F., *Lincoln, Nebraska*

Sliding Doors

Make sliding doors glide easier with...

- **PLEDGE.** "I spray Pledge furniture polish in the track of the patio door. It helps keep dirt out, and the door slides so much easier."

  —KATHLEEN M., *Glen Ellyn, Illinois*

Spackle

Fill holes in walls with...

- ■ **ARM & HAMMER BAKING SODA** AND **MCCORMICK** OR **SCHILLING FOOD COLORING.** "I have used baking soda and food coloring (to match the color of paint on a wall) to fill nail holes in walls."

  —PAT C., *Lemon Grove, California*

- ■ **COLGATE TOOTHPASTE.** "Use Colgate Toothpaste to spackle tiny holes in painted drywall."

  —MICHELE B., *Southaven, Mississippi*

Real-Life Story

SOFTEN THE BLOWS

"Using a Stanley knife, make a two-inch slice in a tennis ball, then make a second two-inch slit perpendicular to the first, creating an X. Place the ball over the head of a hammer, which can then be used to hammer items you don't want to damage."

—RON R., *Camarillo, California*

Stereo Speakers

Dampen vibrations from stereo speakers with...

- ■ **WILSON TENNIS BALLS.** "Instead of buying expensive fabricated dampers, just cut Wilson Tennis Balls in half and set the speakers on top of four tennis ball halves. This way, you get much higher sound performance while doing your neighbors a favor (especially if your speakers are placed on the floor in an apartment building)."

  —ROMAN S., *VIENNA, AUSTRIA*

Repair a damaged speaker with...

- ■ **MR. COFFEE FILTERS** AND **MAYBELLINE CRYSTAL CLEAR NAIL POLISH.** "When my sister put her fingers through the center of my woofers, a friend suggested that I trim down a Mr. Coffee Filter to an appropriate size, place it over the hole, then coat it with clear nail polish. I like my music loud and my bass pumping. It's been seven years and the original patch is still holding strong."

—RICKY W., *Atlanta, Georgia*

Swimming Pools
Control alkalinity in a swimming pool with...

- **20 MULE TEAM BORAX.** "If you don't have any Arm & Hammer Baking Soda, you can use 20 Mule Team Borax in a swimming pool to control the alkalinity."

—TRACEY R., *Sardinia, Ohio*

Table Leafs
Lubricate the metal runners under a leafed table with...

- **WESSON CORN OIL** OR **PAM NO STICK COOKING SPRAY.** "Many years ago, I had a kitchen table with a removable leaf. From frequent cleaning, and from the kids spilling milk, juice, and other foods, the metal runners under the table rusted, making it difficult to pull the table apart to insert or remove the leaf. I applied Wesson Corn Oil to the runners with a paper towel to make them slide easily. It really worked. I have also used Pam No Stick Cooking spray."

—MADELINE F., *Cleveland, Ohio*

Table Saws
Prevent rust on a table-saw top with...

- **PAM NO STICK COOKING SPRAY.** "I use Pam No Stick Cooking Spray to keep my table-saw top from rusting. It also works as a lubricant to allow the wood to glide across the saw's tabletop. Apply and wipe. Reapply after every use."

—SEAN M., *Hillsborough, North Carolina*

- **VASELINE PETROLEUM JELLY.** "To remove rust from a table saw, rub Vaseline Petroleum Jelly on the rust, let set overnight, and wipe clean."

—SUE S., *Aitkin, Minnesota*

Toilets

Determine whether a toilet tank is leaking with...

■ **MCCORMICK** OR **SCHILLING FOOD COLORING.** "Put enough food coloring in the toilet tank to change the color of the water. Let sit overnight. If the water in the bowl has changed color in the morning, your tank is leaking into the bowl and wasting water."

—Marilyn V., *Cedar Rapids, Iowa*

Tread Mills

Prolong the life of a tread mill motor with...

■ **PAM NO STICK COOKING SPRAY.** "Spray Pam No Stick Cooking Spray between the belt and the flat plate on your tread mill to reduce the stress on the motor."

—Bruce R., *Summerville, South Carolina*

Utensils

Help handicapped people hold utensils with...

■ **WILSON TENNIS BALLS.** "Cut a small slit in a Wilson Tennis Ball and insert an eating utensil, pen, or pencil so a person with Parkinson's disease, arthritis, or any impairment that causes crippled or shaky hands, can grip the ball and be able to stabilize their hand."

—Susan H., *West Gardiner, Maine*

Walkers

Prevent a walker from dragging along the floor with...

■ **WILSON TENNIS BALLS.** "My grandmother has a walker with the wheels on the front and the legs on the back. It isn't easy to push the walker because the bottoms of the rear legs have rubber stoppers that slow her down (especially on carpet). We cut slits into two tennis balls and put them on the bottom of the back legs. She can now push the walker with ease."

—Trish S., *Camillus, New York*

Wallpaper
Reglue fallen wallpaper corners with...

- **COLGATE TOOTHPASTE.** "When wallpaper falls down in spots, Colgate Toothpaste works just as well holding it up as glue."

—TERRIE L., *Wichita, Kansas*

Water Pumps
Seal water pump covers to prevent leaks with...

- **VASELINE PETROLEUM JELLY.** "Coat water pump covers or other water pipe connections with Vaseline Petroleum Jelly."

—BRAD L., *Dallas, Texas*

Window Shades
Improvise window shades with...

- **REYNOLDS WRAP.** "Do you work the night shift? Are you a night-owl who just happens to sleep better by day? Place Reynolds Wrap foil over windows to keep out the daylight."

—TERRY V., *Riverside, California*

Windows
Lubricate windows with...

- **VASELINE PETROLEUM JELLY.** "If you have an old house with wooden windows that are difficult to raise and shut, open the window and put Vaseline on the runners along the inside of the window frame. The windows will go up and down like a charm for years."

—LIZ G., *Mesa, Arizona*

Wristwatches
Remove scratches from the glass face of a watch with...

- **CUTEX NAIL POLISH REMOVER.** "Just dip a Q-Tips Cotton Swab in Cutex Nail Polish Remover and delicately wash over the glass face of the watch."

—CATHY K., *Chula Vista, California*

Zippers

Lubricate zippers with...

- **VASELINE PETROLEUM JELLY.** "Applying Vaseline to zippers makes them slippery, saves frequent repairs, and reduces stress."

  —GORDON M., *Columbia, Maryland*

- **ZEST.** "To make an old, stubborn zipper zip better, just rub a bar of Zest soap on the teeth."

  —TERESA E., *Kansas City, Kansas*

Flush It

Bathtubs

Clean a bathtub with...

- **CASCADE.** "Fill the bathtub with warm water, add two table-spoons Cascade, let stand for about ten minutes. Use an abrasive sponge to lightly scour, then rinse with water. Turns the dingiest fixture bright white. Repeat if needed."
  —LYNN H., *Port Charlotte, Florida*

- **CLAIROL HERBAL ESSENCES SHAMPOO.** "Pour Clairol Herbal Essences Shampoo on soap scum in tub, let sit overnight, and rinse. This is a gentle way to clean older tubs whose finish is wearing off."
  —BETH L., *High Point, North Carolina*

- **COCA-COLA.** "I used Coca-Cola to get rid of rust in my bathtub. I couldn't believe it really worked."
  —GWEN R., *Covington, Louisiana*

- **EASY-OFF OVEN CLEANER.** "Spray Easy-Off on and let set for thirty minutes. Then just lightly scrub and rinse with warm water. Your tub will be whiter than expected. Make sure the room is well ventilated."
  —JILL S., *Lompoc, California*

- **HEINZ VINEGAR.** "Fill the bathtub with hot water, pour in a couple cups of vinegar, let soak for a few hours. This softens the hard water buildup, making it easier to remove."
  —MARJORIE G., *Tustin, California*

- **SKIN-SO-SOFT.** "Skin-So-Soft removes grease and dirt marks from the bathtub. Fill the tub with hot water and a couple capfuls of Skin-So-Soft and the ring wipes right off."
  —PATRICIA G., *Amsterdam, New York*

- **SNO BOL.** "I use Sno Bol for everything. It safely cleans fiberglass tubs."
  —MERLIN O., *Fenwick, Michigan*

Shine a bathtub or shower with...

- **TURTLE WAX.** "After cleaning your bathtub, use Turtle Wax to polish your tub, making it virtually self-cleaning. Just be sure to use a rubber bath mat to avoid slipping in the tub."
  —DIANE M., *Calumet, Michigan*

Remove decals from a bathtub with...

- **JIF PEANUT BUTTER.** "If you leave Jif Peanut Butter on your decals in the bottom of the tub, it helps dissolve the glue between decal and the tub. Give it a try."
  —KARLA K., *South Euclid, Ohio*

Drains

Plug a drain with a...

- **WILSON TENNIS BALL.** "If you lose the drain plug for your shower, sink, or bathtub, use a Wilson Tennis Ball to block the drain."
  —PHYLLIS P., *Bellwood, Pennsylvania*

Fixtures

Clean fixtures with...

- **COLGATE TOOTHPASTE.** "Use Colgate Toothpaste to shine faucets in the kitchen and bathroom. Just apply toothpaste and wipe with a dry cloth."
  —JOYCE H., *Mequon, Wisconsin*

- **HUGGIES BABY WIPES.** "Use Huggies Baby Wipes to clean the chrome faucets in the bathroom."
  —RUTH E., *Richmond, Virginia*

- **TURTLE WAX.** "Prevent water spots on bathroom fixtures with Turtle Wax. Rub Turtle Wax into bathroom fixtures and buff well with a clean cloth."
  —TRACY M., *Anaheim, California*

Grout

Clean grout with...

■ **HEINZ WHITE VINEGAR.** "Fill a plastic, sixteen-ounce trigger spray bottle with Heinz White Vinegar and spray the grout in the shower. Let sit for five minutes, then scrub with a clean, used toothbrush."

—LISA W., *Wilsonville, Oregon*

■ **LISTERINE.** "Use Listerine to clean the grout in the bathroom. It helps to reduce the mold that can grow."

—BONITA N., *Arlington, Massachusetts*

Hairbrushes and Combs

Clean hairbrushes and combs with...

■ **CINCH.** "When you're about to launder a load of work clothes, towels, and such (no delicate items), gather up all the plastic combs and brushes in your household. Spray each one well with Cinch and wash them along with the clothes. Just be sure to take them out before transferring the load to the dryer."

—JANET H., *Conway, New Hampshire*

Hair Spray

Clean hair spray from walls or doors with...

■ **DOW BATHROOM CLEANER.** "I tried everything to remove hairspray from my bathroom door that had a build-up from spraying my hair. I tried everything from wood cleaner, to soapy water, to bleach; but then one day I sprayed soap-scum remover for the tub on it and it wiped off with ease."

—RHONDA D., *Kingsland, Georgia*

Mirrors

Prevent mirrors from fogging up with...

■ **BARBASOL SHAVING CREAM.** "Before you get into a shower, coat the mirror with Barbasol Shaving Cream, and then wipe it off with a dry cloth. No matter how hot and steamy the shower is, the mirror will not be covered with steam. This will last for about one week."

—MATT U., *Burlington, Ontario*

■ **COLGATE TOOTHPASTE.** "Colgate Regular Toothpaste is also a great defogger. Coat the bathroom mirror with toothpaste, then rinse off to prevent the mirror from fogging up when you take a shower."

—BRETT B., *Dallas, Texas*

■ **TURTLE WAX.** "I use Turtle Wax on my mirrors to prevent them from steaming up."

—STEPH R., *Nipomo, California*

Shower Curtains

Clean soap scum off vinyl shower curtains with...

■ **HEINZ VINEGAR.** "Place the vinyl shower curtain in the washing machine, set for warm rinse with your regular laundry detergent, and add one cup Heinz White Vinegar. When the rinse cycle finishes, immediately remove and rehang the shower curtain."

—LOREEN S., *Houston, Texas*

Showers

Clean a shower stall with...

■ **CASCADE.** "Just mix up a paste of Cascade and water. Wet down the tub area and apply the paste. Let sit, then watch the dirt just wash away. This tip has saved me loads of money on expensive cleansers."

—TANYA F., *Staunton, Virginia*

Clean mineral deposits from shower heads with...

■ **HEINZ VINEGAR.** "Once a month, soak your shower heads in a cup of Heinz White Vinegar and they will continue to run beautifully. The vinegar takes out all mineral deposits."

—BARBARA L., *Kenosha, Wisconsin*

Clean shower door tracks with...

- **HYDROGEN PEROXIDE.** "Just pour hydrogen peroxide into the tracks, let sit for a few minutes, then wipe and rinse. To keep them clean, just pour in some hydrogen peroxide once a week, let sit and rinse."

  —AMY M., *Granada Hills, California*

Shine a shower stall with...

- **TURTLE WAX.** "Clean your shower, then apply Turtle Wax and buff. From then on, you'll only have to rinse your shower to clean. It's easy, fast, and saves time and money. Just be sure to use a rubber mat so you don't slip on the waxed floor."

  —DIANE M., *Calumet, Michigan*

Sinks

Clean the bathroom sink with...

- **CASCADE.** "Sprinkle a little Cascade in your sink with a little water to make a paste, gently rub over the sink with a sponge, and let sit for a while, then rinse clean to remove tea stains."

  —ELAINE W., *Forest Hills, New York*

- **CREST TOOTHPASTE.** "To clean the bathroom sink, apply Crest Toothpaste (not gel), then scrub away. Toothpaste is safe for any type of finish. The results are great and the smell is delightful."

  —CHARLENE R., *Cortland Manor, New York*

- **SNO BOL.** "Sno Bol takes rust out of sinks."

  —MERLIN O., *Fenwick, Michigan*

Clean stainless steel sinks with...

- **CANADA DRY CLUB SODA.** "Club soda cleans stainless steel sinks."

  —NANCIE P., *Van Nuys, California*

- **EFFERDENT.** "I use Efferdent to shine my sinks. I put a few tablets in the water, let it sit for an hour, and the stainless steel looks shiny and new.

  —RITA K., *Chicago, Illinois*

■ **JOHNSON'S BABY OIL.** "A drop of Johnson's Baby Oil for stainless steel sinks keeps them nice and shiny."

—KAREN N., *Enfield, Connecticut*

Soap Scum

Clean soap scum and hard-water stains from shower doors and walls with...

■ **BOUNCE.** "Wipe the shower doors with a used sheet of Bounce."

—ANGIE L., *Norman, Oklahoma*

■ **CASCADE.** "The ingredients in Cascade cut through soap scum and that nasty ring around the tub. Just make sure you have good ventilation in the room. Wear rubber gloves if you are sensitive to the detergent. Rinse well."

—DAVID H., *Oklahoma City, Oklahoma*

■ **DOWNY.** "Mix one teaspoon of Downy Fabric Softener in a gallon of water, and wipe down the shower doors with a sponge."

—DIANE M., *Blasdell, New York*

■ **EASY-OFF OVEN CLEANER.** "I clean houses for a living, and I use Easy-Off Oven Cleaner to clean shower walls, tub walls, and glass shower doors. Spray and let set for approximately ten minutes. Wearing rubber gloves, wipe clean with a wet cloth and rinse well with very hot water. Clean away any leftover Easy-Off with regular cleanser. This cleans years of soap scum that you can never get off with regular cleansers. Do not spray any of the metal surfaces; Easy-Off will eat away the chrome."

—BRENDA E., *Falls Church, Virginia*

■ **HEINZ WHITE VINEGAR** AND **PLEDGE.** "Fill a spray bottle with white vinegar, spray on doors, and let set a few minutes. Wipe clean with a sponge. Rinse, then spray Pledge on the glass doors to prevent soap scum from building up again."

—TRICIA R., *Southgate, Michigan*

■ **JET-DRY SPARKLE.** "Dilute Jet-Dry Sparkle (liquid rinse agent) with water, wipe down glass shower doors with a mildly abrasive scrub pad (no scrubbing necessary), and rinse."

—BETTY S., *Killarney, Manitoba*

■ **JOHNSON'S BABY OIL.** "Use a few drops of baby oil on a clean cloth to wipe soap scum from shower doors."

—ROSE V., *Lewisville, Texas*

■ **LISTERINE.** "Clean water deposits from the bathroom sink and tub with Listerine. Sponge with Listerine. It makes the bathroom smell good, too."

—BETH P., *Hamilton, Ohio*

■ **MORTON SALT** AND **HEINZ VINEGAR.** "Measure three-quarters cup salt and add Heinz White Vinegar to top off the cup. Using a sponge, spread the abrasive mixture on bathroom tiles and shower doors to remove hard-water stains and soap scum."

—JILDA T., *Englewood, New Jersey*

■ **PLEDGE.** "Spraying Pledge on shower walls and wiping it off removes soap scum build-up easily and effortlessly."

—ELLEN D., *Las Vegas, Nevada*

■ **REALEMON** AND **BOUNCE.** "Sponge ReaLemon lemon juice on a glass shower door, then wipe clean with a used sheet of Bounce."

—FRAN G., *Calabasas, California*

■ **SPRAY 'N WASH.** "Spritz Spray 'n Wash on the glass, wipe with a sponge, then rinse."

—AUDREY W., *Pembroke Pines, Florida*

Prevent hard-water stains on shower doors with...

■ **ARMOR ALL.** "The stuff you use to clean the inside of your car can be used on the bathtub, tile, and glass doors to prevent soap scum from sticking to everything. Just be careful using it on your floors unless you're going for that skating effect."

—BELINDA M., *Richland, Washington*

- **BON AMI** AND **RAIN-X.** "Are your glass shower doors white from hard water? Clean them with Bon Ami and then treat them with Rain-X. *Voila!* Clear glass."

  —KIM B., *Fresno, California*

- **PRESTONE WINDSHIELD RAIN RELIEF.** "After cleaning soap scum from a bathtub or shower, use a felt cloth to apply Prestone Windshield Rain Relief to the walls, following the instructions on the bottle as if putting the formula on your car windows. (Do not let the formula touch the caulking, as it may dissolve some brands.) Wipe off the excess haze as instructed. After I shower, I go over the walls with a squeegee to remove the excess water. You can even clean the tub while you're showering. The soap film easily wipes off with a damp washcloth. Looks like it took hours, but it only takes minutes."

  —MARY M., *Scarborough, Ontario*

- **TURTLE WAX.** "I use liquid car wax on my glass shower door to prevent water spots. There's no need to squeegee the glass after showering."

  —STEPH R., *Nipomo, California*

Tile

Clean tile with...

- **LISTERINE.** "I have found that Listerine is excellent for cleaning tile."

  —JANICE S., *Copperopolis, California*

- **MAXWELL HOUSE COFFEE.** "Just pour hot, brewed Maxwell House Coffee straight from the pot on the tile. The coffee penetrates grease and soap scum. Then wipe clean with a damp sponge. Be careful not to leave the coffee on light-colored grout too long or it will stain."

  —DANA C., *Sunland, California*

Toilets

Clean a toilet with...

- **ALKA-SELTZER.** "Drop two tablets in the toilet and let dissolve. Wash the bowl with a toilet brush. *Voila!*"

  —JEAN W., *Daytona Beach, Florida*

- **CASCADE GEL.** "We had a difficult water stain in our toilet bowl. I put Cascade Gel into the bowl, just like other toilet bowl gels. I let it sit for about fifteen minutes. *Presto!* The toilet bowl was clean and sparkled like a new one."
  —SUE H., *Garner, North Carolina*

- **EFFERDENT.** "Did you know that you can clean your toilet with Efferdent tablets? Just drop two or three into the bowl and watch it clean that ring like never before."
  —VICKI L., *Lebanon, Oregon*

- **HUGGIES BABY WIPES.** "After scrubbing the bowl with a cleaner and brush, wipe down the toilet with a Huggies Baby Wipe. Start with the top of the toilet tank and work your way to the rim and under the seat (the dirtiest spots) and then toss out the wipe. No streaking or dripping."
  —FRAN L., *Old Tappan, New Jersey*

- **KOOL-AID.** "My husband is in the Navy and the guys on his boat use military-issued 'bug juice' (Kool-Aid, essentially) to clean toilets, metal parts, and the sight tubes for the various tanks on board ship."
  —MARILYN T., *Canterbury, Connecticut*

- **LISTERINE.** "Pour one-quarter cup Listerine into the toilet, let sit for thirty minutes, then brush and flush."
  —PAT A., *Holiday, Florida*

- **TANG.** "Put two tablespoons of Tang in the toilet, wait fifteen minutes, then brush and flush."
  —MICHAEL F., *Wilmington, Delaware*

Groom It

Aftershave Lotion

Substitute for aftershave lotion with...

- **SMIRNOFF VODKA.** "While staying in a hotel and having forgotten to bring along my aftershave, I used a little bottle of Smirnoff Vodka from the bar fridge instead. It did a really great job, I have to say, and would be an excellent substitute for aftershave for those who don't react well to the crappy perfumes in a lot of aftershaves."

  —DILLON B., *Lismore, Australia*

Astringent

Clean your face with...

- **HEINZ WHITE VINEGAR.** "I dilute vinegar down for an astringent because it is the proper pH."

  —RITA G., *Joshua Tree, California*

- **HYDROGEN PEROXIDE.** "Use hydrogen peroxide as an astringent to clean your face. Put a small amount on a cotton ball and rub on your face."

  —CHARLOTTE C., *Rowland Heights, California*

Blackheads

Remove blackheads with...

- **ELMER'S GLUE-ALL.** "Instead of buying expensive Bioré strips to remove oil and blackheads from your face, apply a small amount of Elmer's Glue-All to your face (avoiding your eyes), let dry, then gently peel off to reveal soft smooth skin. If the glue dries to your eyebrows, just use a warm washcloth to remove the excess glue."

  —CINDY H., *Austin, Texas*

- **EPSOM SALT.** "Add one teaspoon Epsom Salt and three drops iodine to one-half cup boiling water. After the mix has cooled a bit, dip strips of cotton into the solution and apply to the problem area. Repeat three or four times, reheating the solution if necessary. Then, gently unclog the pores and go over the area with an alcohol-based astringent."

  —JULIET D., *Jackson, Mississippi*

Contact Lenses

Clean soft contact lenses with...

- **ARM & HAMMER BAKING SODA.** "Pour a small amount of Arm & Hammer Baking Soda in the palm of your hand, add your disinfectant solution to make a paste. Then rub each contact lens in the paste with your finger. It works as well as enzyme cleaner, but quicker and less expensively."

  —LEE C., *Nashville, Tennessee*

- **LEMON JOY.** "I use Lemon Joy to clean hard or gas-permeable contact lenses."

  —CASSANDRA H., *Washington, D.C.*

Dentures

Clean dentures with...

- **CLOROX BLEACH.** "One part bleach to three parts water will clean your false teeth quicker than any commercial product. Just be sure to rinse and brush the dentures before you re-install them."

  —BRUCE C., *St. Petersburg, Florida*

Douche

Douche with...

- **HEINZ VINEGAR.** "Use four teaspoons of Heinz White Vinegar to one pint of water for feminine douching."

  —MARY G., *Marine City, Michigan*

Dry Shampoo
Give yourself a dry shampoo with...

- **ARM & HAMMER BAKING SODA.** "Sprinkle Arm & Hammer Baking Soda on hair, wait ten minutes, then brush off hair. The baking soda absorbs the oil from your hair. Great for camping (but doesn't work well on long hair)."
  —THOMAS S., *Inman, South Carolina*

- **GOLD MEDAL FLOUR.** "I've given myself a dry shampoo by sprinkling Gold Medal Flour in my hair, working it in, and then brushing it out."
  —DARLENE M., *Bushnell, Florida*

- **KINGSFORD'S CORN STARCH.** "If you have oily hair and don't have time to wash it, use Kingsford's Corn Starch. Sprinkle some on your hand and apply to the oily parts of your hair (usually the roots). Work in well, then comb it out. It will get rid of the oily look."
  —KELLY L., *Burnaby, British Columbia*

Earrings
Prevent earrings from irritating skin with...

- **MAYBELLINE CLEAR NAIL POLISH.** "Inexpensive earrings sometimes cause skin irritations. I simply paint a protective coating of clear fingernail polish over the post and let it dry completely. Every two weeks I remove the polish with Cutex Nail Polish Remover, and apply a fresh coat of clear nail polish to the post. It makes a huge difference. Try it and see."
  —CINDY, *Jacksonville, Florida*

Eyebrows
Pluck your eyebrows with...

- **ORAJEL.** "To reduce the pain when plucking your eyebrows, dab on some liquid Orajel first to anesthetize your skin."
  —ERIN P., *Joshua Tree, California*

Eyeglasses

Keep eyeglasses on your nose with...

■ **LADY SPEED STICK.** "Put a little dab of Lady Speed Stick (invisible deodorant) on the bridge of your nose to prevent sunglasses from slipping off in hot weather when you get sweaty. I know it sounds crazy, but it really does work."

—FRAN G., *Vancouver, British Columbia*

Prevent the nosepiece of eyeglasses from leaving indents on your nose with...

■ **DR. SCHOLL'S MOLESKIN.** "Rather than buying expensive little glue-on pads that stick for about a week, buy Dr. Scholl's Moleskin, the stuff made for corns. For a couple bucks, you get three sheets of the stuff, and if you use your scissors adroitly, that's enough raw material for two years' worth of nosepiece protectors—even if you use one pair a week."

—ED C., *Nyack, New York*

Facial

Give yourself a rejuvenating facial with...

■ **COLGATE TOOTHPASTE.** "Use Colgate as a facial wash. Dab a small amount on wet hands and lather. Apply on the face and rinse thoroughly."

—LUISA A., *Quezon City, Philippines*

■ **ELMER'S GLUE-ALL.** "Apply Elmer's Glue-All moderately to your face, let set for about twenty minutes, then wash it off. It'll be the smoothest your skin will ever feel."

—CATHY K., *Chula Vista, California*

■ **PEPTO-BISMOL.** "Treat yourself to an instant facial mask treatment with liquid Pepto-Bismol. Cover your face (avoiding your eyes), let dry, then rinse with cool water."

—LORI W., *Coalgate, Oklahoma*

■ **PHILLIP'S MILK OF MAGNESIA.** "Sponge Phillip's Milk of Magnesia on your face with a cotton ball, allow to dry, then rinse off. It's an inexpensive facial mask for people with oily skin. The magnesium in the product dries the skin and, done as many times a week as you can stand it, reduces breakouts."

—VALERIE K., *Brooklyn, New York*

■ **QUAKER OATS** AND **SUE BEE HONEY.** "Oily skin? Mix a batch of warm oatmeal, add a little honey to thicken, and apply to dry face. The heat from the mixture along with the honey will draw out the oils, and the oatmeal will absorb them."

—KRISTEN S., *Bay St. Louis, Mississippi*

■ **REDDI-WIP.** "I use whipped cream as a facial mask. I find that it makes my skin softer and healthier looking."

—MONICA T., *Brampton, Ontario*

■ **SUEBEE HONEY CARNATION EVAPORATED MILK, HEINZ VINEGAR,** AND **GOLD MEDAL FLOUR.** "Mix three tablespoons SueBee Honey, one-half cup Carnation Evaporated Milk, and four tablespoons Heinz Apple Cider Vinegar in a bowl with an egg beater and slowly add Gold Medal Flour to form a very thick paste. Apply to face and let dry. Rinse with warm water and wash face as usual. The honey softens and moisturizes your skin, the vinegar closes your pores, and the milk moisturizes."

—MEGAN H., *St Marys, Kansas*

■ **TIDY CAT.** "I create a deep cleansing mud mask by making a paste with unused Tidy Cat and water. I then smear it all over my face, let set for twenty minuntes, then rinse clean with water. This clears the skin of dirts and oils."

—LAURA S., *Houston, Texas*

Real-Life Story

FLAKES AT KELLOGG'S

"John Harvey Kellogg, M.D., and Reverend Sylvester Graham believed that masturbation resulted in the loss of fluids that were vital to the body. Kellogg's Corn Flakes were originally developed as a food to extinguish sexual desire and to help an individual curb masturbation desires."

—PLUNK, *Studio City, California*

Fingernails

Whiten finger- and toenails with...

■ **EFFERDENT.** "Remove yellow from fingernails by soaking in two Efferdent tablets dissolved in a small bowl of water."

—Sheila J., *Maplewood, Minnesota*

■ **REALEMON.** "Use a cotton ball to wipe ReaLemon lemon juice on your fingernails to remove the yellowing due to nail polish."

—Melanie L., *Wilsonville, Oregon*

Condition cuticles with...

■ **HEINZ WHITE VINEGAR.** "Fill a small bowl with vinegar, and soak your fingers in it for one minute to keep your cuticles soft."

—Elaine B., *Fallbrook, California*

■ **STAR OLIVE OIL.** "Soak your cuticles in warm olive oil to moisturize them."

—Morgan J., *Las Vegas, Nevada*

Strengthen fingernails with...

■ **JELL-O.** "Mix strawberry-flavored Jell-O powder with enough water to make a paste. Then paint the mixture on your fingernails. The gelatin in the Jell-O makes your nails grow longer and stronger. Also the strawberry powder stains your nails red so you don't have to paint them with polish, and they smell great all day."

—Kate M., *Upper Sandusky, Ohio*

Make nail wraps with...

■ **MR. COFFEE FILTERS** AND **KRAZY GLUE.** "Cut a piece of a coffee filter to the size of your fingernail, add a drop of Krazy Glue, and you're on your way to an inexpensive set of wraps."

—Valerie H., *Chestnut Ridge, New York*

Hair

Give your hair a shine with...

- **VASELINE PETROLEUM JELLY.** "After brushing your hair, take a very small dab of Vaseline, rub it between your hands, and then run your hands through your hair for an amazing shine."

  —MICHELLE C., *Parma, Ohio*

End the frizzies with...

- **AUNT JEMIMA ORIGINAL SYRUP.** "For frizzy dry hair, apply Aunt Jemima Original Syrup to the ends of hair, massage in, wait thirty minutes, then shampoo and rinse hair."

  —MAUREEN H., *Evart, Michigan*

Hair Coloring

Prewash your hair before dying with...

- **TIDE.** "Washing your hair with Tide detergent before coloring it will prevent the hair dye from turning your hair that brassy red color."

  —TAMMY L., *Hackett, Arizona*

Dye your hair with...

- **FOLGER'S INSTANT COFFEE.** "Add a packet of Folger's Instant Coffee with your regular conditioner and mix well. Apply the mixture to your hair, let set for one minute, then rinse clean, and you'll have brown hair."

  —KIRSTEN L., *Cambridge, Minnesota*

- **HEINZ KETCHUP.** "Put Heinz Ketchup in your hair, then rinse clean to achieve natural-looking red highlights."

  —TARA C., *London, England*

- **JELL-O.** "Did you know you can color your hair with Jell-O? Make a thick paste from Jell-O powder and cold water, then color your hair. It works great on light hair and washes out after a few shampoos. I especially love the lime Jell-O for that extra special Halloween color."

  —GRETCHEN E., *San Clemente, California*

■ **KOOL-AID.** "Mix Kool-Aid powder with a little water to make a paste and apply to hair—instant funky hair color. Best of all, it's inexpensive and nontoxic."
—STEPHANIE P., *Norwich, Connecticut*

■ **MCCORMICK** OR **SCHILLING FOOD COLORING.** "To make your hair blue or green, squeeze drops of food coloring into your hair and comb it through until you achieve the desired color."
—CASSANDRA, *Houston, Texas*

■ **TANG.** "Mix Tang and water into a paste and apply to your hair."
—JASON O., *West Springfield, Massachusetts*

Remove hair dye from skin with...

■ **CREST TOOTHPASTE.** "Crest is abrasive enough to remove the dye, but gentle enough not to irritate the skin. Apply the toothpaste with a damp cloth and rub the stain in a light, circular motion. Darker dyes (black, dark brown) may require a few attempts."
—MELISSA F., *Akron, Ohio*

Hairbrushes

Clean hairbrushes with...

■ **ARM & HAMMER BAKING SODA.** "Just soak the brush in warm water and about three heaping tablespoons of baking soda and swish around in the water until clean."
—DENISE S., *Phoenix, Arizona*

Hair Cuts

Cut hair in short layers with...

■ **DIXIE CUPS.** "Make a pony tail in the crown of the head, and fasten it with a rubber band. Cut the bottom of the Dixie Cup, place the pony tail through the cup, and cut the exposed hair back to the rim of the cup."
—FREDA H., *Grand Falls-Windsor, Newfoundland*

Make a haircut smock and shield with a...

■ **GLAD TRASH BAG.** "When I give my husband a haircut, I cut some Glad Trash Bags and lay them on the floor. Then I cover the chair with one. But most importantly, I cut a hole in the bottom of a trash bag, put it over my husband's head (to keep the hair off him), and when I'm done I cut the bag off him and throw away the hairy mess."

—CHRISTINE H., *Logan, Utah*

Hair Setting
Set your hair in curlers with...

- **BUDWEISER.** "When I was a teenager, I always set my hair in curlers with stale Budweiser beer which I kept in the refrigerator in a nozzle-type squeeze bottle. When the beer dried, I would have stiff curls. When I brushed them out, all that remained of the beer was a really great set—without any beer smell."

  —LINDA J., *Mountain View, California*

- **CARNATION NONFAT DRY MILK.** "My mom used Carnation Nonfat powdered milk as a hair-setting solution with regular curlers. She reconstituted the milk according to the instructions on the box, then saturated each strand of hair with the milk before rolling it up in curlers. Her curls were great and long-lasting."

  —LARA H., *Newport Beach, California*

Hair Spray
Substitute for hair spray with...

- **NIAGARA SPRAY STARCH.** "I found myself without hair spray one morning before work, so I used spray starch. It worked like a charm and held my hair in place all day."

  —AUDREY P., *Leonardo, New Jersey*

Hair Straightener
Straighten your hair with...

- **CRISCO ALL-VEGETABLE SHORTENING.** "Crisco can be used to straighten your hair. Some people use pressing combs to straighten their hair. If you run out of hair oil, use Crisco."

  —BETTY S., *Nacogdoches, Texas*

- **MARSHMALLOW FLUFF.** "Marshmallow Fluff makes really wicked hair straightener or dressing if you thin it first with a little cooking oil."

  —MICHAEL Y., *Somerville, Massachusetts*

Hands

Clean hands after playing slot machines with...

- **HUGGIES BABY WIPES.** "If you frequent gambling casinos, you know how black your hands get from playing slot machines. The casinos provide hand-wipe packets that do absolutely nothing. Even soap doesn't work. Carry Huggies Baby Wipes in a Ziploc Storage Bag. They clean hands thoroughly."

  —MIRIAM F., *Scarborough, Maine*

Hot Wax

Remove hot wax from skin with...

- **CUTEX NAIL POLISH REMOVER.** "I use Cutex Nail Polish Remover to remove wax from my face or anywhere I have used it to remove unwanted hair. Once the wax is on your skin and gets cold, it is beyond impossible to get the excess that you might have missed when you stripped the area of hair. The nail polish remover stings a little, but it works like a charm."

  —JANET D., *Silver Spring, Maryland*

- **SKIN-SO-SOFT.** "After using a hot waxer to remove unwanted hair, apply Skin-So-Soft sparingly to remove the excess wax from your skin."

  —MARCIA J., *Indianapolis, Indiana*

Lips

Moisturize your lips with...

- **JOHNSON'S BABY OIL.** "Johnson's Baby Oil makes lips silky smooth. I constantly had chapped lips until my doctor told me to use a little baby oil. It works."

  —DAVID W., *Tully, New York*

Lipstick

Blot lipstick with...

- ■ **MR. COFFEE FILTERS.** "Use coffee filters to blot lipstick. The filters won't break apart and stick to your lips like tissues do."

  —KALYNDA B., *Fryeburg, Maine*

Real-Life Story

YOU'RE IN THE ARMY NOW

"My son-in-law, who is in the Army, says he uses Huggies Baby Wipes to clean the camouflage off his face while they are out in the field and good old Coca-Cola to clean the carbon off his weapons."

—KERMIT B., *Waianae, Hawaii*

Makeup

Apply makeup with...

- ■ **STAYFREE MAXI PADS.** "In a pinch a Stayfree Maxi Pad makes a great makeup sponge."

  —JANET M., *Ridgeland, Mississippi*

Remove makeup with...

- ■ **CRISCO ALL-VEGETABLE SHORTENING.** "Use a dab of Crisco All-Vegetable Shortening to remove makeup and leave skin feeling soft and silky."

  —DEBBIE G., *Columbia, South Carolina*

- ■ **HUGGIES BABY WIPES.** "Huggies Baby Wipes are safe for sensitive skin and even remove waterproof makeup. I am a mother of three so I always have them on hand and I have used them for makeup removal for years."

  —DANA G., *Houston, Texas*

- ■ **JOHNSON'S BABY OIL.** "Johnson's Baby Oil is superb for cleaning off waterproof mascara. Also, if you mix a little baby oil with water in the palm of your hand, it makes a very pleasant skin moisturizer that is economical and nonallergenic."

—CHARLES B., *Greenville, Mississippi*

■ **JOHNSON'S BABY SHAMPOO.** "I've found that the most inexpensive makeup remover in the known universe is Johnson's Baby Shampoo. I wondered one day 'Hey, couldn't I use tearless shampoo to remove eye makeup?' Well, the answer is yes. It doesn't burn and it removes all of your makeup. A bottle of this stuff lasts forever. I don't even buy the big bottle, I just use the trial size. Plus, of course, it makes you smell good."

—LAURA E., *Barboursville, West Virginia*

■ **REDDI-WIP.** "Use Reddi-wip whipped cream to remove eye makeup."

—JENN D., *Washington, New Jersey*

Massage Oil
Substitute for massage oil with...

■ **JOHNSON'S BABY POWDER.** "Use Johnson's baby powder instead of massage oil. It works as a lubricant without the greasy mess of oil. Also, it softens skin and smells great."

—RENEE S., *Menasha, Wisconsin*

Moisturizer
Moisturize skin with...

■ **CRISCO ALL-VEGETABLE SHORTENING.** "I have been using Crisco All-Vegetable Shortening for years to help with the dry skin on my hands. I usually put on a good coat, then put on a pair of Playtex Living Gloves, and leave the Crisco on overnight. Crisco is less costly than most hand lotions, doesn't contain any perfumes, and also prevents dry skin from cracking in the winter months."

—KATE B., *Springfield, Oregon*

■ **DANNON NONFAT PLAIN YOGURT.** "Before I take a shower I cover my body—especially the extra-dry areas—with Dannon

Plain Yogurt. I leave it on my skin for about ten minutes and then I take a warm shower. It keeps my skin smooth and moist. I am fifty years old and have been using it for the past twenty-five years. I have been told I look like I am thirty-five."

—JUANITA R., *Bluefield, West Virginia*

■ **STAR OLIVE OIL.** "Heat up Star Olive Oil and soak hands and feet, then save the oil to use again."

—VIE L., *Concord, California*

■ **VASELINE PETROLEUM JELLY.** "I use Vaseline as an all-over body moisturizer. I swim quite often and the chlorine makes my skin itch terribly. I slather myself with Vaseline after showering and beat the itch. I usually swim in the evenings and find that by morning my skin is very soft but not at all greasy or slimy."

—JULIE D., *Yankton, South Dakota*

Mousse

Mousse your hair with...

■ **ALOE VERA GEL.** "Use Aloe Vera Gel as hairstyling gel. It works great and doesn't contain any alcohol."

—FRANKIE C., *Lebanon, Kentucky*

■ **BARBASOL SHAVING CREAM.** "A small dab of shaving cream will keep your hair in place—especially if you use a hair dryer."

—KEVIN D., *Des Moines, Iowa*

■ **COCA-COLA.** "A can of Coke, diluted with a little water, in a spray bottle and squirted onto damp hair will leave your locks with a sexy, tousled texture. *Dawson's Creek* star Michelle Williams is a big fan of this technique."

—MIRANDA C., *Asheville, North Carolina*

■ **DOMINO SUGAR.** "Mix one part Domino Sugar with two parts warm water in a spray bottle and use it as hair spray."

—SHAUNNA K., *Yellowknife, Northwest Territory*

■ **KNOX GELATIN.** "We use Knox Gelatin for my daughter's hair. It keeps it in place while she performs in the pool for synchronized swimming."

—CINDY G., *Northbrook, Illinois*

Nail Polish

Avoid getting nail polish on your skin with...

■ **JET-PUFFED MARSHMALLOWS.** "Place Jet-Puffed Marshmallows between your toes when polishing your toenails. If your feet are clean, you can eat afterwards."
—CAROL W., *Metairie, Louisiana*

■ **VASELINE PETROLEUM JELLY.** "Put Vaseline on the skin around your fingernails before painting your nails."
—SUSAN J., *Statesville, North Carolina*

Polish your nails with...

■ **LIQUID PAPER.** "When you're all out of nail polish, you can use Liquid Paper to give yourself a French manicure."
—ISABEL T., *Brantford, Ontario*

Prevent nail polish from drying up with...

■ **CUTEX NAIL POLISH REMOVER.** "Add a drop or two of Cutex to an old bottle of nail polish to keep it from drying up."
—ANDREA W., *Fremont, California*

Remove nail polish with...

■ **BOUNCE.** "A used Bounce sheet dipped in Cutex Nail Polish Remover doesn't leave any lint and moisturizes your cuticles as well."
—NATALIE G., *Brossard, Quebec*

■ **L'EGGS SHEER ENERGY PANTY HOSE.** "Panty hose that have been used and abused are great for removing fingernail polish. Just add a drop of Cutex Nail Polish Remover and the polish will come off with ease. No more messy cotton balls or toilet paper."
—KYM A., *Waterbury, Vermont*

Perfume

Perfume yourself with...

■ **DOWNY FABRIC SOFTENER SHEETS.** "Out of perfume? Rub a Downy Fabric Softener Sheet all over your body and smell springtime fresh. (It's inexpensive, too.)"
—JULIE S., *Gallipolis, Ohio*

Dilute perfume with...

■ **SMIRNOFF VODKA.** "Smirnoff Vodka is excellent for diluting perfume that is too strong. It makes the intensity milder without changing the actual fragrance of the perfume."
—KARIMA P., *Pittsburgh, Pennsylvania*

Make perfume last longer with...

■ **VASELINE PETROLEUM JELLY.** "Applying a thin coat of Vaseline Petroleum Jelly to your wrist before putting on your favorite fragrance will make the scent last longer."
—PAM H., *Shenandoah,Virginia*

Perspiration

Prevent underarm sweat stains with...

■ **STAYFREE MAXI PADS.** "If you have a problem with excessive underarm sweat, use self-adhesive Stayfree Maxi Pads under your clothing. Simply adhere the pads in the armpits of your undergarments and—*voila!*—no more embarrassing wetness for all to see."
—MICHELLE G., *North Hollywood, California*

Razors

Prolong the life of razors with...

■ **SMIRNOFF VODKA.** "Simply soak the razor blade in Smirnoff Vodka when not in use. The vodka keeps the blade clean, sharp, and bacteria-free."
—AARON L., *Lexington, Kentucky*

■ **VASELINE PETROLEUM JELLY.** "Dipping your shaving razor blade in Vaseline Petroleum Jelly after every use can make it last for weeks. The jelly rinses off completely with a little warm water."

—TED E., *Miami, Florida*

Real-Life Story

BACK IN THE GAME

"Use Chloraseptic Spray to treat premature ejaculation. A couple of spritzes and the anesthetic partially numbs the nerves. Wait thirty seconds and wipe off excess spray (to avoid transmitting the same effect to your partner). Pleasure can be increased to thirty minutes (or more with further applications). Please don't ask how I discovered this. It's kind of embarrassing."

—JERALD M., *Cleveland, Ohio*

Shaving

Shave with...

■ **CLAIROL HERBEL ESSENCES CONDITIONER.** "Cream rinse is an excellent lubricant for women shaving their legs or men shaving their faces. It leaves skin feeling soft and sensuous."

—CHERYL O., *Niskayuna, New York*

■ **CLOSE-UP TOOTHPASTE.** "I have very sensitive skin and I am allergic to most shaving creams. I've found that the best shaving cream is regular, no-frills Close-Up Toothpaste. It's a shaving cream and aftershave lotion built into one. With a quality razor, Close-Up helps give one of the closest and smoothest shaves ever."

—JASON K., *Fairport, New York*

■ **MIRACLE WHIP.** "Using Miracle Whip to shave your legs hydrates your skin and prevents razor burn."

—CRYSTAL W., *High Point, North Carolina*

■ **REDDI-WIP.** "Simply apply Reddi-wip on your legs and leave on for about two minutes before shaving. Ladies, it moisturizes as you shave."
—SUZANNE L., *Homewood, Alabama*

Prevent skin irritations from shaving your bikini area with...

■ **ABSORBINE JR.** "Apply Absorbine Jr. to the skin after shaving the bikini area to avoid itching and red bumps. It burns slightly for a second, but saves you uncomfortable grief later."
—LORNA S., *Houston, Texas*

Soothe legs after shaving with...

■ **JOHNSON'S BABY OIL.** "After shaving your legs, use Johnson's Baby Oil. They will feel softer than ever."
—KARLA B., *West Fargo, North Dakota*

Skin

Cleanse skin with...

■ **CRISCO ALL-VEGETABLE SHORTENING.** "Use Crisco All-Vegetable Shortening the same way you would use any cleansing cream on your face. It moisturizes and cleanses the skin."
—GENEVIEVE W., *Freeport, Texas*

Tone your skin with...

■ **HEINZ VINEGAR.** "Mix one tablespoon Heinz Apple Cider Vinegar with two cups water. Use after you wash your face as a finishing rinse or toner."
—DEBBIE G., *Columbia, South Carolina*

Spike Hair

Spike your hair with....

■ **CLOSE-UP CLASSIC RED GEL TOOTHPASTE.** "Use Close-Up Gel Toothpaste to get the spiky look in your hair. Works well for other hard-to-hold styles too, and leaves your hair kissably fresh."
—MICHELLE J., *East Hartford, Connecticut*

- **ELMER'S GLUE-ALL.** "Put a dab of Elmer's Glue-All the size of a quarter in your palm, rub in your hands, and apply evenly to your hair. Comb your hair with the fine teeth of the comb to remove the excess glue. Now style spiked hair and let dry. (Elmer's Glue-All is water soluble and washes out of hair with regular shampoo.)"
  —CATHY K., *Chula Vista, California*

Static Electricity

Prevent static electricity in combs and brushes with...

- **BOUNCE.** "Simply stroke a used sheet of Bounce over the flyaway strands of hair and magically the static disappears. This trick is especially helpful for moms dealing with little girls' hair disasters."
  —MARTHA C., *Lewisville, North Carolina*

- **STATIC GUARD.** "I spray Static Guard on the hairbrush before brushing my daughter's hair. It takes the static out of her hair. It doesn't leave a bad smell either."
  —JUDY T., *Tompkinsville, Kentucky*

Weird Fact

SMOKEY AND THE VASELINE

"In the movie *Striptease,* starring Demi Moore, Burt Reynolds coats his entire body with Vaseline."
  —CHRIS S., *Stow, Massachusetts*

Tan

For an instant tan, use...

- **LIPTON TEA.** "For a healthy-looking color on pale skin, brew two strong cups of Lipton tea, let cool, and pour into a plastic spray bottle. Spray the tea on clean, dry skin and let dry. Repeat as desired. This also works for men after they have shaved off a beard."
  —CLAUDIA T., *Huntsville, Alabama*

Teeth

Whiten teeth with...

- **HYDROGEN PEROXIDE.** "Simply gargle for one to two minutes a day for gleaming white teeth."

  —MURRAY W., *Honolulu, Hawaii*

- **VEGEMITE.** "Smear Vegemite on teeth to whiten, then brush off."

  —BOB D., *Nashville, Texas*

Temporarily reglue a loose crown with...

- **COLGATE TOOTHPASTE.** "Put a dab of Colgate Toothpaste inside the crown and press back in place. See your dentist promptly."

  —SUSIE P., *Gush Etzion, Israel*

Toothbrushes

Sanitize toothbrushes with...

- **EFFERDENT.** "Fill a glass with water, drop in two Efferdent tablets, and let toothbrushes sit in the solution overnight."

  —SUSAN Q., *Naperville, Illinois*

Grow It

Cut Flowers

Prolong the life of cut flowers in a vase with...

- **BAYER ASPIRIN.** "Drop two Bayer aspirin tablets into a vase of freshly cut flowers and they will stay fresh longer."

  —JULIE W., *Marietta, Georgia*

- **HYDROGEN PEROXIDE.** "Add a capful of hydrogen peroxide every time you change the water of your fresh-cut flowers. It kills stem-clogging bacteria which wilts the flowers prematurely."

  —RICHARD M., *Studio City, California*

- **7-UP OR SPRITE.** "Filling a vase of cut flowers with 7-Up or Sprite instead of water makes the flowers last longer and look better."

  —SHELLEY M., *Dublin, Ohio*

Keep flowers upright in a vase with...

- **SCOTCH TAPE.** "Put pieces of Scotch Tape crisscross over the mouth of the vase."

  —RITA H., *San Bernardino, California*

Seal cut flowers with...

- **CRAYOLA CRAYONS.** "Melt a green Crayola Crayon and dip the end of the stem of a cut flower into the hot wax to seal the stem and keep the flower looking fresh longer."

  —HILDA R., *Laredo, Texas*

Fertilizer

Enrich plant soil with...

- **BUDWEISER.** "Whenever my husband and his friends have leftover Budweiser beer, I dilute it with water (one part beer to two parts water). I pour this mixture on my azaleas, shrubs, and ornamental grasses. It makes a great plant food. My yard looks better all the time."

—DONNA H., *Hammond, Louisiana*

■ **EPSOM SALT.** "For every foot of a plant's height, sprinkle one teaspoon of Epsom Salt evenly around the base for better blossoms and deeper greening. Adding Epsom Salt to any plant food will also enrich the color of any flowering plants and aid in disease resistance."

—MARY K., *Scranton, Pennsylvania*

■ **KELLOGG'S FROSTED MINI-WHEATS.** "Add leftover crumbs in cereal boxes such as Kellogg's Frosted Mini-Wheats to your garden soil or planter mix. The sugar adds nitrogen and the cereal adds potassium and other nutrients."

—CAROLYN B., *Yorba Linda, California*

Fungus

Kill fungus in trees with...

■ **CLOROX BLEACH.** "Do you have mistletoe or a fungus in your tree? Does the tree surgeon say there is no hope? Before you cut down the tree, pour one or two gallons of Clorox around the base of the tree. Repeat every four months. I have done this for oak, pine, and pecan trees. One of my friends used this technique on his oak tree that was rotting from the inside out. The tree healed, and five years later he still has his beautiful tree."

—SHERRY F., *De Ridder, Louisiana*

Gardenias

Make gardenias bloom with...

■ **HEINZ VINEGAR.** "Use one-quarter teaspoon of white vinegar in a gallon of water to get gardenias to bloom. Don't overdo it or you can kill the plant. I water the gardenia bush with this solution about once a week until it blooms."

—BOB B., *Millville, New Jersey*

Germinating

Germinate seedlings with...

- **DANNON YOGURT CUPS.** "Using a large nail and hammer, try to poke a hole in the center of the bottom of each [empty, clean] cup. This will usually yield a three-pronged crack radiating out from the center, just the right amount of drainage for a seedling cup. Line the bottom with a small square of newspaper, add your preferred potting mix, and plant your tomato, pepper, or other seeds. An eight-ounce yogurt cup has plenty of room for two or three seedlings of most vegetables, but only one of most cucumber family varieties (squash, pumpkin, or melon). Don't hesitate to put in three or more seeds, figuring at least one won't germinate. With plants such as the cucumber family that have delicate roots and don't transplant easily, plan to thin down to one plant per cup."

—JOHN P., *Albuquerque, New Mexico*

Grass

Kill grass in crevices with...

- **MORTON SALT.** "Simply sprinkle the cracks and crevices with Morton Salt to kill unwanted grass and weeds."

—ROBIN R., *Pearl River, New York*

Houseplants

Water houseplants more efficiently with...

- **HUGGIES DIAPERS.** "When potting plants in hanging baskets, pots, or window boxes, remove plastic cover from a pair of Huggies disposable diapers, then alternate potting soil with the diaper stuffing. This really cuts down on how often you'll need to water your container plants, and the gel capsules also store plant food and slowly feed the plants."

—KIM R., *Fort Wayne, Indiana*

- **KNOX GELATINE.** "Sprinkle Knox Gelatine into pots of houseplants to absorb water so you don't have to water the plants as often. The gelatin will hold onto water instead of letting it run through soil."

—JAMES M., *Thaxton, Virginia*

Prevent houseplant pots from leaking water with...

- **HUGGIES PULL-UPS.** "Put a pair of Pull-Ups on the bottom of leaky plants to catch the water. To cover up the Pull-Up, place the first pot in a second, larger pot."
  —JAMIE D., *Tonawanda, New York*

Insecticide

Repel insects from plants with...

- **LISTERINE AND DAWN.** "Mix one teaspoon of Listerine (regular flavor) and one teaspoon of Dawn dishwashing liquid in a quart spray bottle to use once every two weeks as an insecticide on garden plants, especially fruits and vegetables."
  —TED B., *Boise, Idaho*

Lawn Mowers

Prevent cut grass from sticking under a lawn mower with...

- **PAM NO STICK COOKING SPRAY.** "Spray Pam on the underside of your lawn mower when mowing wet grass, and the grass will not stick to the blades. I get by with one application for both my front and back yards."
  —BRIAN P., *Tulsa, Oklahoma*

Filter sediment from a gas can when filling a lawn mower with...

- **MR. COFFEE FILTERS.** "I place a Mr. Coffee Filter over the mouth of my plastic portable gas canister (for my lawn mower), then screw on the threaded cap. Over time sediment sinks to the bottom of the gas can, but the paper filter prevents me from pouring these particles into the gas tank of the lawn mower. The gas pours slowly, but at least it's filtered. I recommend changing the Mr. Coffee Filter once a year."
  —PETER S., *Deltona, Florida*

Lubricate a lawn mower with...

- **JIF PEANUT BUTTER.** "I put a dollop of peanut butter on the blade shaft of my lawn mower. It provides great lubrication."
  —ROBERT T., *Orlando, Florida*

Moss

Grow moss with...

- **DANNON YOGURT.** "I mix one cup of Dannon Plain Yogurt, one cup of water, and a handful of common lawn moss in my blender for thirty seconds. Then I paint this mixture on my flower pots or pour it between the cracks in my stone sidewalk. Soon I have beautiful new moss decorating my flower pots or a lovely green moss carpet growing between the sidewalk stones. This is not only pretty but also prevents weeds from taking root."

  —MARIE C., *Silver Creek, New York*

Plant Leaves

Shine plant leaves with...

- **HELLMANN'S** OR **BEST REAL MAYONNAISE.** "Rub Hellmann's Real Mayonnaise on your plant leaves to make them shiny and healthy-looking all year round."

  —SUZANNE B., *Dartmouth, Massachusetts*

- **MIRACLE WHIP.** "When I was younger my mother used to have me take a paper towel and rub our plant leaves with Miracle Whip. It really makes the leaves shine and keeps dust from settling on them."

  —CHERYL V., *Winchester, Kentucky*

- **STAR OLIVE OIL.** "Put a little olive oil on a paper towel and lightly coat each leaf, then wipe the excess off."

  —JENNY E., *Washington, Illinois*

Planters

Clean planters with...

- **CLOROX BLEACH.** "Mix three-quarters cup Clorox Bleach per gallon of water in a bucket and soak recycled plastic and clay pots, planters, and seed-starter trays."

  —JAC W., *Bloomingdale, New Jersey*

Poison Ivy

Kill poison ivy with...

- **CLOROX BLEACH.** "Spraying Clorox on poison ivy kills the plant."
  —FRAN A., *Hutchinson, Kansas*

- **MORTON SALT.** "Pour Morton Salt on poison ivy on a dry sunny day and the poison ivy will die."
  —CLIFF C., *Boone, North Carolina*

Pruning Shears

Clean pruning shears with...

- **CLOROX BLEACH.** "Mix three-quarters cup Clorox Bleach per gallon of water in a bucket. This solution is invaluable for disinfecting pruning equipment to halt the spread of diseases, if not between cuts, at least between plants."
  —JAC W., *Bloomingdale, New Jersey*

Tomatoes

Stake tomato plants with...

- **L'EGGS SHEER ENERGY PANTY HOSE.** "I cut one inch strips of L'eggs Panty Hose and use them as ties to support plants and vegetables on stakes. The strips are like a firm elastic that stretches as the plant grows. I also fill the foot of the panty hose with diatomacious earth and then dust my plants and vegetables. Sock it to 'em!"
  —SANDRA Z., *Raleigh, North Carolina*

Fertilize tomato plants with...

- **KNOX GELATINE.** "Knox Gelatine diluted with water adds nitrogen to tomato plants in the garden."
  —WANDA B., *Bristol, Tennessee*

- **20 MULE TEAM BORAX.** "When I lived in Georgia, a tomato farmer told me to put a teaspoon of 20 Mule Team Borax in the ground and mix with the soil before planting the tomato plants in the early spring. This helps the blossoms set on the first cool nights and helps bring on an early tomato crop."

  —RONNIE C., *Patterson, Louisiana*

Water tomato plants more efficiently with...

- **CLOROX BLEACH BOTTLES.** "To conserve water, cut the bottoms off clean, empty Clorox bottles and bury them, neck down, next to the tomato plant. Then water the plant by filling up the plastic bottle with water. The water goes to the roots where it's needed. (This technique doesn't work for plants with shallow roots, such as basil or azaleas; those should be watered from above ground.)

  —STEVE H., *Swedesboro, New Jersey*

Tools

Prevent tools from rusting with...

- **PAM NO STICK COOKING SPRAY.** "After cleaning your garden tools, spray them with a light coat of Pam No Stick Cooking Spray to keep them from rusting."

  —LAURIE D., *Phoenix, Arizona*

Weeds

Kill weeds with...

- **HEINZ WHITE VINEGAR.** "Pour vinegar on weeds and the grasses that grow up in the cracks in the sidewalk and driveway. It's an environmentally-safe weed killer that really works well."

  —ROBERTA B., *Dayton, Ohio*

- **SPRAY 'N WASH.** "Spray 'n Wash kills weeds without hurting the soil. You'll also get those nasty stains out of the weeds."

  —SYDNEY B., *Amarillo, Texas*

Worms

Breed worms with...

■ **MAXWELL HOUSE COFFEE.** "My grandfather put used Maxwell House Coffee grounds in his worm bed and had the best worms around. It keeps the worms awake, too."

—LANCE M., *Ward Cove, Alaska*

Heal It

Acne

Dry up acne pimples with...

- **COLGATE TOOTHPASTE.** "Put a dab of Colgate Toothpaste on your pimples and the next day wash your face and they will be gone."

  —MIKE A., *Vancouver, British Columbia*

- **CORTAID.** "Using an allergy cream like Cortaid on your pimples reduces the swelling and tenderness."

  —IVAN H., *Cerritos, California*

- **CREST TOOTHPASTE.** "Crest Regular Toothpaste, applied to a pimple and covered with a Band-Aid before bed, will reduce the pimple by the next morning."

  —DANIELLE B., *Grand Island, New York*

- **NEOSPORIN.** "Use Neosporin for pimples or blemishes. Dab a little on the blemish. The antibiotic helps to clear it up."

  —TRICIA R., *Wyandotte, Michigan*

- **PHILLIP'S MILK OF MAGNESIA.** "I've had acne for years and I find using Phillip's Milk of Magnesia as a facial mask or blemish treatment greatly decreases the amount of oil on my face. It also helps take the redness away from blemishes and makes them go away faster."

  —STACIE H., *Valley City, North Dakota*

- **PREPARATION H.** "Preparation H is the best cream for reducing the swelling of acne pimples."

  —MARLENE M., *Denver, Colorado*

- **SUEBEE HONEY.** "I had a serious pimple which could not be steamed or medicated. I tried for a week. It was embedded. I put

140

SueBee Honey on it and covered that with a Band-Aid. The pimple came to the surface and disappeared in one day."

—RITA G., *Joshua Tree, California*

■ **VISINE.** "Applying Visine to pimples or other skin irritations removes the redness. Visine is a vasoconstrictor that works fast. Be sure not to touch the tip of the bottle to the skin if you plan to use it on your eyes again."

—CHRISTINA F., *New York, New York*

Allergies

Eliminate allergic reactions to metal buttons on clothing with...

■ **MAYBELLINE CRYSTAL CLEAR NAIL POLISH.** "Paint the backs of fly buttons on jeans with Maybelline Crystal Clear Nail Polish to prevent skin irritation for those who are allergic to nickel and other metals."

—DANNII R., *Christie Downs, South Africa*

Arthritis

Relieve arthritis pain and joint immobility with...

■ **HEINZ APPLE CIDER VINEGAR.** "Drink two tablespoons of Heinz Apple Cider Vinegar daily. It really works."

—JANA C., *Crawfordsville, Indiana*

■ **WD-40.** "If you suffer from occasional joint pain in knees or wherever, spray on WD-40 and rub it in. It really makes movement easier."

—DONNA E., *Fennville, Michigan*

Asthma

Stop asthma attacks with...

■ **HEINZ APPLE CIDER VINEGAR.** "Do you have asthma? When you feel congested and start to wheeze, take a teaspoon of Heinz Apple Cider Vinegar. It will stop an attack."

—SHERRY F., *De Ridder, Louisiana*

Athlete's Foot

Cure athlete's foot with...

- **HEINZ VINEGAR.** "Soak your feet in Heinz White Vinegar four times daily for several weeks."

  —David S., *Atlanta, Georgia*

- **PREPARATION H.** "Everyone knows the benefits of Preparation H to the posterior; however, it is also excellent for athlete's foot and itchy toes."

  —Aubrey B., *Fairhope, Alabama*

Baby Injections

Relieve a baby from the pain of an inoculation with...

- **LIPTON TEA.** "Dampen a Lipton Tea bag in warm water and apply to the skin to relieve the pain from baby shots. The tannic acid in the tea does the trick. I used tea bags with both my kids and I never even had to give them Tylenol."

  —Jennifer A., *Fort Pierce, Florida*

Bee and Wasp Stings

Relieve bee and wasp stings with...

- **ADOLPH'S ORIGINAL UNSEASONED TENDERIZER.** "Make a paste from water and Adolph's Tenderizer, and apply to the bee sting. Within two minutes, the sting is relieved, and the skin heals within an hour."

  —Rob W., *Rocky River, Ohio*

- **ARM & HAMMER BAKING SODA.** "When you get a bee sting, put some moist baking soda on it and cover with a Band-Aid. It will draw out the poison."

  —Flo J., *Hollandale, Minnesota*

- **BAN DEODORANT.** "Applying Ban stick deodorant directly on a bee or wasp sting stops the pain and swelling immediately. Excellent for the first-aid box."

  —R. S., *Pender Island, British Columbia*

- **DOMINO SUGAR.** "To stop the pain of a bee or wasp sting, make a paste from water and a teaspoon of Domino Sugar. Rub the mixture over the bite for a few minutes. The sugar neutralizes the poison from the sting."

  —BILL N., *Shingleton, Michigan*

- **LISTERINE.** "I got stung by a wasp and had no anesthetics, so I grabbed a bottle of Listerine mouthwash and dabbed it on the sting. Wow! The pain was instantly gone."

  —HARRIET F., *Lansing, Michigan*

- **MCCORMICK OR SCHILLING MEAT TENDERIZER.** "Make a paste from meat tenderizer and water, then apply the mixture on a bee sting, making sure you've removed the stinger. The enzymes in bee venom are broken down by the enzymes in meat tenderizer."

  —TRISTAN A., *Sunrise, Florida*

- **PREPARATION H.** "To remove the stinger and provide immediate relief from a bee sting, simply apply a liberal coat of Preparation H to the area."

  —SAM S., *Copenhagen, New York*

- **SUEBEE HONEY.** "Applying SueBee Honey to a bee sting reduces the swelling within about twenty minutes. Especially great for those allergic to bee stings."

  —JANET D., *North Charleston, South Carolina*

- **WD-40.** "Spray WD-40 directly on a bee sting. It takes the sting right out."

  —ALTA D., *Archer, Florida*

- **WINDEX.** "Use regular blue Windex on bee stings. It lessens the pain and the ammonia draws the poison out, thus reducing the swelling."

  —BARB P., *Dover, Ohio*

Bleeding

Stop a bleeding wound in an emergency with...

- **PAMPERS.** "When my son cut his knee badly, I used the cleanest thing I could find to protect it and stop the bleeding during the trip to the hospital. What was it? A Pampers disposable diaper! I also used Pampers when my other son cut his head. He was quite a sight with a diaper on his head."

—JACQUE H., *Tucson, Arizona*

- **SOFTSOAP INSTANT ANTIBACTERIAL HAND GEL.** "If you accidentally scratch a scab open, Softsoap Instant Antibacterial Hand Gel stops bleeding."

—SHERYL L., *Clearlake, California*

- **SURE-JELL.** "To stop bleeding, just sprinkle a little Sure-Jell on the wound and it will jell right up. Great for camping, boating, and hiking."

—TINA R., *Bradley, West Virginia*

Blisters

Prevent blisters from new shoes with...

- **VASELINE PETROLEUM JELLY.** "Apply Vaseline Petroleum Jelly on new shoes where there is friction against your feet."

—GINA S., *Niagara Falls, Ontario*

Boils

Soothe a boil with...

- **ARM & HAMMER BAKING SODA.** "When I have a boil in an uncomfortable spot, I use a hot compress with some Arm & Hammer Baking Soda to take the soreness away. The compress also opens the boil so the head can be removed."

—KAREN P., *Massapequa, New York*

- **LIPTON TEA.** "If you cover a boil with a wet tea bag overnight, the boil drains by the next morning without any pain."

—JIM V., *Dedham, Massachusetts*

Bruises

Soothe a bruise with...

- **HEINZ VINEGAR.** "Soak a piece of cotton in Heinz Vinegar, then apply it to a bruise for an hour to remove the blueness and quicken healing."

—KIRSTY R., *Bristol, England*

- **ORAJEL.** "Using Orajel on and around a bruise apparently tells the brain that there is no injury at that particular location, so the brain stops constricting the blood vessels that would otherwise cause discoloration."

  —DENIS R., *Ottawa, Ontario*

- **PREPARATION H.** "Preparation H is great for speeding up the healing and disappearance of bruises."

  —GINNY W., *Summerdale, Alabama*

- **STAR OLIVE OIL.** "When you hit your thigh on a table and antici-pate a bruise, rub Star Olive Oil on the spot and the bruise will not appear."

  —JULIE P., *St. Thomas, Virgin Islands*

Burned Tongue

Soothe a burned tongue with...

- **DOMINO SUGAR.** "Just a few granules of Domino Sugar on the tongue relieves the pain."

  —MONICA J., *Seattle, Washington*

Burns

Heal burns with...

- **ARM & HAMMER BAKING SODA.** "Make a paste of baking soda and water (like thick cake batter) and apply to the burn. Cover with gauze and tape."

  —SUSAN T., *Parma Heights, Ohio*

- **AUNT JEMIMA ORIGINAL SYRUP** AND **GOLD MEDAL FLOUR.** "Mix equal amounts of Aunt Jemima Original Syrup and Gold Medal Flour into a paste and apply it to a burn. Cover with a gauze bandage, and wait ten minutes. Somehow it draws the burning sensation out of the burn."

  —LYNN J., *Melrose Park, Illinois*

- **CARNATION CONDENSED MILK.** "If you burn yourself, pour Carnation Condensed Milk on the burn to relieve the pain and prevent scarring."

  —FRANCOISE G., *Yellowknife, New Territory*

■ **COLGATE TOOTHPASTE.** "Spread a generous quantity of Colgate Toothpaste on the skin immediately after burning. Let it dry and keep it on for a few hours. You can use a bandage to protect it. After washing the toothpaste off, the burnt skin should appear red but dry, without blisters. The toothpaste seems to isolate the skin from oxygen (making the burn less painful right away) and prevents the formation of blisters. It also seems to dry out the skin deeply, preventing liquid from building up under the skin. The skin remains 'sealed' and heals more easily. I have used toothpaste to relieve a burn many times, once on a pretty harsh oven-grid burn which healed very quickly."

—DANIEL C., *Montreal, Quebec*

■ **CREST TOOTHPASTE.** "When my son was a year old, he spilled extremely hot espresso on his hand, causing an immediate blister. After the usual first-aid treatment of an ice cube, he was still screaming, so an elderly woman got Crest Regular Toothpaste and smeared it all over the burn. He stopped screaming immediately. The next time I burned myself, I tried Crest and it worked."

—LINDA H., *Glenolden, Pennsylvania*

■ **DESITIN.** "To soothe minor scrapes and first-degree burns, apply Desitin cream to the area."

—KIMBERLY M., *Baltimore, Maryland*

■ **FRENCH'S MUSTARD.** "Burn yourself? Immediately apply French's Yellow Mustard to the burn, and the burn will stop stinging and will not blister."

—JUDI F., *Peabody, Massachusetts*

■ **KIKKOMAN SOY SAUCE.** "Kikkoman Soy Sauce quickly relieves the pain from a burn. I burnt my thumb on a hot pie plate, enough to blister. I placed my thumb in soy sauce. After three minutes, I had no pain from the burn."

—CLARK S., *APO, AP*

■ **MCCORMICK** OR **SCHILLING VANILLA EXTRACT.** "A Chattanooga fireman told me to use McCormick Vanilla Extract on a kitchen burn. I keep a bottle in the cabinet and whenever I burn myself frying or by accidentally touching a hot item, I apply the extract. I thought he was nuts until I tried it. I learned this hint over fifteen years ago, and I have not had a painful burn since then."

—JUDY L., *Chattanooga, Tennessee*

■ **NOXZEMA.** "Use Noxzema skin cream to soothe burns and keep them from blistering."

—TRACIE M., *Southfield, Michigan*

■ **ORAJEL.** "Orajel relieves the pain of small burns if used immediately. I have even seen fairly large burns disappear when I used Orajel right away."

—DENIS R., *Ottawa, Ontario*

■ **PREPARATION H.** "Immediately apply Preparation H on mild burns and they won't blister. Depending on the severity of the burn, you may even be able to prevent any marks whatsoever."

—SHARON M., *Arlington, Virginia*

■ **SMUCKER'S CONCORD GRAPE JELLY.** "Just rub a little Smucker's Jelly on a mild burn to relieve the pain."

—KEITH P., *Orlando, Florida*

■ **SUEBEE HONEY.** "Put SueBee Honey on burns to help the healing."

—DENISE N., *Mt. Prospect, Illinois*

■ **SUNLIGHT** AND **HEINZ WHITE VINEGAR.** "Combine Sunlight dishwashing liquid with white vinegar and apply to a burn. It works like magic to take away the pain and prevent blisters and scarring."

—LORNA M., *Downsview, Ontario*

Cactus

Remove cactus spines from the skin with...

■ **ELMER'S GLUE-ALL.** "Spread a thin layer of Elmer's Glue-All over the spines and let dry. Peal off the dry glue. This should remove a large number of the hard-to-see spines from the skin."

—REBECCA A., *Marietta, Georgia*

Calluses

Prevent calluses from splitting open with...

- **KRAZY GLUE.** "Guitar players on tour use Krazy Glue to hold split calluses on their fingers together."
  —KEVIN M., *Toronto, Ontario*

Heal a callus with...

- **VICKS VAPORUB.** "Apply Vicks VapoRub on a callus, then cover it with a Band-Aid. Repeat over a few days and the callus will disappear."
  —VICKI S., *Lynwood, California*

Canker Sores

Soothe and heal a canker sore with...

- **ARM & HAMMER BAKING SODA.** "Moisten the end of your finger, dip in baking soda, and put the powder on the canker sore. The baking soda helps the sore heal much faster. My grandfather taught me that."
  —LYNN M., *Plano, Texas*

- **LIPTON TEA.** "Hold a wet Lipton tea bag on a canker sore and the tannin in the tea will help the healing process."
  —CATHERINE P., *Scotch Plains, New Jersey*

Chaffing

Soothe chaffing skin with...

- **VASELINE PETROLEUM JELLY.** "If you wear skirts, just smear a small amount of Vaseline Petroleum Jelly on the part of your thighs that touch to prevent chaffing on the inner thigh."
  —HARRIET W., *Clearwater, Florida*

Chapped Lips

Soothe chapped lips with...

- **NOXZEMA.** "To relieve chapped lips, put some Noxzema on your lips before going to bed. The taste is pretty bad, but your lips will be smooth in the morning."
  —JULIE S., *Washington, Missouri*

Chicken Pox

Relieve itching from Chicken Pox with...

■ **PHILLIP'S MILK OF MAGNESIA.** "Use Phillip's Milk of Magnesia as a lotion to soothe Chicken Pox."

—CAROLYN C., *Colorado Springs, Colorado*

■ **QUAKER OATS** AND **L'EGGS SHEER ENERGY PANTY HOSE.** "Cut off the foot from a clean pair of L'eggs Panty Hose and fill with one-half cup Quaker Oats. Tie a knot in the nylon and hang it from the tub's spigot while filling the tub with water for an inexpensive and soothing oatmeal bath. Once the tub is filled with water, use the oatmeal sack as a washcloth to wash with soap."

—DEBBIE G., *Columbia, South Carolina*

Chiggers

Repel chiggers and soothe chigger bites with...

■ **MAYBELLINE CRYSTAL CLEAR NAIL POLISH.** "Just brush Maybelline Clear Nail Polish over chigger bites and the chiggers, which have burrowed into the skin, die. Finally, no more itching."

—NICOLE A., *Seadrift, Texas*

■ **PREPARATION H.** "Do your chigger bites itch? Put Preparation H (cream or gel) on the bites and rub it in to reduce the swelling and itching."

—ROBERT S., *Maryland Heights, Missouri*

■ **SELSUN BLUE SHAMPOO.** "My Nana used to put dabs of this amazing blue stuff directly on any chigger bites I ever had and it works. No more itching and they heal faster."

—LISA B., *Newcastle, Oklahoma*

Colds

Cure a cold with...

■ **HEINZ VINEGAR.** "I take two tablespoons of Heinz White Vinegar straight, not watered down, the first sign of a cold coming on. The cold usually disappears within the next day or two."

—YVONNE B., *Yatesville, Georgia*

Cold Sores

Heal a cold sore with...

- **HEINZ VINEGAR.** "Applying Heinz Vinegar liberally to a cold sore the moment it appears dries it up and keeps it from swelling and hurting."
  —AMY M., *Deming, New Mexico*

- **MYLANTA.** "Dabbing cold sores with Mylanta dries up the acid in the sore."
  —AMY S., *Toledo, Ohio*

- **PREPARATION H.** "For years I have used Preparation H hemorrhoid cream to stop cold sores in their tracks. The minute you feel a cold sore coming on your lips, start dabbing Preparation H on the spot and your cold sore will be a thing of the past."
  —BARBRA P., *Naples, Florida*

- **PURELL.** "Wash the area around the cold sore and gently pat dry. Put Purell no-wash antiseptic hand cleaner on the sore. The cold sore will dry up in a day or so. It's much cheaper than those prescription ointments and there isn't any need for a trip to the doctor for a prescription."
  —MARY ELISE L., *Richmond, Virginia*

Corns

Remove corns with...

- **CHAPSTICK.** "Rubbing a little ChapStick lip balm on corns softens them and eases any pain."
  —BARRY S., *Rego Park, New York*

- **KARO CORN SYRUP.** "Karo Corn Syrup softens corns."
  —VIRGINIA H., *Eagle River, Alaska*

- **TIDE.** "Soak your feet in liquid Tide detergent, rinse well, then coat the corn with Vaseline Petroleum Jelly."
  —TRACIE M., *Southfield, Michigan*

Cuticles

Condition cuticles with...

- **CHAPSTICK.** "Use ChapStick lip balm to relieve dry, cracked cuticles."

  —FONNIE M., *El Paso, Texas*

- **VASELINE PETROLEUM JELLY.** "The cuticles on my nails are horrible. When I want my hands to look good for a special occasion, I massage Vaseline into the cuticles before going to bed. Then I put on a pair of white cotton gloves to keep the Vaseline on my hands and off the sheets, which don't need moisturizing, thank you. A few nights of this and my cuticles look really nice."

  —MADELEINE, *Dublin, Ohio*

Dandruff

Cure dandruff with...

- **HEINZ WHITE VINEGAR.** "Rinsing your hair with Heinz White Vinegar is not only good for the scalp, it can also cure dandruff."

  —TIM A., *South Whitley, Indiana*

- **LISTERINE.** "I have been a hairdresser for thirty-five years and the best dandruff medication is Listerine mouthwash. Wash hair, rinse with Listerine, leave in, and style."

  —VIE L., *Concord, California*

Diaper Rash

Soothe diaper rash with...

- **BAG BALM.** "Use Bag Balm on your baby's behind."

  —CHRISTY M., *Ashtabula, Ohio*

- **CRISCO ALL-VEGETABLE SHORTENING.** "Smear the baby's butt completely with Crisco and the rash will clear up faster than any store-bought remedy."

  —LISA D., *Bolingbrook, Illinois*

- **KINGSFORD'S CORN STARCH.** "Use Kingsford's Corn Starch for diaper rash. It works great."

  —MARIA P., *Meridian, Mississippi*

■ **MYLANTA.** "My pediatrician recommended dabbing liquid Mylanta on my baby's bottom to get rid of diaper rash. It works."

—DIXIE H., *Madison, Tennessee*

■ **PALMOLIVE.** "Palmolive dishwashing liquid works great to prevent diaper rash or to clear it up quickly. Put a few drops of Palmolive in a bathtub of warm water and let baby play for a few minutes in the bubbles. Rinse well, dry, and diaper. Within two baths, the rash will clear up. My family and close friends have used this tip. Not one of my four kids ever had a diaper rash, and I never used Desitin."

—SANDY G., *New Castle, Delaware*

■ **PAM NO STICK COOKING SPRAY.** "When my husband came home from the nursing home, he had a severe diaper rash. Looking around for something to use, I found Pam No Stick Cooking Spray. Figuring it could not hurt him, I used it. It worked. The rash is gone. It took about a week."

—JEWEL, *West Palm Beach, Florida*

■ **PHILLIP'S MILK OF MAGNESIA.** "Two pediatricians told me to make a paste from Phillip's Milk of Magnesia and corn starch or sponge the Milk of Magnesia directly on the skin. If you think about it, this is an obvious cure, but little known. Inexpensive, too."

—LAUREL P., *Acworth, Georgia*

Diarrhea

Prevent diarrhea while taking antibiotics with...

■ **DANNON NONFAT YOGURT.** "Taking antibiotics not only kills disease-bearing bacteria but often kills the healthy bacteria necessary for proper digestion, resulting in diarrhea. Eating Dannon Yogurt with active cultures (*Lactobacillus acidophilus*) produces bacteriocins necessary for proper digestion."

—MADELEINE J., *Burlington, Vermont*

Dry Hands

Moisturize dry hands with...

- **NEOSPORIN.** "Neosporin antibiotic is great as a hand cream for really dry hands."
  —KEREN H., *Port Angeles, Washington*

- **PREPARATION H.** "For dry, chapped hands use Preparation H."
  —JEANMARIE S., *Tilden, Nebraska*

Ears

Protect newly pierced ears from infection with...

- **PREPARATION H.** "If you use Preparation H on newly pierced ears, it will protect them from infection."
  —YVONNE L., *Kokomo, Indiana*

Eczema

Heal eczema with...

- **CRISCO ALL-VEGETABLE SHORTENING.** "Rubbing Crisco on the skin of a baby who has eczema will improve the condition."
  —RACHEL K., *White Plains, New York*

Eyes

Soothe tired eyes with...

- **LIPTON TEA.** "Take two Lipton tea bags, soak with warm water, and cover your eyes for twenty to thirty minutes to remove puffiness and revitalize tired eyes."
  —PAUL F., *Akron, Ohio*

Eliminate bags under eyes with...

- **PREPARATION H.** "Makeup artists swear by Preparation H to get rid of puffiness around the eyes. Rub it into the skin under the eyes and wait. It acts as a vasoconstrictor and really works. Just be careful not to get it in your eyes. Of course, you should avoid using it frequently for this purpose."

—RACHAEL K., *Skokie, Illinois*

Feet

Soften dry feet with...

- **BOUNCE.** "Put one Bounce sheet in a small bucket of warm water and soak your feet in it for ten minutes. It makes a great foot moisturizer."

  —JENNIFER C., *Montgomery, Alabama*

- **HELLMANN'S** OR **BEST REAL MAYONNAISE.** "If you warm up Hellmann's Real Mayonnaise in the microwave and then soak your feet in it, you can get your feet ready for sandals for the summer."

  —DIANE L., *San Diego, California*

- **QUAKER OATS.** "Mix one cup of Quaker Oats, one-third cup of honey, and one-half cup of milk. Put the mixture in a dish pan and place your feet in it for twenty minutes, working them back and forth in the mixture. I guarantee your feet have never had it so good."

  —PAULA S., *Paint Rock, Alabama*

- **VICKS VAPORUB.** "To soften and soothe dry aching feet, apply a generous amount of Vicks VapoRub to feet before going to bed and cover with a pair of heavy socks. By morning, your feet will feel ultra smooth and rejuvenated."

  —LAURA Z., *Fort Worth, Texas*

Deodorize smelly feet with...

- **HEINZ VINEGAR.** "Soaking your smelly feet in Heinz White Vinegar will get rid of that bad stink for about three months."

  —KEN H., *Clover, South Carolina*

- **JELL-O.** "I soak my smelly feet in strawberry Jell-O (already made) for twenty minutes, then rinse. My hubby will lap my toes for hours after that."

  —JULIE B., *Minneapolis, Minnesota*

Fever

Relieve a fever with...

■ **SMIRNOFF VODKA.** "Smirnoff Vodka can be used as a liniment on your chest and back when you have a fever. (This is supposedly an old Ukranian remedy.)"
—DARRYL P., *Edmonton, Alberta*

Fire Ants

Relieve bites from fire ants with...

■ **COLGATE TOOTHPASTE.** "If neighbors, family, or friends see me running to the house after being bitten by fire ants, they know I am heading for the Colgate Toothpaste. It works and I don't get any blisters the next day."
—BAYOU SIS, *Baton Rouge, Louisiana*

Genital Warts

Locate genital warts with...

■ **HEINZ WHITE VINEGAR.** "Dermatologists, urologists, and gynecologists use white vinegar to find genital warts. The warts appear bright white after a vinegar-soaked towel has been applied to the genital area for five minutes."
—TERRY C., *Boston, Massachusetts*

Hangovers

Prevent a hangover with...

■ **SUEBEE HONEY.** "Honey contains a large amount of fructose which helps the body metabolize alcohol, flushing the alcohol from the body and lessening the effects."
—CHRIS N., *Pittsburgh, Pennsylvania*

Hemorrhoids

Soothe hemorrhoids with...

■ **ORAJEL.** "If you have hemorrhoids and you're out of Preparation H, reach for the Orajel. Orajel is a pain reliever for teeth and works great for hemorrhoids, too."
—ELOISE W., *Jacksonville, North Carolina*

Hiccups

Cure hiccups with...

▪ **DOMINO SUGAR.** "Take a full teaspoon of granulated Domino Sugar and swallow it dry, without water."

—LOIS W., *Bluffton, South Carolina*

▪ **JIF PEANUT BUTTER.** "As soon as those pesky hiccups begin, immediately grab a jar of Jif Peanut Butter and eat one heaping spoonful. This is a sure way to cure them."

—SHERA A., *West Jefferson, North Carolina*

▪ **REALEMON.** "To cure hiccups, pour yourself a jigger of ReaLemon lemon juice, and down it quickly. It really works."

—BRENDA C., *Catlettsburg, Kentucky*

Hot Water Bottles

Improvise a hot water bottle with a...

▪ **ZIPLOC STORAGE BAG.** "Fill a Ziploc freezer bag with water, seal well, pop it in the microwave for thirty seconds, and use it as a hot water bottle."

—MICHELLE L., *East Meadow, New York*

Ice Packs

Use an ice pack that molds to the contours of your body with...

▪ **BIRDS EYE SWEET GREEN PEAS.** "Next time you have a toothache from dental work, a black eye, a sprained ankle, or any other soreness that requires an ice pack, use a plastic bag of Birds Eye frozen peas instead. It works great, and you can still eat the peas after they've thawed out."

—CARL T., *Portland, Oregon*

▪ **ZIPLOC STORAGE BAG** AND **SMIRNOFF VODKA.** "Pour one-half cup Smirnoff Vodka and one-half cup water into a Ziploc freezer bag (add food coloring for easy identification), and freeze. The alcohol doesn't freeze, so you have a great, slushy ice pack."

—RENEE B., *Danville, Iowa*

Indigestion

Relieve indigestion with...

- **ARM & HAMMER BAKING SODA.** "It used to say on the box of Arm & Hammer Baking Soda, feel the 'burp of relief.' It no longer does, but it still tells you to take it for heartburn or indigestion. One-half teaspoon dissolved in one-half glass of water really does give you the 'burp of relief.' I have taken it for years and it gets rid of heartburn immediately." (Arm & Hammer Baking Soda does neutralize an acid stomach, but read the instructions on the side of the box carefully.)
  —JUDY S., *Danville, Illinois*

- **COCA-COLA.** "Pediatricians often recommend that patients with an upset stomach drink a glass of flat Coca-Cola, served at room temperature, to relieve the upset."
  —MADELINE V., *Sarasota, Florida*

Insect Bites

Relieve insect bites with...

- **ALBERTO VO5 HAIR SPRAY.** "I use hair spray to stop the itching from bug bites."
  —EMILY B., *St. Louis, Missouri*

- **ALKA-SELTZER.** "Mix two Alka-Seltzer tablets in a glass of water and dab the mixture on the insect bite. This also works on Fiddle Back spider bites. I was bitten by one last summer and the Alka-Seltzer worked."
  —BEV F., *Midwest City, Oklahoma*

- **BAN DEODORANT.** "I was suffering miserably from mosquito bites and had nothing to put on them. It occurred to me that antiperspirants might work to stop the itching. I was right. Ban works better than the usual medications."
  —CASEY C., *Portland, Oregon*

- **COLGATE TOOTHPASTE.** "Use a dab of Colgate Toothpaste on insect bites. It relieves the itch instantly."
  —SUSAN B., *Tustin, California*

■ **IVORY SOAP.** "To get rid of the itch from a mosquito bite, apply Ivory soap on the area. Instant relief."

—GRAHAM B., *West Richland, Washington*

■ **LISTERINE.** "Apply Listerine mouthwash to mosquito and other bug bites to stop itching."

—CHERYL D., *Salem, Oregon*

■ **MAYBELLINE CRYSTAL CLEAR NAIL POLISH.** "Use Maybelline Crystal Clear Nail Polish to stop mosquito bites from itching and getting larger. The polish seals off the air from the puncture. Later you can remove it with Cutex Nail Polish Remover."

—LUCILLE D., *Forest Hills, New York*

■ **MIRACLE WHIP.** "Rubbing Miracle Whip on mosquito bites really stops the itching."

—MONA W., *Fayetteville, Arkansas*

■ **ORAJEL.** "To relieve the itch from insect bites, dab some Orajel directly onto the bite. It stops the itching almost instantly."

—RAMONA M., *Ewa Beach, Hawaii*

■ **PARSONS' AMMONIA.** "Workers at the local sawmill carry a small bottle of household ammonia with them when working around the lumber piles. Lumber piles are notorious for attracting hornets and wasps. The workers rub a little ammonia into the sting and it disappears almost immediately."

—BILL N., *Shingleton, Michigan*

■ **PHILLIP'S MILK OF MAGNESIA.** "I use Milk of Magnesia as an inexpensive substitute for calamine lotion. It works wonderfully on insect bites and rashes to take away the itching."

—STACIE H., *Valley City, North Dakota*

■ **PREPARATION H.** "We keep a tube of Preparation H in the refrigerator for bites from bees, deer flies, and other flying insects. Just a dab usually helps take away the sting and welts."

—PAUL B., *Algonac, Michigan*

■ **ROLAIDS.** "The best remedy for an insect bite is Rolaids. Just crush a Rolaids antacid tablet, mix it with a little water to make a paste, put it on the bite, and within a few seconds the itch is gone. It's great for chiggers. Trust me, I know."

—SCOTT S., *Independence, Missouri*

■ **SECRET.** "Apply Secret deodorant to the bite, allow the deodorant to dry, and within a few minutes, the bite will stop itching."

—JAN B., *Hamden, Connecticut*

■ **VICKS VAPORUB.** "Rub the insect bite with Vicks VapoRub and it will instantly stop stinging or itching."

—GENE L., *Baxter, Minnesota*

Jellyfish Stings
Soothe a jellyfish sting with...

■ **ADOLPH'S ORIGINAL UNSEASONED TENDERIZER.** "Don't go to the beach without Adolph's Original Unseasoned Tenderizer. Scuba divers and lifeguards have known for years that a paste made from tenderizer and water and applied to the skin will take the sting right out of a jellyfish or Portuguese Man o' War sting."

—MOE P., *Del Valle, Texas*

■ **ARM & HAMMER BAKING SODA.** "Make a paste from a tablespoon of Arm & Hammer Baking Soda and water. Apply to the jellyfish sting. It instantly kills the pain."

—RANDY P., *Stockton, California*

■ **CLOROX BLEACH.** "Pour some Clorox bleach onto a jellyfish sting to take away the pain. We always bring a small bottle with us to the beach."

—DEBRA V., *Moberly, Missouri*

■ **COCA-COLA.** "Just pour Coke over the jellyfish sting."

—CLIFF D., *Ft. Lauderdale, Florida*

Lacerations
Soothe lacerations with...

■ **KRAZY GLUE.** "I am a hairdresser, and working with scissors all day, I inevitably cut myself. The fastest, easiest, least painful way to stop the bleeding is to glue the wound shut with Krazy Glue. It truly works great."

—CARRIE R., *Marysville, Michigan*

■ **PREPARATION H.** "For cuts and scrapes I use Preparation H. They heal faster than using any other product."

—DYANA E., *Baytown, Texas*

Lice

Prevent head lice with...

■ **ALBERTO VO5 HAIR SPRAY.** "To stop lice from even getting into your hair or your children's hair, spray a light coat of hair spray on hair before leaving the house. The lice won't even attempt to jump into the smell of the hair spray."

—KRISTEN C., *Pana, Illinois*

■ **HEINZ VINEGAR.** "When my children were little and there was an outbreak of lice at school, I rinsed their hair with Heinz White Vinegar after shampooing and they never got lice. My grandmother used to do this, too."

—SUE N., *Detroit, Michigan*

■ **PAUL MITCHELL TEA TREE SHAMPOO.** "Tea Tree Oil repels head lice naturally, as does shampooing regularly with Paul Mitchell Tea Tree Shampoo."

—TAMMY R., *Wahiawa, Hawaii*

Kill head lice with...

■ **JOHNSON'S BABY OIL.** "When you have head lice, you can soak your head with Johnson's Baby Oil overnight. The lice drown in the oil. The next morning, use Dawn dishwashing liquid to wash the oil from your hair."

—WENDY M., *Independence, Missouri*

■ **STAR OLIVE OIL.** "Saturate hair with olive oil, cover with a shower cap, and leave in overnight to kill head lice and make removing nits easier. Spray hair daily with white vinegar or Listerine, and comb through to help keep head lice away."

—ARLINE S., *East Jewett, New York*

THE MIRACLE ALL-NATURAL LICE TREATMENT

Medicated lice shampoos are often ineffective and may cause brain damage in children if left in their hair even ten minutes longer than the manufacturer's recommended time. Mayonnaise costs much less, is completely safe, and will kill all lice on the head as well as their nits (eggs). The oils in the mayonnaise do the trick. Plus, mayonnaise is a great hair conditioner. To kill the head lice completely, follow these simple instructions:

STEP 1

Saturate hair completely with Hellmann's Real Mayonnaise, Best Real Mayonnaise, or Kraft Real Mayonnaise. Be sure to work the mayonnaise in the hair and roots well. Hair must be extremely greasy with mayonnaise to drown the lice.

STEP 2

Wrap hair as tightly as possible with Saran Wrap or Handi-Wrap (or a shower cap), then wrap with a towel.

STEP 3

Allow to remain on head for two hours. During this time take all pillow cases, towels, blankets, sheets and clothes that have come into contact with any lice-infested hair and run them through the washing machine and dryer.

STEP 4

Shampoo hair thoroughly. Rinse hair with Heinz White Vinegar, then rinse clean with water. Comb hair with a nit comb. No nits should survive this treatment if done properly.

Congratulations! You're done! There's no need to repeat the treatment in seven days as with medicated shampoos (although it can't hurt).

Marital Relations

Improve marital relations with...

■ **CRISCO ALL-VEGETABLE SHORTENING.** "My husband and I use Crisco All-Vegetable Shortening as a lubricant."

—PEGGY E., *Syracuse, New York*

Nasal Passages

Open nasal passages with...

■ **BAND-AID BANDAGES.** "Wear a Band-Aid bandage across your nose to breathe easier."

—OLIVER P., *Newark, California*

Nipples

Soothe sore nipples from breastfeeding with...

■ **CHAPSTICK.** "I work in obstetrics and we advise all of the breast-feeding mothers to use cherry-flavored ChapStick on their nipples to prevent cracking. It really works, and it is safe for the babies. The moms don't have to wash off the ChapStick before feeding the baby like some of the products on the market. Plus, the babies seem to like the taste and tend to latch on quicker."

—CONNIE E., *Creston, Iowa*

■ **LIPTON TEA.** "If you have sore nipples from breastfeeding, make a cup of Lipton Tea, remove the tea bag, let it sit in a cup of ice for roughly one minute, then place the tea bag on your sore nipple and cover with a nursing pad under your bra for about five minutes. The tannic acid in the tea helps soothe and heal your nipple (while you get to enjoy a cup of tea)."

—TRISHA C., *Spokane, Washington*

Nosebleeds

Stop nosebleeds with...

■ **AFRIN.** "When I managed the high school wrestling team (Go Mounties!), I learned that when a wrestler gets a nosebleed, he soaks a cotton ball with Afrin nasal spray and stuffs it up his nose. Somehow the Afrin helps clot the blood faster. A few months later,

I cut my leg shaving, so I squirted some Afrin on the cut and the bleeding stopped in a matter of seconds."

—WENDY L., *Rainier, Washington*

■ **JELL-O.** "One tablespoon of Jell-O powder placed on the tongue and then raised to the roof of the mouth to dissolve slowly will stop a nosebleed."

—BRENDA P., *Nyssa, Oregon*

Paper Cuts

Heal paper cuts with...

■ **CHAPSTICK.** "I rub the original ChapStick on paper cuts. It stops the sharp pain immediately and heals the cut."

—JANET T., *Arlington, Massachusetts*

Weird Fact

A GENUINE LIFESAVER

"Lifesavers candies have a hole in the middle so that if a child accidentally swallows the candy and it gets stuck in his or her throat, the child can still breathe through the hole."

—STEVE H., *Phoenix City, Alabama*

Pepper Spray or Mace

Relieve the pain caused by pepper spray or Mace with...

■ **MIRACLE WHIP.** "If for some reason you or your child accidentally get sprayed in the face with pepper spray or Mace, rub Miracle Whip on the area and the pain and discomfort disappears (from experience . . . I used to deal in it)."

—CORY L., *Louisville, Kentucky*

Poison Ivy

Relieve the itch of poison ivy with...

■ **HEINZ VINEGAR** AND **MORTON SALT.** "Wet the affected area with white vinegar and sprinkle lightly with table salt. Let this mixture dry, then brush off the salt. Repeat if the itching begins again or if the affected area begins weeping. The rash should dry up in one to two days."

—CAROL G., *Jeffersonville, Indiana*

■ **LIPTON TEA.** "Strongly brewed Lipton Tea, dabbed on the affected area, will help dry up a poison ivy rash."

—VICKIE H., *Deweyville, Texas*

■ **PREPARATION H.** "I didn't believe it, but Preparation H actually does help clear up poison oak rash. This came straight from my mother."

—SANDRA P., *Durham, North Carolina*

■ **QUAKER OATS AND L'EGGS SHEER ENERGY PANTY HOSE.** "Cut off the foot from a clean pair of L'eggs Panty Hose and fill with one-half cup Quaker Oats. Tie a knot in the nylon and hang it from the tub's spigot while filling the tub with water for an inexpensive and soothing oatmeal bath. Once the tub is filled with water, use the oatmeal sack as a washcloth to wash with soap."

—DEBBIE G., *Columbia, South Carolina*

Rashes

Prevent rashes with...

■ **NEUTROGENA BODY MOISTURIZER.** "I use Neutrogena Body Moisturizer on my legs and arms because I get a rash that itches like mad and bleeds when I scratch it. As long as I use Neutrogena cream, the rash stays away. Dermatologists have never been able to help me."

—DOUGLAS M., *Washington, D.C.*

Skin

Heal cracked skin with...

■ **KRAZY GLUE.** "For those irritating cracks in your fingers which occur in cold weather, use Krazy Glue instead of Newskin. It works much better."

—GENE M., *Jamesville, New York*

Prevent concrete or plaster from cracking skin with...

■ **HEINZ VINEGAR.** "After working with plaster or concrete, rub Heinz White Vinegar on your hands. The acetic acid in vinegar neutralizes the alkaline from the concrete or plaster which can crack the skin or cause eczema in the long-run."

—XAVIER S., *West Hollywood, California*

Sore Muscles

Soothe sore muscles with...

■ **HEINZ APPLE CIDER VINEGAR.** "I pour two or three cups of Heinz Apple Cider Vinegar in a bathtub of hot water to soak away sore muscles. (To get more than one use out of the vinegar, I use the vinegar as a hair rinse in the shower and then fill the tub and soak.)"

—DEBI M., *Erlanger, Kentucky*

■ **UNCLE BEN'S CONVERTED BRAND RICE.** "Put uncooked rice in the foot of a sock, tie a knot in the end, and heat in a microwave oven for three or four minutes. Use the rice-filled sock as a heating pad for sore neck, back, or muscle."

—SHEILA H., *Coats, North Carolina*

Sore Throat

Banish a sore throat with...

■ **COCA-COLA.** "Gargle with Coca-Cola. The fizz in the cola loosens phlegm."

—LINDA T., *Toledo, Ohio*

■ **CUTTY SARK SCOTCH WHISKEY.** "Here's an old Scottish remedy: Mix four tablespoons of Cutty Sark Scotch Whiskey and four tablespoons of honey in a saucepan and warm over a stovetop. Gargle with the potion, then swallow it."

—RIC M., *Gold Coast, Australia*

■ **HEINZ APPLE CIDER VINEGAR.** "Mix one teaspoon of Heinz Apple Cider Vinegar in one cup of warm water. Gargle, swish, and swallow three mouthfuls whenever you feel a sore throat coming on. In a few days, you'll feel great. This tip has kept my kids and me out of the doctor's office many times. NOTE: Heinz uses all of the apple peelings and seeds—which contain the healing properties—to make its apple cider vinegar. My kids' pediatrician told me this."

—SUZEE N., *Kuna, Idaho*

■ **HYDROGEN PEROXIDE.** "Gargle with hydrogen peroxide."

—TRACIE M., *Southfield, Michigan*

Spider Veins

Reduce spider veins with...

■ **PREPARATION H.** "Rubbing a dab of Preparation H into the skin is great for reducing or getting rid of those nasty little veins showing on the back of legs."

—GINNY W., *Summerdale, Alabama*

Splinters

Remove a splinter with...

■ **ELMER'S GLUE-ALL.** "To remove a splinter that is partially exposed, pour Elmer's Glue-All over the splinter and let it dry, then slowly peel it from your skin. The splinter will stick to the glue."

—CARMEN S., *Panama City, Florida*

■ **ORAJEL.** "Put Orajel on the spot where you have a splinter to alleviate the pain while removing the splinter with tweezers or a needle. The Orajel numbs the skin."

—CHRISTINE H., *Virginia Beach, Virginia*

■ **SCOTCH TAPE.** "Stick a piece of Scotch Tape over the splinter, then pull the tape off in the opposite direction from the way the splinter went in. It should come right out."

—JACQUE H., *Tucson, Arizona*

Sprained Ankle

Relieve pain from a sprained ankle with...

■ **HEINZ VINEGAR.** "Soak a paper towel in Heinz Apple Cider Vinegar and wrap it around foot and ankle. Cover with a plastic grocery bag. Elevate the foot for at least one hour. It smells really bad and causes your foot to sweat, but it helps to relieve the pain."

—REGINA P., *Mt. Sterling, Kentucky*

Sties

Heal a sty on your eye with...

■ **LIPTON TEA.** "Make a cup of tea with a Lipton tea bag, let the tea bag cool, and place the bag on the infected eye for fifteen minutes. Repeat until the swelling goes down. This should require two or three applications."

—CATHERINE B., *Sebastian, Florida*

Stuffy Nose

Clear congested sinuses with...

■ **MORTON SALT.** "Mix one teaspoon of Morton Salt in two cups of warm water. Sniff up one nostril at a time, then gently blow your nose. It's an old remedy for clearing the sinuses."

—LARRY S., *Rio, Wisconsin*

Sunburn

Soothe sunburn pain with...

■ **HEINZ VINEGAR.** "Saturate a washcloth with white vinegar and lay the washcloth on the sunburn, pressing down lightly. Repeat over the entire sunburn to relieve the pain."

—ALEXANDRA C., *Long Beach, California*

■ **MENNEN AFTA.** "Dab on Mennen Afta. It works especially fast to relieve sunburn pain."

—KATHY P., *Beaver, Pennsylvania*

■ **NESTEA.** "Nestea soothes a sunburn when you put it in your bath water."

—VICKIE C., *Gulfport, Mississippi*

■ **PREPARATION H AND DESTIN.** "Mix equal amounts of Preparation H and Desitin baby rash ointment and rub into the affected area immediately after getting a sunburn. The pain and redness will be almost nonexistent."

—BARBARA A., *Rison, Arkansas*

Sunspots

Get rid of sunspots with...

■ **HEINZ APPLE CIDER VINEGAR.** "Some women get brown spots on their face from hormone changes and menopause. These spots are unsightly and hard to cover up with makeup. I saw a few plastic surgeons and used many expensive prescription creams, exfoliating creams, and gels. Applying Heinz Apple Cider Vinegar cleared up the spots. Just apply apple cider vinegar to the spots at least twice a day with a cotton ball. The more frequently you apply it, the faster the spots disappear. After the spots vanish, apply the vinegar once a week to keep them away."

—JOHNNA P., *Hamilton, Ohio*

Swimmer's Ear

Cure swimmer's ear with...

■ **HEINZ VINEGAR.** "Use an eyedropper to put Heinz White Vinegar in the affected ear four times daily for five days."

—DAVID S., *Atlanta, Georgia*

Teething

Soothe a teething baby with...

■ **CHLORASEPTIC.** "Spray Chloraseptic Throat Spray on your finger and rub on the baby's gums. It numbs gums to stop teething pain."

—ALISON H., *Indian Springs, Ohio*

Ticks

Remove ticks from skin with...

■ **JIF PEANUT BUTTER.** "Simply cover the tick with Jif. The tic begins to suffocate underneath and backs out of the skin."

—RENEE S., *Menasha, Wisconsin*

Toenail Fungus

Cure toenail fungus with...

■ **LISTERINE.** "Soak your feet in Listerine four times daily for a couple of weeks."

—DAVID S., *Atlanta, Georgia*

- **VICKS VAPORUB.** "Simply apply Vicks VapoRub on nail fungus several times a day. It worked on toenail fungus that my husband has been fighting ever since the jungles of Vietnam."

  —ANN R., *Humble, Texas*

Toothache

Relieve a toothache temporarily with...

- **LISTERINE.** "Listerine works as an immediate analgesic for any toothache due to an air-exposed nerve (such as a cavity, lost filling, or broken tooth). Swish a mouthful of Listerine around the trouble spot. The Listerine relieves the pain for an amazingly long time, and is easily reapplied when needed."

  —JOHN C., *Cahaba Heights, Alabama*

Urinary Tract Infection

Cure urinary tract infection with...

- **ALKA-SELTZER.** "I know from personal experience that Alka-Seltzer, when dissolved in a glass of water and drunk immediately, will start eliminating urinary tract infection almost as soon as it is swallowed. This is a lifesaver in the middle of the night when the doctor is not in his office. It really works well."

  —DURINDA W., *Durand, Michigan*

Warts

Remove warts with...

- **BLISTEX.** "When my husband and I got married, he had numerous warts on his hands. On a whim, he put some of Blistex medicated lip balm on them. Presto! They disappeared."

  —SUSAN W., *Jefferson, Maryland*

- **ELMER'S GLUE-ALL.** "Remember peeling dried Elmer's Glue from your hands in grade school? My sister would intentionally put the glue on her warts and they miraculously disappeared. She began telling people to cure warts by applying Elmer's Glue-All in the morning, peeling it off in the afternoon, applying it again at night, and peeling it again upon waking up. It worked within weeks."

  —TIM H., *Bloomington, Illinois*

- **HYDROGEN PEROXIDE.** "I use hydrogen peroxide over several days. Dab it on the wart and let dry."

  —CHRIS M., *Perth, Australia*

- **VASELINE PETROLEUM JELLY.** "I am a pharmacist, and I recommend outlining a wart with Vaseline before applying Compound-W (or other wart removal liquids). This prevents the surrounding skin from burning since applying Compound-W to a wart without inadvertently getting some on the surrounding skin is extremely difficult."

  —JOHN M., *Jupiter, Florida*

Wounds

Heal wounds with...

- **MAALOX.** "Just apply Maalox once or twice a day to cure open sores."

  —BARBARA N., *Starke, Florida*

Disinfect wounds with...

- **LISTERINE.** "Listerine antiseptic is great for disinfecting cuts and scrapes."

  —ANNE T., *Columbia, Maryland*

Wrinkles

Eliminate wrinkles with...

- **PREPARATION H.** "Rub Preparation H cream into your face. It moisturizes dry skin and keeps wrinkles away, leaving your skin looking younger."

  —MARY D., *Lake Worth, Florida*

Yeast Infection

Cure yeast infections with...

- **DANNON YOGURT.** "Yeast infection? Why go to the doctor when all you need to do is add another product to your grocery list. Yogurt contains a live organism (*Lactobacillus acidophilus* cultures) that will actually heal *Candida albicans* if vaginally inserted."

  —POLO R., *Monterey Park, California*

Make It

Alka-Seltzer Rockets

Make a paper rocket with...

- **ALKA-SELTZER.** "Find a 35-mm film canister where the lid snaps inside the body. Take a sheet of paper and roll it around the film canister so the open end of the film canister sticks out. Tape the paper onto the film canister. Add a paper cone to the top of the paper tube. Turn the rocket upside-down so the open end of the film canister is facing up. Fill it halfway with cold tap water. Drop in half an Alka-Seltzer tablet. Snap on the lid, turn the rocket rightside-up and set it down on the ground. Stand back and count 5-4-3-2-1. The rocket will blast off about six feet high."

  —Sue K., *Menlo Park, California*

Artwork

Protect artwork with...

- **ALBERTO VO5 HAIR SPRAY.** "Preserve pictures drawn and colored with chalk. Just spray the hair spray lightly over the paper and chalk and let it dry."

  —Andrea C., *Lake City, Florida*

Baby Wipes

Make homemade Baby Wipes with...

- **BOUNTY** AND **DICKINSON'S WITCH HAZEL.** "Tear off twenty individual sheets of Bounty paper towels. Cut each square in half and fold each half into thirds (like a Baby Wipe). Place all the folded sheets in a pan. In a jar, combine one cup witch hazel and one teaspoon glycerin (optional). Drizzle the mixture over the paper towels, allowing the towels to absorb the liquid. Stack the towels in a plastic container."

  —Debbie G., *Columbia, South Carolina*

Ball Catchers

Make a ball-and-bucket game with...

■ **CLOROX BLEACH BOTTLES.** "Cut the bottoms and one side diagonally up to the handle on two clean, empty Clorox bleach bottles. Put a ball in one catcher and toss to your partner who catches it in the other bleach bottle. You can also let children decorate the catchers."

—Dorothy C., *Willits, California*

Banks

Make a bank with a...

■ **CLOROX BLEACH BOTTLE.** "A clean, empty Clorox bleach jug makes a great bank for spare change."

—Lisa H., *Weymouth, Massachusetts*

Beer

Clear beer when home brewing with...

■ **KNOX GELATIN.** "Dissolve a packet of Knox Gelatin in hot water (do not boil it) and add one packet per five-gallon batch of beer."

—Paul G., *Hinesville, Georgia*

Strain whole leaf hops from beer wort when home brewing with...

■ **CHORE BOY SCOURING PADS.** "Simply sanitize a scouring pad (stainless or copper) by boiling it in water, then attach it to the end of the siphon tube with a rubber band."

—Paul G., *Hinesville, Georgia*

Bread Beads

Make beads with...

■ **WONDER BREAD, ELMER'S GLUE-ALL,** AND **ORAL-B DENTAL FLOSS.** "Remove the crust from three slices of Wonder Bread. Crinkle up the bread in a bowl and add three teaspoons Elmer's Glue-All. Knead until the dough is no longer sticky. Roll the dough into little balls, then pierce each with a toothpick. Let dry for twelve hours, then string with dental floss."

—MEG F., *Carson City, Nevada*

Body Paints

Make body paints with...

■ **CRISCO ALL-VEGETABLE SHORTENING** AND **MCCORMICK** OR **SCHILLING FOOD COLORING.** "Mix Crisco All-Vegetable Shortening with food coloring to make body paint."

—JAKE B., *San Francisco, California*

Boots

Make impromptu boots with...

■ **GLAD TRASH BAGS.** "When the toilet overflows, flooding the bathroom floor with water, simply wear a Glad Trash Bag on each foot and secure in place with masking tape to make emergency flood boots."

—CHRISTINE H., *Logan, Utah*

■ **ZIPLOC STORAGE BAGS.** "Put each foot inside a one-gallon Ziploc freezer bag before putting on shoes to keep feet dry and warm when out in wet weather. I learned this while playing backyard football in the snow."

—CHRIS B., *Novato, California*

Bubbles

Make huge soap bubbles with...

■ **KARO LIGHT CORN SYRUP** AND **DAWN.** "Mix one teaspoon Karo Light Corn Syrup, one cup Dawn dishwashing liquid, and ten cups of water to make bubble formula for the kids to use with big bubble wands."

—SHERRY U., *Glen Burnie, Maryland*

Candles

Make candles with...

■ **DIXIE CUPS.** "Tie one end of a four-inch string of wick to the middle of a pencil, set the pencil across the rim of a Dixie cup so the wick hangs to the bottom of the paper cup, pour melted paraffin wax to fill the cup, let harden, and you have an instant candle."

—MARJORIE S., *Savannah, Georgia*

Dye candles with...

- **CRAYOLA CRAYONS.** "Broken bits of Crayola Crayons make a great dye for wax when making candles. Simply melt the crayons in with the paraffin wax."

—MARJORIE S., *Savannah, Georgia*

Chalk String
Make a chalk tape line with...

- **CRAYOLA CHALK.** "Place a stick of colored Crayola Chalk in a Ziploc bag and crush the chalk into a powder with a hammer. Place a piece of string in the bag and shake well to cover the string in chalk."

—MATTHEW K., *Columbus, Ohio*

Crystal Paintings
Make crystal paintings with...

- **EPSOM SALT.** "Have kids use crayons to draw pictures on construction paper. Then mix together equal parts Epsom Salt and boiling water. Using a wide paintbrush, have the kids paint their picture with the salt mixture. When the picture dries, frosty crystals will appear."

—JULIET D., *Jackson, Mississippi*

Weird Fact

KRAZY CRIME FIGHTING

"I am a Police Officer. In Law Enforcement we use Krazy Glue to raise latent fingerprints off of items. The item is placed inside a closed area, such as a fish tank, with the Krazy Glue. To accelerate the process, the glue can be placed in a small tin dish on a heating tray. Within minutes the prints will appear."

—R.W. R., *Houston, Texas*

Curtain Rods

Make lively curtain rods with...

■ **WILSON TENNIS BALLS.** "For my living room curtains, I bought a wooden dowel and mounted it above the window. Then I took two tennis balls, cut a circle the diameter of the dowel in each one, covered the balls with fabric, and popped them on each end of the dowel for a perfect decoration. Nobody knows the curtain rod is made with tennis balls."

—PAGE W., *Weston, Massachusetts*

Feed curtain rods through curtains easily with...

■ **REYNOLDS WRAP.** "Tear off a small piece of Reynolds Wrap and secure it around the end of the curtain rod before inserting the rod through the curtain. No tears or snags along the way."

—JANET H., *Conway, New Hampshire*

Dry Flowers

Dry flowers with...

■ **MR. COFFEE FILTERS.** "When drying flowers, I place a Mr. Coffee Filter flat on one of my eight-inch squares of thin fiberboard, lay a flat flower or a bud on the filter, lay a second coffee filter flat on top of the flower, and then place a second wooden square on top, securing it closed by tightening the screws on all four corners. After a week or so, I check to see whether the flower is dry enough to make a picture. I use cheap wooden frames, place velvet material on the frame cardboard, lay flowers in whatever design I want, then place the glass in the frame and hang. These make beautiful gifts, but the real fun is in drying the flowers."

—IDA B., *Connellsville, Pennsylvania*

Dryer Sheets

Make your own reusable dryer sheets with...

■ **DOWNY.** "Dip a clean, light-colored washcloth in Downy Liquid Fabric Softener, wring it out, and throw it in the dryer with your next load. The cloth can be reused several times before re-dipping."

—GEORGIE M., *Trail, British Columbia*

Fingerpaint

Make fingerpaint with...

- **BARBASOL SHAVING CREAM.** "In small bowls, mix Barbasol Shaving Cream with a few drops of food coloring."

    —SUZIE B., *Davie, Florida*

- **CARNATION CONDENSED MILK.** "Mix one-quarter cup Carnation Condensed Milk with your choice of food coloring to make a great glossy paint for the kids. Add more coloring for more intense color."

    —CINDY S., *Nashville, Tennessee*

- **DANNON YOGURT.** "Mix Dannon Plain Yogurt with food coloring and let young children fingerpaint with it, without having to worry about them eating real paint."

    —PAIGE M., *Montpelier, Vermont*

Fireplace

Make the flames in your fireplace glow pink with...

- **NOSALT.** "For special, romantic occasions I sprinkle NoSalt on the wood logs in my fireplace. NoSalt contains potassium chloride rather than sodium chloride. The potassium gives the flame a beautiful pinkish-lavender color and adds a lovely ambience."

    —DEB D., *Tulsa, Oklahoma*

Glue

Make rice glue with...

- **UNCLE BEN'S CONVERTED BRAND RICE.** "Mix one-half cup Uncle Ben's Converted Brand Rice with one-half cup of water and after stirring for a while you get glue. Perfect for wallpaper, envelopes, or your in-laws' eyelids while they sleep."

    —FAUSTO G., *Fresno, California*

Apply glue with...

- **Q-TIPS COTTON SWABS.** "A Q-Tips Cotton Swab makes an excellent brush to dab on glue for crafts projects or when working around the house."

    —LOIS F., *Wichita, Kansas*

Ice Sculptures

Make colorful ice sculptures with...

- **MCCORMICK** OR **SCHILLING FOOD COLORING.** "Put colored water into buckets, dishpans, and other containers. Leave outside overnight in freezing weather. Unmold and create your own private little colorful Stonehenge in your yard."

  —MARILYN V., *Cedar Rapids, Iowa*

Lip Gloss

Make lip gloss with...

- **CRISCO ALL-VEGETABLE SHORTENING** AND **KOOL-AID.** "Mix three tablespoons of Crisco All-Vegetable Shortening and a package of Kool-Aid (whatever flavor you like most) in a coffee cup. Place in a microwave oven for one minute. Carefully pour the colored liquid into a clean empty 35-mm film canister, cap tightly, and refrigerate overnight. In the morning, you've got homemade lip gloss that's great for little girls."

  —KIMBERLY G., *Bakersfield, California*

Mail Box

Make a toy mail box with a...

- **QUAKER OATS CANISTER.** "Use the round Quaker Oats canister, colored construction paper, glue, crayons, and sprinkles to make your child a toy mail box."

  —STACEY S., *New Melle, Missouri*

Newspaper Clippings

Preserve newspaper clippings with...

- **PHILLIP'S MILK OF MAGNESIA.** "To preserve a newspaper clipping, dissolve one Phillip's Milk of Magnesia tablet in a quart of club soda. Let set in refrigerator eight hours. Shake well and pour into a shallow pan or tray to accommodate the flat newspaper clipping. Soak the clipping for one hour, then blot and let dry. This prevents yellowing by neutralizing the acid in the paper."

  —JULIE F., *Hollister, Missouri*

Padded Hangers
Pad hangers with...

- **L'EGGS SHEER ENERGY PANTY HOSE.** "Sew clean, used L'eggs Panty Hose to cover wire coat hangers with a half hitch macrame stitch. Great for recycling panty hose and saving sweaters from getting hanger marks and slipping off hangers."

  —LINDA H., *Glenolden, Pennsylvania*

Plastic Bag Holder
Recycle plastic bags with a...

- **CLOROX BLEACH BOTTLE.** "Cut a hole in the side of a clean, empty Clorox Bleach bottle and stuff it full of plastic grocery bags for easy storage."

  —KARI P., *Deming, New Mexico*

Posters
Hang posters with a...

- **BAND-AID BANDAGES.** "Use Band-Aid bandages instead of Scotch Tape to hang up posters."

  —SUSAN S., *Baltimore, Maryland*

- **VELCRO.** "I teach junior high school and my posters always come off the walls. I've used a hot glue gun to make them stick, but I've found that Velcro strips on the wall and the back of the poster work much better. My posters stay up, and I can change them and move them around easily without the trouble of putting on tons of tape and then having to remove it."

  —SHERYL V., *Roseville, Michigan*

- **WRIGLEY'S SPEARMINT GUM.** "Instead of tape or blue tack, chew a piece of Wrigley's Spearmint Gum, and apply a small piece to each corner of a poster to hang it on the wall."

  —SUZANNE V., *Albrightsville, Pennsylvania*

Potpourri

Make potpourri with...

■ **BOUNCE.** "Fill a clean, used Bounce sheet with either fresh coffee grounds or potpourri, gather up the edges, and tie with a ribbon."

—CHRIS M., *Revere, Massachusetts*

Rubber Stampers

Clean rubber stampers with...

■ **HUGGIES BABY WIPES.** "I use Huggies Baby Wipes for cleaning off rubber stampers while making crafts. It saves having to get up and wash stampers. Just put the stamper on the Baby Wipe and rub it a bit."

—GAIL P., *Adrian, Michigan*

■ **PURELL.** "Gel hand sanitizer works every bit as well as expensive cleaners to clean indelible ink from rubber stampers."

—IRIS R., *Carbondale, Pennsylvania*

Weird Fact

SPAM SPAM SPAM

"Seattle, Washington holds a yearly Spam carving contest. Each contestant is given one can of Spam and fifteen minutes to carve it into anything they like (cars, animals, people's faces, the list goes on and on)."

—CRIS H., *Seattle, Washington*

Scratch-and-Sniff Artwork

Make scratch-and-sniff artwork with...

■ **JELL-O.** "Put just enough water in Jell-O powdered mix to make a thick paste. Let kids fingerpaint with it on poster board, allow to dry, then scratch and sniff. It can also be licked off poster board."

—ELSPETH D., *Dayton, Ohio*

Sepia-Tone Photographs
Make sepia-tone photographs with...

■ **COCA-COLA.** "While in a photography class years ago, a friend had some prints sitting on a table. There was a Coke sitting nearby. Somebody bumped the Coke and spilled it onto his photos. Where the Coke landed, the photos turned a nice shade of sepia, which is the color that makes old photos look so warm. The trick is to place the photos (color or black and white) in a tray with some Coca-Cola, then carefully wash and dry the pictures (pat them with a dry towel and then use a blow-dryer set on high)."

—LEE R., *West Covina, California*

Straw Tower
Build towers with...

■ **GLAD FLEXIBLE STRAWS** AND **SCOTCH TAPE.** "I work in a job that relies on teamwork. As a teambuilding exercise, we are divided into teams of four to six people, given a box of flexible drinking straws and a few rolls of tape, and instructed to build the tallest freestanding tower possible within twenty minutes—without talking. It is absolutely out-of-control and crazy. You quickly learn that success requires proper communication, because everyone has their own ideas of how things work."

—SERA M., *Warner Robins, Georgia*

Tie-Dying
Tie-dye clothes in reverse with...

■ **CLOROX BLEACH.** "Mix two cups of Clorox Bleach in a bucket of hot water. Use traditional tie-dying techniques (rubber bands or string) to prepare a dark-colored t-shirt. Place the shirt in the bleach solution, stirring occasionally until the color of the shirt lightens considerably. Launder the shirt in the washing machine with your regular detergent. Remove the rubber bands or string and dry as usual."

—SUSAN M., *Newark, Delaware*

- **LIQUID CASCADE.** "Dip chunky stampers from a craft shop in Liquid Cascade, then stamp a dark-colored t-shirt. Let the t-shirt dry for 72 hours, then wash as usual."

  —MICHELE K., *Hartford, Connecticut*

Time Capsule

Make a toy time capsule with a...

- **QUAKER OATS CANISTER.** "Let your child decorate the round Quaker Oats canister and use it as a time capsule."

  —STACEY S., *New Melle, Missouri*

Toast Rack

Hold toast with a...

- **SLINKY.** "A Slinky makes a great expandable toast rack. Simply place the pieces of toast between the coils."

  —LYNDA D., *St. Andrews, England*

Toilet Paper Holder

Make a toilet paper caddy with...

- **MAXWELL HOUSE COFFEE CANS.** "Cut the top and bottom off two coffee cans and cut only the top from a third coffee can. Stack the cans with the third can at the bottom. Tape the cans together with Scotch Clear Packaging Tape. Cover all three cans with Con-Tact Paper. Store four rolls of toilet paper inside and cover with a plastic lid from one of the coffee cans."

  —BERNADETTE B., *Woodbine, New Jersey*

Wallpaper Paste

Make wallpaper paste with...

- **GOLD MEDAL FLOUR** AND **DOMINO SUGAR.** "Mix one-half cup Gold Medal Flour, one-half cup Domino Sugar, and one cup cold water in a large saucepan. Slowly add two cups boiling water and stir continuously until stiff. Remove from heat and cool. Store in a tightly sealed container. I have been using this for years."

  —JACKIE S., *Pierceton, Indiana*

Mop It

Carpet

Deodorize carpet with...

- **BOUNCE.** "Putting a sheet of Bounce in your vacuum cleaner bag before vacuuming will get rid of the stale smell in the house."

  —SUE K., *Lawrenceville, Georgia*

- **DOWNY.** "Mix one part Downy and two parts water into a spray bottle. Spray the mixture on your carpets after you've cleaned them. The Downy smells terrific and, since it's an antistatic formula, you can vacuum up lint and pet hair much easier."

  —JULIE N., *Steilacoom, Washington*

- **GAIN.** "For a quick carpet freshener, I use Gain powdered clothes detergent. Just sprinkle it on the carpet, then vacuum it up. It makes your vacuum smell fresh, too."

  —BRANDI S., *Troy, Alabama*

- **HEINZ WHITE VINEGAR.** "I add a cup of Heinz White Vinegar to the carpet cleaner when I shampoo my carpets. I make it strong and the carpet smells like vinegar for an hour or so after cleaning, but then the smell fades, along with any other odors in the carpet."

  —ROBIN T., *Archer, Florida*

Chair Legs

Prevent chair legs from scratching floors with...

- **WILSON TENNIS BALLS.** "I know a middle school science teacher who cuts an *X* on one side of four Wilson Tennis Balls and puts the balls on all four legs of the desk chairs. Not only do the tennis balls keep the chair legs from making noise when a student moves, but they also look like small planets in a decorated science classroom."

  —ELSPETH D., *Dayton, Ohio*

Dance Floors

Increase friction on slippery dance floors with...

■ **COCA-COLA.** "If you don't have any rosin to make a slick dance floor less slippery, mix Coca-Cola in a pail with water and mop the stage floor. Do not use too much Coke or the floor will be too sticky—making it difficult to do glissades as well as making a sticky sound every time you lift your foot. This solution can be applied quickly (rosin takes time to spread around evenly and makes dust at first, which may bother the musicians). The Coke solution works well whenever the local powers nix the use of rosin to avoid dulling the shiny stage surface. Coke can be mopped up afterwards without any major damage to the floor."

—CHARLES G., *Akron, Ohio*

Floors

Clean hardwood floors with...

■ **HEINZ VINEGAR.** "Mix two parts Heinz White Vinegar to one part water for cleaning hardwood floors. Use a soft cloth and wring it so it's just damp. It leaves a shine not to be believed."

—KATHY M., *Germantown, Maryland*

■ **LIPTON TEA.** "Mopping hardwood floors with Lipton Tea (unsweetened) makes them shine like crazy."

—BETTY S., *College Park, Georgia*

Clean tile floors with...

■ **CASCADE.** "Mix one-quarter cup Cascade in a bucket of hot water. Scrub floors with a scrub brush, then rinse clean with a mop and water."

—CARRIE P., *New Hartford, New York*

■ **CLING FREE.** "I put a Cling Free sheet on the bottom of my dry sponge mop and dust my floor with it. It clings to the dry sponge mop without having to secure it to any part of the mop. This works just as well as those new dust mops sold on television, and a box of Cling Free contains a lot more sheets."

—KATHY R., *Spokane, Washington*

- **DOWNY.** "To get rid of the tacky feeling on your floors left by cleanser, add one-half capful of Downy Fabric Softener (Mountain Spring Downy is my favorite). I not only get a well-rinsed floor, but a fresh scent as well."

  —BARB H., *Ludlow Falls, Ohio*

- **LISTERINE.** "Listerine cleans your floors and kills the germs."

  —MICKEY S., *Dupo, Illinois*

Remove wax build-up from floors with...

- **MR. MUSCLE.** "The manufacturer won't recommend it, but an oven cleaner like Mr. Muscle can be used to remove wax build-up on flooring (cautiously!). My son tried every product known to mankind, and when I recommended Mr. Muscle with plenty of ventilation, he was surprised at how well it worked. Now his wife is prohibited from waxing the floor and it looks as good as new."

  —JANET H., *Conway, New Hampshire*

Real-Life Story

A REALLY BIG SHOW

"Years ago, we were doing a television special from the Ed Sullivan Theater in New York City. The girls rehearsed a dance number, then we took a dinner break. When we came back to tape the number, we learned they had polished the stage and the girls kept slipping. We bought a case of Coke and poured it on the stage, which made it sticky enough to proceed."

—CHARLES W., *New York, New York*

Grout

Clean tile grout with...

- **COCA-COLA.** "I recently spilled Coca-cola on my kitchen floor. Immediately the grout was immaculate."

  —ROZ S., *West Hills, California*

Knees

Protect your knees when scrubbing floors with...

- **STAYFREE MAXI PADS.** "Stayfree Maxi Pads make excellent knee pads. Just peel the adhesive strips and stick the pads to your knees."

  —MARY R., *Georgetown, Texas*

Scratches

Hide scratches in hardwood floors with...

- **FOLGER'S INSTANT COFFEE.** "Just take a teaspoon of Folger's Instant Coffee and mix it with warm water into a paste. Then take a cloth, dip it in the paste, and wipe over the scratches in the floor. The scratches disappear immediately. Works really well with darker wood."

  —JODI W., *Burlington, Massachusetts*

Scuff Marks

Clean scuff marks from floors with...

- **KIWI SCUFF AND STAIN REMOVER.** "Use Kiwi Scuff and Stain Remover (for shoes) to get black marks off linoleum floors. Rub on the mark, then wipe with a paper towel."

  —PETER O., *Phoenix, Arizona*

- **MIRACLE WHIP.** "Use a dab of Miracle Whip to clean black shoe marks from tile floors."

  —JAMES B., *Cantonment, Florida*

- **PAM NO STICK COOKING SPRAY.** "I use Pam No Stick Cooking Spray to get scuff marks off the floor. Just spray and wipe clean."

  —MAUREEN H., *Evart, Michigan*

- **SKIN-SO-SOFT.** "Use Skin-So-Soft to remove black skid marks left by shoes on tile or linoleum."

  —RHONDA H., *Hartford, South Dakota*

- **VASELINE PETROLEUM JELLY.** "Vaseline Petroleum Jelly takes scuff marks off tile and linoleum floors."

  —GAYLE T., *Chicago, Illinois*

- **WD-40.** "For really tough black scuff marks on vinyl floors try spraying a little WD-40 before rubbing with a paper towel. Helps loosen the mark."

  —SHERI H., *Alturas, California*

- **WESSON CORN OIL.** "Put a little Wesson Oil on a clean rag or paper towel and gently rub the scuff."

  —CARL T., *Portland, Oregon*

Vinyl Floors

Clean discolored vinyl floor tile with...

- **WESTLEY'S WHITEWALL TIRE CLEANER.** "We had extensive water damage to the tile floor in our basement due to flood water. Mud had discolored the vinyl tile. The solution? Westley's Whitewall Tire Cleaner spray and a scrub brush."

  —PETER H., *Philadelphia, Pennsylvania*

Organize It 13

Envelopes

Seal envelopes with...

- **CRAYOLA CRAYONS.** "Melt a Crayola Crayon over the seal on the envelope."

  —MICHAEL H., *Austin, Texas*

Files

Protect files while on vacation with...

- **SCOTCH TAPE.** "Place small pieces of Scotch Tape from the file drawers to the main frame. If someone were to go through your private files, the tape will be broken when you return."

  —SPENCER W., *Lakeville, Pennsylvania*

Important Papers

Protect important papers with...

- **ZIPLOC STORAGE BAGS.** "Place all of your vital papers (passports, birth certificates, immunization papers, stock certificates) in a gallon-size Ziploc freezer bag and put it in your freezer. Robbers rarely look in the freezer and if your house catches on fire, the refrigerator is almost always left standing."

  —AMY W., *Arlington, Texas*

Letter Holder

Make a letter holder with a...

- **SLINKY.** "Simply attach both ends of the Slinky to two ends of your desk and insert letters into the springs."

  —BARB H., *Cincinnati, Ohio*

Packing

Pack fragile objects in...

■ **GLAD TRASH BAGS.** "I wrapped my Christmas presents (breakable drinking glasses) by wrapping each glass in its own Glad Trash Bag, then stuffing the rest of the box with lots of trash bags. Everyone got a good laugh and a supply of reusable trash bags to boot."

—LORRIE S., *Houston, Texas*

■ **MAXWELL HOUSE COFFEE CANS.** "Pack valuables inside a coffee can stuffed with paper or Styrofoam peanuts. You can also tape two or more cans together with electrical tape."

—MARY LOU B., *Port St. John, Florida*

■ **ORVILLE REDENBACHER'S GOURMET POPPING CORN.** "When sending off boxes through the mail, pack your items in air-popped popcorn (no grease). It's environmentally safe, and the recipient can throw it out for birds to eat."

—DONNA S., *Monmouth, Illinois*

■ **ZIPLOC STORAGE BAGS.** "Place a drinking straw in the opening of a Ziploc Storage Bag, seal the bag shut up to the straw, and blow air through the straw to fill the bag. Quickly remove straw and seal the bag shut before the air escapes. Place the protective, air-filled bags in a box around the fragile item to be shipped."

—CAROLYN B., *Yorba Linda, California*

Paperclips

Clip papers together with...

■ **FORSTER CLOTHES PINS.** "Use clothes pins instead of paper clips. Works great when several papers need to be clipped together."

—GERALDINE P., *Cantonment, Florida*

Pens

Prevent pens from leaking in a purse with...

■ **ZIPLOC STORAGE BAGS.** "I keep pens in a Ziploc Storage Bag in my purse to stay organized and prevent a leaky pen from ruining my purse or other valuables." —DEBORAH W., *Jonesboro, Arkansas*

Photographs

Carry photos while traveling with...

■ **ALTOIDS.** "Use an empty Altoids can as a travel picture frame. Put the pictures inside and paint or decorate the outside. Great for travelers." —DONNA B., *Altus, Oklahoma*

School Supplies

Identify school supplies with...

■ **COVER GIRL NAILSLICKS CLASSIC RED.** "Use red nail polish to mark your child's name on his or her school supplies." —JOANN B., *Manhattan, Illinois*

Storage

Store small items with a...

■ **DANNON YOGURT CUP.** "Clean, empty Dannon Yogurt cups make excellent storage cups for small items, especially if you also save the lids." —JOHN P., *Albuquerque, New Mexico*

■ **KODAK FILM CANISTER.** "Empty film containers are great for storing beads, safety pins, push pins, earrings, or as a travel case for pills, toothpaste, shampoo, conditioner, or hair gel." —LISA H., *Weymouth, Massachusetts*

Suitcases

Freshen suitcases with...

- **BOUNCE.** "When you go on holiday, put three sheets of Bounce in your suitcase, one on the bottom, one in the middle, and one on the top. When you reach your destination, you won't need to air out your clothes for hours, because they'll already be smelling fresh and clean."

  —KENNIE Y., *Aveley, England*

Thumb Tacks

Store thumb tacks with...

- **COCA-COLA.** "Fill a clean, empty Coke bottle with thumb tacks. Need a tack? Turn the bottle on an angle. It dispenses only a few tacks at a time. With the cap on the bottle, you never have to worry about spilling tacks again."

  —ROD N., *Florence, South Carolina*

Paint It

Cleaner

Clean oil-based paint from hands with...

- **JOHNSON'S BABY OIL.** "To clean fresh paint off your hands (or anywhere else), use Johnson's Baby Oil instead of turpentine. It's gentler on the skin."
  —JUDITH A., *Les Lilas, France*

- **SKIN-SO-SOFT.** "A few drops of Skin-So-Soft removes latex or oil-based paint from skin."
  —CATIE M., *New York, New York*

- **VASELINE PETROLEUM JELLY.** "Before I paint a room, I coat my hands and arms with Vaseline Petroleum Jelly. When I'm done painting, I wipe the splattered paint from my arms and hands. Clean-up is a breeze."
  —WILLIAM S., *Huntington, West Virginia*

Concrete

Age concrete with...

- **COCA-COLA.** "Pour Coke on new concrete to 'age' it, so it blends in with existing material."
  —CARMEN T., *Berkeley, California*

Deodorize

Deodorize the smell of paint with...

- **MCCORMICK OR SCHILLING VANILLA EXTRACT.** "If you put a tablespoon of vanilla extract in one gallon of paint and stir well, you won't have that nasty paint smell all through your house. Instead, your house will smell like you've been baking cookies."
  —FAITH O., *Sheffield Lake, Ohio*

Galvanized Metal

Prepare galvanized metal for a new coat of paint with...

- **HEINZ WHITE VINEGAR.** "Wipe down galvanized metal with Heinz White Vinegar and let dry before painting. Vinegar neutralizes ('pickles') the galvanized surface so that normal paint will stick and be less likely to flake off."
  —HOWARD C., *Yorktown, Virginia*

Latex

Color latex paint with...

- **KOOL-AID.** "I use Kool-Aid to color latex paint for my home decorating projects. Just mix with a couple teaspoons of water and add to the paint."
  —SHANNON B., *Lantzville, British Columbia*

Paint

Substitute for paint with...

- **CLAIROL HAIR COLORING.** "Mix up hair coloring to paint on cardboard or poster board to create a masterpiece."
  —HEATHER S., *Commerce, Georgia*

Paint Stripper

Strip paint or varnish from wood furniture with...

- **DOW BATHROOM CLEANER.** "Use Dow Bathroom Cleaner to strip furniture for refinishing. Spray on, let it sit, and the paint or varnish will bubble up. The paint can then be scraped off with a putty knife or wiped off with an old rag. As a bonus, the piece will be cleaned in the process."
  —TERRY S., *Mims, Florida*

Paintbrushes

Improvise a paintbrush with...

- **Q-TIPS COTTON SWABS.** "Use a Q-Tips Cotton Swab as a paintbrush for touch-ups on appliances or picture frames."
  —HARRY J., *Albuquerque, New Mexico*

Avoid cleaning oil-based paint from a wet paintbrush with...

- **ZIPLOC STORAGE BAGS.** "Seal the wet paintbrush (handle and all) inside a Ziploc Storage Bag if you intend to use the brush again by the next day. You can also use large bags for paint rollers."

—JUDITH W., *Yucca Valley, California*

Plastic

Help paint adhere to plastic with...

- **BOUNCE.** "Wipe the plastic with a used Bounce sheet before painting so the paint will adhere better. This is especially useful when painting decorative details on plastic items."

—MOLLY F., *Metairie, Louisiana*

Poster Paints

Make poster paints easy to clean from clothes with...

- **DAWN.** "Mix a few drops of Dawn dishwashing liquid into poster paint and mix well. This way, if you get the paint on your clothes, it will wash out easily."

—PAMELA P., *Philadelphia, Pennsylvania*

Rust

Remove rust from wrought iron to prepare for painting with...

- **COCA-COLA.** "Simply saturate a Scotch-Brite sponge with Coca-Cola and scrub the rusty spot on the wrought iron."

—IRV S., *Philadelphia, Pennsylvania*

Spills

Clean wood stain from carpeting with...

- **GOLD MEDAL FLOUR.** "If you spill stain on carpeting, pour a small pile of Gold Medal Flour over the spill. Brush up the flour the next morning. Repeat several times if necessary. The flour soaks up most of the stain."

—ANITA P., *Wassaic, New York*

Splatters

Clean up paint splatters with...

- **HUGGIES BABY WIPES.** "After painting, I found dried white specks all over my television console. I grabbed a Huggies Baby Wipe and—wow!—it really did a great job. In just a little time, all the paint was gone."
  —DAVID N., *Ashland, Oregon*

Stain

Stain wood with...

- **KIWI SHOE POLISH.** "Use Kiwi Shoe Polish to stain wood to a high polish. Repeat to achieve a deeper color. It's cheaper than stain, easier to apply, and leaves a high gloss finish."
  —T. L., *Crane, Texas*

- **NESTEA.** "Nestea Ice Tea Mix makes an interesting wood stain. Use spray lacquer to seal."
  —JOHN C., *Henderson, Nevada*

- **RIT DYE.** "Mix up Rit dye according to the directions on the box, and use a sponge brush to give wood one coat. Let dry. Using sandpaper, sand the wood to achieve an antique look. Applying a lot of pressure to the edges adds an older look."
  —ROBIN D., *Elkton, Maryland*

Stain unfinished cherry wood with...

- **RED DEVIL LYE.** "Mix three tablespoons Red Devil Lye in one gallon warm water, and wearing rubber gloves and eye protection, sponge this solution on unfinished cherry wood in a well ventilated area. Rinse off after one minute or so and dry. The more lye, the redder the cherry wood will get. The results are permanent."
  —BUCK J., *Scotia, New York*

Wallpaper

Remove wallpaper with...

- **AJAX.** "Ajax all-purpose cleanser takes stubborn wallpaper off the walls."
  —SAM S., *Newcastle Upon Tyne, England*

- **DOWNY.** "I used Downy Fabric Softener diluted with water to soften and remove old wallpaper. I applied the solution with a spray bottle, let it sit for a few minutes, then easily stripped the paper from the wall. I used a wide putty knife to get under the edge of the paper."

  —BRENDA S., *Longbow Lake, Ontario*

- **HEINZ VINEGAR.** "Heinz Vinegar can be used to remove wallpaper and wallpaper paste. I have used it several times instead of wallpaper-removing chemicals (which can be expensive) to remove wallpaper and borders. I think it works best if you heat it up a little first. The best way I've found is to score the wallpaper (as you would with a store-bought remover). Warm the vinegar in the microwave and then spray it on the paper. I have also tried using a mop to apply the vinegar, but that seemed to be a little messier (easier to reach high places though)."

  —HEATHER A., *Atlanta, Georgia*

- **RESOLVE CARPET CLEANER.** "I've sprayed Resolve Carpet Cleaner on wallpaper that was difficult to peel off the wall. After spraying with Resolve, the wallpaper was much easier to scrape off with a plastic scraper."

  —PAMELA H., *Jerico Springs, Missouri*

Wood Restoration

Restore weathered wooden fences, decks, railings, and tables with...

- **CLOROX BLEACH.** "Spray Clorox Bleach directly on the wood surfaces using a garden pressure sprayer, and—poof!—it looks new again. Use straight from the bottle. Be sure to wear adequate protection (goggles, rubber gloves, boots, and rain gear). Bleach works faster than painting and it never peels."

  —ED L., *Grand Prairie, Texas*

Pet It

Aquariums

Clean aquarium plants and decor with a...

- **WATER PIK.** "I can't do without my Teledyne Water Pik as my 'mini-high-pressure sprayer.' It was nearly impossible to clean the small leaves of the plastic plants in my aquarium. People buy high-pressure sprayers to clean cars and houses, so I figured I'd use my Water Pik as my own personal high-pressure cleaner. I haven't tried the Water Pik on anything else, but I suppose it could be used for fine detail on jewelry as well."

  —TODD C., *Bowling Green, Kentucky*

Bathing

Bathe your dog with...

- **DOWNY.** "Mix one cap of Downy Fabric Softener in one-half gallon of water and use as final rinse when bathing your dog or cat. Rinse again after using Downy. This will leave your pet's coat feeling soft and smelling fresh."

  —SHERRY B., *Hallsville, Texas*

- **HUGGIES BABY WIPES.** "Wipe the bottom of your dog's paws with Huggies Baby Wipes after it's been in the garden. I have a Shihtsu and I wipe her face after she's eaten and her ears when they dangle in her food."

  —YVONNE S., *Cleveland, Ohio*

- **JOHNSON'S BABY SHAMPOO.** "When bathing your dog, use baby shampoo. It won't hurt the dog's eyes and it leaves a nice smell."

  —BILL N., *Shingleton, Michigan*

- **MURPHY'S OIL SOAP.** "A few drops of Murphy's Oil Soap in the dog bath helps to moisturize and soften a dog's skin and coat."

  —KATHY P., *Newton, North Carolina*

Birds

Make a toy for your pet bird with...

- **GLAD FLEXIBLE STRAWS.** "Weave several straws through the bars of the cage. Parrots, macaws, and cockatiels love to remove them, chew them, and play with them. The birds don't eat them so the straws make a cheap, easy, and safe toy."

—DENENE V., *Mosinee, Wisconsin*

Bleeding

Stop a pet's claw or nail from bleeding with...

- **GOLD MEDAL FLOUR.** "When my parrot broke a toenail and I didn't have a styptic pencil, I put a pinch of Gold Medal Flour on the broken nail and applied pressure. It stopped the bleeding. I also did this with a dog after clipping its toenail too short."

—RUTH A., *Dorothy, New Jersey*

Burrs

Remove burrs from a horse's mane and tail with...

- **WD-40.** "I use WD-40 on my horses' manes and tails when they get full of burrs. It helps me slide the burr out without tearing out the hair or having to cut it."

—CONNIE S., *Ft. Collins, Colorado*

Cat Food

Cover cat food cans with lids from...

- **FRITOS CHEESE DIP.** "The lid from a small can of Fritos Cheese Dip fits just perfectly on a 5.5-ounce can of cat food, so you can save the leftover cat food in the refrigerator."

—YVONNE B., *Yatesville, Georgia*

Cat Food Bowls

Keep a cat bowl clean with...

- **MR. COFFEE FILTERS.** "I place about five coffee filters in my cat's food dish. When the top filter begins to look disgusting, I simply throw it away, leaving a clean filter underneath."

—WADINE T., *Philadelphia, Pennsylvania*

Cat Litter Boxes
Line a cat box with...

- **GLAD TRASH BAGS.** "Tired of cleaning the cat box? Open a Glad Trash Bag, place the cat litter box inside, and pour litter on top of the plastic covering the open side of the box. To clean, lift out the bag, turn it inside-out, and throw away."

  —MARJORIE S., *Savannah, Georgia*

Coprophagy
Prevent coprophagy with...

- **ACCENT FLAVOR ENHANCER.** "Accent Flavor Enhancer is actually a digestive enzyme that can be used by pet owners to prevent coprophagy (when a pet eats its own bowel movements). Giving the pet one teaspoon in its food twice daily for three days should put an end to a rather nasty habit."

  —MATTHEW C., *Ipswich, Massachusetts*

Dander
Reduce dander with...

- **DOWNY.** "Add a capful of Downy Fabric Softener to the bath water when washing your pets to reduce animal dander. It works."

  —MARK R., *Charlotte, South Carolina*

Deodorize
Deodorize a dog or pet with...

- **BOUNCE.** "Rub a sheet of Bounce over your dog's coat to make it smell fresh and avoid bathing it as often."

  —PAULA S., *Paint Rock, Alabama*

- **FEBREZE.** "I use Febreze on my dog. It removes the funky smell from his coat. (Some dogs may have an allergic reaction to Frebreze.)"

  —BARBARA S., *Columbia, Tennessee*

- **HUGGIES BABY WIPES.** "Wipe the dog or cat with a Huggies Baby Wipe. It will take away the smell along with the loose fur."

  —LISA W., *Forest Lake, Minnesota*

Dry Shampoos
Give a dog a dry shampoo with...

- **ARM & HAMMER BAKING SODA.** "Tired of that smelly dog? Sprinkle with Arm & Hammer Baking Soda, work into the coat, then brush clean for a dry shampoo that removes the smell."

—MARJORIE S., *Savannah, Georgia*

Ear Mites
Kill ear mites with...

- **STAR OLIVE OIL.** "If your dog or cat gets ear mites, put a few drops of olive oil in the infected ear to smother the ear mites."

—BRENDA W., *Novato, California*

Fish
Feed fish with...

- **CHEERIOS.** "Cheerios dyed with red food coloring make great fish chum. Fish will eat Cheerios and the red coloring attracts because it looks like blood."

—KARA L., *San Antonio, Texas*

Flatulence
Reduce flatulence with...

- **DANNON YOGURT.** "Use a tablespoon of plain, non-fat, non-flavored yogurt in your dog's food once a day to avoid flatulence."

—KATHY F., *Pleasant Prairie, Wisconsin*

Fleas
Prevent fleas on dogs with...

- **SKIN-SO-SOFT.** "When I worked in a grooming shop, we used Skin-So-Soft as an organic flea dip. After bathing the dogs, we would rinse them with diluted Skin-So-Soft, which repels fleas and ticks and leaves dogs' coats shiny."

—WENDY M., *Concord, New Hampshire*

Kill fleas on dogs or cats with...

■ **ALBERTO VO5 CONDITIONER.** "I use Alberto VO5 Conditioner to kill fleas and ticks on dogs and cats. Simply wash the animal, pour conditioner on the animal, and rinse. This treatment kills fleas, and it sure doesn't hurt the animal's coat."

—BRENDA C., *Checotah, Oklahoma*

■ **PALMOLIVE.** "Use a small amount of Palmolive dishwashing liquid to give a dog, cat, or other pet a flea shampoo. This works better than some prescribed flea shampoos."

—JIMME R., *East Greenbush, New York*

Clean a cat and repel fleas with...

■ **HELLMANN'S** OR **BEST REAL MAYONNAISE.** "I use Hellmann's Mayonnaise to wash and shine my cat. She hates water but loves mayonnaise. I rub the mayonnaise into her skin and fur, then wipe her down with a damp towel. She helps me by licking. The mayonnaise makes her coat shine and the fleas hate it."

—JANET G., *Drexel, North Carolina*

Furniture

Keep cats off furniture with...

■ **BOUNCE.** "I've tried everything to keep my cats off the backs of my chairs. While I was folding clothes, a sheet of Bounce fell to the floor. I tossed it on the back of a chair. I haven't seen a cat on it since."

—CINDI N., *Cabot, Arizona*

Goats

Prevent bloat in goats with...

■ **ARM & HAMMER BAKING SODA.** "Another use for baking soda, one I use all the time, is to feed it to goats to prevent bloat." (High-grain diets typically increase acid formation in the ruminant animals, interfering with the bacteria that aid digestion. Adding baking soda to cow and goat feed increases the pH in the animals' rumina, which lowers the acidity, making for a more favorable environment for the microbacteria that aid digestion, thus elevating the rate of feed intake and increasing milk production and the butterfat content of the milk.)

—PATTI E., *Topeka, Kansas*

LION WASHING

"As a producer for a Madison Avenue advertising agency, I had to make the arrangements for photographing a print advertisement featuring a lion and a lamb lying next to each other in the Hollywood hills. Before we shot any pictures, the owner of the lion shampooed the animal's mane with Johnson's Baby Shampoo so it would look clean, natural, and fluffy."

—DEBBIE W., *Forest Hills, New York*

Hair

Make vacuuming up pet hair a snap with...

■ **DOWNY.** "Mix two tablespoons Downy Fabric Softener in one cup of water in a spray bottle, shake well, then spray carpet liberally. Let dry a few minutes and vacuum."

—DENENE V., *Mosinee, Wisconsin*

Hairballs

Prevent cat hairballs with...

■ **VASELINE PETROLEUM JELLY.** "Place a dab of Vaseline Petroleum Jelly on the cat's paw. The cat will lick it off and it prevents hairballs. The Vaseline collects hairs and they travel naturally out the proper end."

—MAGGIE P., *Tillamook, Oregon*

Hamster Wheels

Lubricate a hamster wheel with...

■ **PAM NO STICK COOKING SPRAY.** "Since my hamster licks off anything I spray to get rid of the squeak on the wheel in his cage,

I decided to use something that won't hurt him—Pam No Stick Cooking Spray."

—PAULA E., *Louisville, Kentucky*

Heat

Protect a cat in heat with...

- **PAMPERS.** "I use duct tape to secure a Pampers disposable diaper on my cat when she goes in heat. It definitely works, although I have one mad cat."

  —ROBERT C., *Kannapolis, North Carolina*

Horses

Scrub stains from a horse's coat with...

- **EFFERDENT.** "When my white horse gets yellow stains all over his legs, I use watered-down Efferdent to scrub the stains out."

  —JESSICA B., *Pleasant Prairie, Wisconsin*

Stop a horse from rubbing its tail with...

- **LISTERINE.** "Apply Listerine to your horse's tail. Only regular flavor Listerine works. The other flavors attract insects. This has been a horse person's trick for as long as I can recall."

  —KIMBERLY L., *Youngstown, Ohio*

Give a horse's coat a shine with...

- **WESSON CORN OIL.** "Add one-quarter cup Wesson Corn Oil to your horse's grain daily."

  —PAT F., *Eldon, Missouri*

Clean dust from a horse's coat before entering a show with...

- **BOUNCE.** "Use a new sheet of Bounce to wipe the dust off a horse just before entering the show arena. It works great."

  —HELEN L., *Jefferson City, Montana*

Prevent snow from sticking inside a horse's hooves with...

■ **PAM NO STICK COOKING SPRAY.** "Spray the bottom of the horses hooves with Pam No Stick Cooking Spray when riding in snow to prevent snow from packing in."

—DEBRA E., *Reading, Pennsylvania*

Repel flies from horses with...

■ **SCOPE COOL PEPPERMINT MOUTHWASH AND JOHNSON'S BABY OIL.** "Mix equal parts Scope Cool Peppermint Mouthwash and Johnson's Baby Oil in a spray bottle, and spray the mixture on your horses."

—SHERRI B., *Norco, California*

■ **SKIN-SO-SOFT.** "I'm an Avon lady, and I have been using Skin-So-Soft for years. Some people use it to rub down their horses to repel flies."

—MARSHA P., *Bay Minette, Alabama*

Medication

Give dogs medication with...

■ **EASY CHEESE.** "Do you have trouble getting your dog to take pills? Tired of jamming your fingers down its throat? Put the pill in the palm of your hand, smother it with Nabisco Easy Cheese (in the aerosol can), and your dog will gulp down the cheese—pill and all."

—RHONDA H., *Wauna, Washington*

■ **JIF PEANUT BUTTER.** "If your dog does not like to eat its heartworm pills, put Jif Peanut Butter on a cracker and bury the pill in it. The dog cannot spit the pill out, and it will look forward to the nightly peanut butter and cracker."

—DAVID H., *Tampa, Florida*

Parakeets

Make a tunnel for a parakeet with a...

■ **SLINKY.** "Stretch a Slinky across the ceiling of a parakeet or parrotlet cage to make a cool tunnel for the bird to explore."

—CAROLYN C., *Colorado Springs, Colorado*

Paw Glove

Protect a dog or cat paw from getting wet with a...

■ **TROJAN NON-SCENTED CONDOM.** "The vet fixed my dog's split toenail and told me to keep the paw dry. When we returned home, it began raining. I knew the dog would have to go outside to relieve itself, so I unrolled a non-lubricated Trojan condom on the dog's foot. It worked like a charm to keep the foot dry."

—CHRIS H., *Lusby, Maryland*

Pet Tags

Prevent metal pet tags from jangling with...

■ **MAYBELLINE CRYSTAL CLEAR NAIL POLISH.** "Our dog has an identification tag, a rabies vaccine tag, and a microchip tag. When he walks, the jangling tags sound like sleigh bells, which can get annoying, especially at night. By coating them with clear nail polish, it deadens the sound."

—RICK A., *Indianapolis, Indiana*

Rabbits

Clean a rabbit with...

■ **HUGGIES BABY WIPES.** "I use Huggies Baby Wipes to wipe my rabbit's fur before showing him at fairs and shows. It cleans his fur and gets rid of any loose hairs. Since he is a Rex breed, brushing or combing his fur will damage it. Huggies Baby Wipes really work well, and I win a lot of blue ribbons."

—JODY W., *Durand, Michigan*

Make a great toy with a...

■ **SLINKY.** "A Slinky is a great pet toy for bunnies. Our bunny loves pulling on it and tossing it around in the cage."

—BOHDANNA M., *Poughquag, New York*

Shedding

Slow a dog from shedding with...

■ **STAR OLIVE OIL.** "Add one tablespoon of Star Olive Oil to your dog's food. The oil will keep your dog's coat shiny and slow down the shedding."

—MARK B., *Orlando, Florida*

Skunk

Deodorize a dog sprayed by a skunk with...

- **FEBREZE.** "When my dog got sprayed by a skunk, I sprayed the dog with Febreze (extra strength) fabric refresher. The skunk odor vanished. Thanks Febreze." (Some dogs may have an allergic reaction to Febreze).
  —KAPUALANI F., *Calhoun, Louisiana*

- **LISTERINE.** "Listerine will remove the smell of skunk spray when applied full strength to the affected areas. Avoid getting Listerine in the dog's eyes or ears. Then rinse or shampoo the animal. It works. I wrote to the company years back to tell them about this wonderful discovery we made."
  —WENDY L., *Gap, Pennsylvania*

- **MASSENGILL DISPOSABLE MEDICATED DOUCHE.** "Remove skunk odor from your dog by washing the animal with Massengill Disposable Medicated Douche."
  —SALLY C., *Saginaw, Michigan*

Skunk

- **REALEMON.** "Wipe down the animal with a sponge soaked in ReaLemon lemon juice. The acid cuts through the odor better than tomato juice."
  —BILL N., *Shingleton, Michigan*

Stains

Eliminate animal urine stains from carpets with...

- **HUGGIES BABY WIPES.** "I use a Huggies Baby Wipe to clean up accidents from our new puppy. They are perfect for cleaning up urine from the carpet."
  —SHANNON B., *Brookston, Indiana*

- **LYSOL** AND **PARSONS' AMMONIA.** "Mix one-half cup of Lysol cleaner, a teaspoon of Parsons' Ammonia , and one quart of water in a bucket, and use this solution to clean the carpet where a pet has had an accident. It also takes the smell away."
  —BEVERLY T., *Greenville, Illinois*

- **PAMPERS** AND **HEINZ WHITE VINEGAR.** "Lay a Pampers diaper on top of the stain, then place something heavy on top of the diaper to keep it pressed flat against the stain for about an hour. The diaper will soak up most of the urine. Then clean the remaining stain with a mixture of vinegar and water which will erase the smell."

  —DIANE B., *Crystal Lake, Illinois*

Prevent a pet from excreting on carpets, floors, and furniture with...

- **HEINZ VINEGAR.** "When a pet excretes on carpets or other spots, spray that area with a misted squirt of vinegar. The scent will ward off dogs and cats from marking the area."

  —DEBBIE T., *Washington, D.C.*

Clean urine stains from waxed floors with...

- **ARM & HAMMER BAKING SODA.** "Just sprinkle Arm & Hammer Baking Soda on the stain, add a little water, and wipe clean."

  —WAYNE L., *Courtright, Ontario*

Static Electricity

Eliminate static electricity on pets with...

- **BOUNCE.** "We have a cat that has very long hair, and in the winter he is miserable because of static electricity. One day we decided to rub him down with a used Bounce sheet. It worked. The cat calmed down quite a bit because petting and brushing no longer gave him a shock."

  —JAMIE B., *Raytown, Missouri*

Play It

Barbie Dolls

Dress Barbie dolls easily with...

- **JOHNSON'S BABY POWDER.** "The legs on Barbie dolls are sometimes sticky with the rubber coating, making it hard to undress or dress them. To make it easier, sprinkle a small amount of Johnson's Baby Powder on the doll's legs. Dresses and pants will slide on or off easily."
  —MELISSA G., *Dickinson, North Dakota*

Baseball

Make practice balls with...

- **WILSON TENNIS BALLS.** "Cut a small slit in a Wilson Tennis Ball just long enough to fit a penny, then fill the ball with pennies so you can throw the ball around before a baseball game to warm your arm up."
  —DAVE D., *Pittsburgh, Pennsylvania*

Bicycle

Make bicycle wheels firmer with...

- **WILSON TENNIS BALLS.** "If you frequently ride your bicycle over rough terrain or if you'd like a softer landing when jumping hills, put four tennis balls between the spokes in each wheel near the hubs."
  —JEREMY F., *Horn Lake, Mississippi*

Prevent a bicycle kickstand from sinking into the ground with a...

- **WILSON TENNIS BALL.** "Poke a hole in a Wilson Tennis Ball and put it on the end of the kickstand of your bike to stop the end of the stand from sinking into grass, sand, or mud."
  —KERRY P., *Venice, Florida*

Goggles and Masks

Prevent goggles and masks from fogging up with...

- **COLGATE TOOTHPASTE.** "Coat the insides of ski goggles, swim goggles, or scuba masks with Colgate Toothpaste, then rinse off to prevent them from fogging up."
  —BRETT B., *Dallas, Texas*

Golf

Give golf balls an added spin with...

- **WD-40.** "Spray WD-40 on your golf ball for that needed spin. This is probably illegal in tournaments, but it sure works well. Wipe golf ball clean afterwards."
  —STACY D., *Kaiser, Missouri*

Guitar

Play guitar with a...

- **MASTERCARD.** "I use an expired MasterCard as a guitar pick. You wouldn't believe how great it works."
  —BRUCE H., *Tampa, Florida*

Real-Life Story

SILLY PHYSICS

"**Materials Engineering professors have used Silly Putty to demonstrate its elastomeric properties. If you rip it apart quickly, it acts as a brittle object and 'fractures.' If you pull it slowly, it acts as a maleable object and 'elongates.'**"
—BONNY C., *Toronto, Ontario*

Ice Skates

Clean rust from ice skate blades with...

- **COCA-COLA.** "I had three figure skaters in my family, and they cleaned the rust from the blades of their skates with Coke. It worked great. Try it."
  —DONNA N., *Bellevue, Washington*

Deodorize smelly ice skates with...

- **BOUNCE.** "I place used Bounce dryer sheets in my son's hockey skates after he wears them for practice and games. The Bounce keeps them smelling fresh."

  —SHERI M., *Sanborn, New York*

Soloflex Machines

Adjust a Soloflex machine with ease with...

- **JOHNSON'S BABY POWDER.** "For those of us with Soloflex machines, sprinkle a little Johnson's Baby Powder on a folded towel and when the weight straps start getting hard to put on, hit the towel with both ends of the weight strap. They almost fly on by themselves."

  —KIM B., *Fresno, California*

Weird Fact

3 DAYS OF PEACE AND PUTTY

"At the 1969 Woodstock, the medics working the First Aid tents gave out Silly Putty to pacify people who were having a bad LSD trip."

—DAVID T., *Milwaukee, Wisconsin*

Sports Bag

Deodorize a smelly sports bag with...

- **BOUNCE.** "Put a Bounce sheet in your kid's hockey or baseball bag and the smell disappears."

  —JACKIE T., *Euclid, Ohio*

Polish It

Bass Cello
Polish a bass cello with...

- **PLEDGE.** "As a musician, I like to keep my bass in good condition, but my wife has now managed to keep me from buying expensive wood products by using Pledge on my bass one day while I was at work. It conditions the wood and allows my hand to slide along the neck easily, making my style smoother."

  —ROBERT P., *San Bernardino, California*

Dents
Repair dents in wood furniture with a...

- **PROCTER-SILEX ULTRA-EASE IRON.** "A dent in wooden furniture results when the moisture is pushed out of the wood. To fix those dents, place a towel over the dent and run a steam iron over it. The dent will disappear as it reabsorbs the moisture."

  —CARMEN S., *Panama City, Florida*

Dusting
Dust furniture and appliances with...

- **HUGGIES BABY WIPES.** "Huggies Baby Wipes are excellent for cleaning the coffee table, the television screen, and the microwave."

  —JULIA M., *Lakewood, Colorado*

Furniture
Polish furniture with...

- **ALBERTO VO5 CONDITIONING HAIRDRESSING.** "I use VO5 to polish my furniture. I squeeze some on a rag, rub the furniture gently, then buff."

  —TRINA C., *Selma, California*

- **BOUNCE.** "Used Bounce sheets dust furniture really well without leaving a dull residue."
  —KATHY M., *Germantown, Maryland*

- **COLGATE TOOTHPASTE.** "Use Colgate Toothpaste to polish your tables instead of regular polish. It removes built-up Pledge or polish."
  —ROBIN H., *Napa, California*

- **SKIN-SO-SOFT.** "Use a drop of Skin-So-Soft as furniture polish and buff with a soft, clean cloth."
  —MARLENE J., *Oceanside, California*

- **WESSON CORN OIL AND HEINZ VINEGAR.** "Mix two-thirds cup Wesson Corn Oil and one-third cup Heinz Vinegar in a trigger spray bottle."
  —HERTA F., *Security, Colorado*

Glass Furniture
Polish glass furniture with...

- **DOWNY.** "Polish your glass furniture by adding a few drops of Downy Fabric Softener to your glass cleaner to reduce static and prevent dust from settling."
  —SHELLEY P., *Delta, British Columbia*

Grease
Clean grease from dining room tables with...

- **HEINZ VINEGAR.** "Here's an old restaurant trick: Wiping down dining room tables with a mixture of equal parts Heinz White Vinegar and water will cut through the thin layer of greasy build-up and also deodorize the table."
  —MAGGIE P., *Tillamook, Oregon*

Lubricate Drawers
Make drawers slide easily with...

- **VASELINE PETROLEUM JELLY.** "Coat the runners on your dresser drawers with Vaseline to make your drawers slide open wonder-fully and stop making scratchy sounds. You can also do this on computer slide-outs, doors, the bottoms of wheeled chairs, and the legs of beds. It stays greased for months."
  —JAMIE D., *Tonawanda, New York*

Patio Furniture

Clean patio furniture with...

▪ **ARMOR ALL.** "Armor All shines up resin patio furniture and prevents the dirt from settling, making it easy to clean."

—GINA S., *Niagara Falls, Ontario*

▪ **BARBASOL SHAVING CREAM.** "Just put shaving cream on the furniture and scrub with a wet rag or sponge. Since shaving cream is nontoxic, you can get your kids to help. They love to lather up the patio table. (Just don't tell them they're really cleaning for you.)"

—BARB H., *Ludlow Falls, Ohio*

▪ **CLOROX BLEACH AND PLEDGE.** "Fill a spray bottle using three-quarters cup Clorox bleach (fresh outdoor scent) diluted with a gallon of water. Simply spray the plastic lawn chairs with the bleach, wipe dry with a paper towel, spray lightly with Pledge, and wipe dry with another paper towel. The Pledge keeps the plastic shiny and smooth so dirt doesn't stick. And to think I used to scrub those puppies by hand to keep them clean. Now it takes less than a minute per chair. Great for tables, benches, planters, and all your outdoor stuff that gets gunky."

—JEANETTE W., *Buffalo, Minnesota*

▪ **HEINZ VINEGAR.** "Here in Florida everything left outside mildews. I used to use bleach to get rid of the mildew stains on furniture and our pool deck, but now all I do is sponge or spray the furniture, deck, and screens with Heinz White Vinegar and then wipe clean. Vinegar keeps newer furniture looking great and cleans the older woven strap furniture without the decay caused by bleach."

—HELEN G., *Naples, Florida*

▪ **PAM NO STICK COOKING SPRAY.** "Pam No Stick Cooking Spray cleans oil and dirt from all kinds of wood. It's great for polishing outdoor furniture that has a natural wood finish."

—RUSSELL W., *Spanaway, Washington*

- **WD-40.** "Spray WD-40 on faded plastic, then wipe with a clean cloth to bring back the color and shine."

  —STEVE M., *West Chester, Ohio*

RUN FOR THE BORDER

"When I was a kid, I would polish pennies in Taco Bell Hot Sauces (boredom, I guess). Now my girlfriend polishes all her jewelry in the mixture by letting the items sit in a short glass filled with the wonder sauce. The chemicals clean away tarnish and goo. The sauce is highly acidic from the pepper oils."

—STEVE B., *Taylor, Michigan*

Scratches

Hide scratches on furniture with...

- **CRAYOLA CRAYONS.** "Use a brown Crayola crayon to cover up scratch marks on furniture."

  —LOUIS P., *Redondo Beach, California*

- **HEINZ VINEGAR.** "Mix Heinz White Vinegar and a few drops of iodine to match the color of the furniture. Then use a Q-Tips Cotton Swab to touch up the furniture."

  —MARILYN R., *Fredericton, New Brunswick*

- **HELLMANN'S** OR **BEST REAL MAYONNAISE.** "Apply a dab of mayonnaise to the scratch, let sit for a few minutes, then rub it in and wipe clean."

  —FLORENCE G., *Perth Amboy, New Jersey*

- **KIWI SHOE POLISH.** "To repair scratches apply Kiwi Shoe Polish. Repeat until you achieve the desired look."

  —T. L., *Crane, Texas*

Stains

- ▪ **OXO LIQUID BEEF CONCENTRATE.** "Oxo Liquid Beef Concentrate, used for making gravy, is a great scratch cover for furniture. Simply apply with a Q-Tips Cotton Swab."

  —DON W., *Glencoe, Ontario*

Clean spills from furniture with...

- ▪ **HUGGIES BABY WIPES.** "Baby Wipes are great for cleaning spills and washable marker from wood furniture. My daughter spends all her time at my coffee table and it is always a disaster."

  —DIANE M., *Concord, New Hampshire*

Teak

Revitalize teak or unfinished furniture with...

- ▪ **WESSON CORN OIL.** "Oil the teak or unfinished furniture with Wesson Corn Oil to give new life to the wood."

  —MARJORIE S., *Savannah, Georgia*

Tombstones

Polish a marble headstone with...

- ▪ **OLD ENGLISH FURNITURE POLISH.** "Rejuvenate a marble headstone at the cemetery by pouring Old English Furniture Polish liberally on the surface around name and numbers, then buffing with terrycloth towel."

  —EMILY W., *Snellville, Georgia*

- ▪ **WD-40.** "I've polished a marble headstone with WD-40."

  —HETTIE R., *Phoenix, Arizona*

Water Rings

Remove water stains from wood furniture with...

- ▪ **COLGATE TOOTHPASTE.** "Plain white Colgate Toothpaste gets water stains off antique furniture without harming the finish. It works like nothing else."

  —GAIL S., *Charlottesville, Virginia*

■ **CREST TOOTHPASTE.** "Crest Regular toothpaste removes water marks on fine wood furniture. Just rub a little toothpaste in, wipe it off, then polish the coffee table."

—PATRICIA, *New Caney, Texas*

■ **LAND O' LAKES BUTTER.** "Mix two tablespoons Land O' Lakes Butter with ashes from the fireplace. Using a soft cloth, rub the mixture with vigorous circular motion over and into the whitened area. A little more elbow grease and—*voila!*—no more stain. And it leaves the wood with a nice shine, too."

—LEE R., *Livingston, Tennessee*

Remove It

Adhesives

Clean construction adhesives from skin with...

- **LISTERINE.** "Listerine can remove some construction adhesives from your skin."
  —BURGE S., *Detroit, Michigan*

Bandage Glue

Clean bandage glue from skin with...

- **ALBERTO VO5 CONDITIONING HAIRDRESSING.** "VO5 Hairdressing works great to get rid of adhesive on skin from Band-Aids and hormone patches."
  —TERESA M., *Belleville, Illinois*

- **JIF PEANUT BUTTER.** "You can remove the black sticky glue left from Band-Aids using a little Jif Peanut Butter."
  —DUSTIN H., *Norwalk, Ohio*

- **SKIN-SO-SOFT.** "To remove the sticky stuff left on your skin from a bandage, use Avon Skin-So-Soft on a rag and rub. It takes a couple of minutes, but it works."
  —RENELLE B., *Houston, Texas*

Bottles

Remove labels from bottles with...

- **CASCADE.** "Dissolved Cascade in water in a large garbage pail quickly removes beer labels from commercial beers."
  —PAUL G., *Hinesville, Georgia*

Dry-Erase Boards

Clean ink from a dry-erase board with...

- **COCA-COLA.** "Coca-Cola removes permanent marker from dry-erase boards."
  —LESLIE B., *Martinez, California*

- **HUGGIES BABY WIPES.** "Huggies Baby Wipes can be used to remove leftover marker stains from a dry-erase message board. Simply wipe clean and it's white again."
  —KIMBERLY W., *Valparaiso, Indiana*

Fiberglass

Clean fiberglass from skin with...

- **VASELINE PETROLEUM JELLY.** "Vaseline is great for getting fiberglass insulation off your skin. Just spread on and wipe off, and those little fibers will miraculously come off."
  —SUE K., *Lawrenceville, Georgia*

Glue

Remove dried glue with...

- **CUTEX NAIL POLISH REMOVER.** "Nail polish remover takes off the glue left over after removing stickers."
  —KEN E., *Narberth, Pennsylvania*

- **HELLMANN'S** OR **BEST REAL MAYONNAISE.** "Hellmann's Real Mayonnaise works wonderfully to remove the glue left behind when pulling stickers off a valuable item that a solvent or scraping would ruin. To remove the glue, put some mayonnaise on the tip of your finger and rub it over the glue. The glue will slowly dissolve. Do not use any abrasive. The mayonnaise is a wonderful solvent."
  —HOWARD G., *Reading, Pennsylvania*

- **JIF PEANUT BUTTER.** "A dab of Jif Peanut Butter removes the sticky residue left by Band-Aids and the sticky labels or price tags on glass items."
  —DEBBY C., *Asheville, North Carolina*

- **PURELL.** "Purell, the soapless, antibacterial hand sanitizer, takes off adhesive from peeled labels."
  —FRAN G., *Calabasas, California*

- **SKIN-SO-SOFT.** "Use Skin-So-Soft to remove masking tape from windows."
  —JULEE G., *Edinboro, Pennsylvania*

- **WD-40.** "Clean dried glue from any hard surface with WD-40. Spray with WD-40, let sit thirty seconds, and wipe clean."
  —JEAN R., *Millsboro, Delaware*

- **WESSON CORN OIL.** "Clean price-tag residue off items with a drop of Wesson Corn Oil, then wipe clean."
  —ED M., *Surrey, British Columbia*

Gum

Remove chewing gum from carpet with...

- **JIF PEANUT BUTTER.** "Use a dab of Jif Peanut Butter to remove gum from carpet."
  —DENISE L., *Vincent, Ohio*

- **SKIN-SO-SOFT.** "A drop of Skin-So-Soft, rubbed into chewing gum, removes it from carpet."
  —KELLI R., *Kansas City, Missouri*

Remove chewing gum from hair with...

- **HELLMANN'S** OR **BEST REAL MAYONNAISE.** "You can use Hellmann's Mayonnaise to get gum out of your hair. Leave it in for ten minutes, then comb clean."
  —BENNETT S., *Santa Clara, California*

- **JIF PEANUT BUTTER.** "Got gum in your hair? Slather some Jif Peanut Butter over the gum and comb it out. The oil in the peanut butter dissolves the gum in the chewing gum. Then just wash your hair with regular shampoo to get rid of the peanut butter."
  —KEITH A., *Los Angeles, California*

- **WD-40.** "Spray the gum with WD-40. It slowly dissolves the gum. Work the gum free with your fingers, then wash hair to get rid of the WD-40."
  —JENNIFER B., *Pueblo, Colorado*

Remove chewing gum from the inside of a dryer with...

■ **JIF PEANUT BUTTER.** "Ever dry clothes in a clothes dryer only to find that someone left bubble gum in their pockets and now it's all over the inside of the dryer? Just apply a dab of Jif Peanut Butter on the bubble gum and wipe clean."

—CHERYL-MARIE W., *Richmond, Texas*

Krazy Glue

Remove Krazy Glue with...

■ **CUTEX NAIL POLISH REMOVER.** "Have you ever Krazy-Glued your fingers together? Using Cutex Nail Polish Remover, the glue comes off in seconds."

—CAROLYN J., *Bassano, Alberta*

Price Tags

Remove price-tag stickers with...

■ **JIF PEANUT BUTTER.** "Jif Peanut Butter removes stickers (price tags) from glass. Works well on chandeliers."

—ROBERT S., *Oceanside, California*

■ **RONSONOL LIGHTER FUEL.** "Use lighter fluid on a Kleenex Tissue to remove stubborn price tags from glass, wood, or metal. It gets rid of the sticky residue really well."

—JOHN O., *Lafayette, Indiana*

■ **SCOTCH TAPE.** "Just press a piece of Scotch Tape over the price tag, pull up, and the price tag will come off with the tape."

—JOYCE V., *Hopewell, New Jersey*

■ **SCOTT'S LIQUID GOLD.** "Spray on Scott's Liquid Gold, let set for a few minutes, and price tags scrape off easily."

—ROBERT M., *Hemet, California*

■ **SKIN-SO-SOFT.** "I use Skin-So-Soft to remove labels on jars. Just apply a dab, rub it into the label, let sit a few minutes, then peel away."

—ANYTA M., *Boca Raton, Florida*

- **WD-40.** "You can spray WD-40 onto glass, metal, or plastic objects to get rid of those nasty price stickers that refuse to come off. After soaking for a minute, they come off easily."

—MARY W., *Gloucester, Virginia*

Remover

Remove paint, ink or Krazy Glue from furniture or skin with...

- **CUTEX NAIL POLISH REMOVER.** "Simply dab the stain with a cotton ball soaked in Cutex Nail Polish Remover."

—KAREN R., *Claremont, New Hampshire*

Rings

Remove a ring stuck on a finger with...

- **JOHNSON'S BABY OIL.** "Use a few drops of Johnson's Baby Oil and a stuck ring will slide off your finger."

—LINDA D., *Cary, North Carolina*

- **MIRACLE WHIP.** "Slather on Miracle Whip and the ring will glide off."

—WILMA T., *Baltimore, Maryland*

- **PREPARATION H.** "Got a ring stuck on your finger? Use Preparation H cream to reduce the swelling and the ring will come right off."

—KRISTEN S., *Bay St. Louis, Mississippi*

- **WINDEX.** "My aunt owns a jewelry store and uses Windex when customers get her expensive antique rings stuck on their fingers. We also use it to clean all of the glass counters."

—SUE N., *Boulder, Colorado*

Tar

Remove tar from skin with...

- **LAND O' LAKES BUTTER.** "Rub in Land O' Lakes butter and tar comes off like magic."

—DOREEN M., *London, Ontario*

Tree Sap

Wash tree sap from skin with...

- **JIF PEANUT BUTTER.** "After making Christmas wreaths with pine boughs, I was left with sticky pine pitch on my hands. I used Jif Peanut Butter as a cleaner. It removed all the pine pitch."

  —PAT H., *Jackson, Michigan*

- **PAM NO STICK COOKING SPRAY.** "If you get pine pitch (tree sap) on your hands, spray on Pam No Stick Cooking Spray, rub it in, then wash in soapy water. The Pam removes the pine pitch completely."

  —NANCY K., *Ione, Washington*

- **JOHNSON'S BABY OIL.** "Johnson's Baby Oil dissolves tree sap from hair, body, and clothes."

  —MARY M., *Scarborough, Ontario*

- **SKIN-SO-SOFT.** "I climbed a huge pine tree to trim it and got fresh sap in my hair and on my arms. Skin-So-Soft dissolved it immediately. I was amazed."

  —MARK F., *Lenox, Massachusetts*

Repel It

Ants

Repel ants with...

- **CRAYOLA CHALK.** "Ants everywhere? They never cross a chalk line. So get out some Crayola Chalk and draw a thick line on the floor or wherever ants tend to march."

  —GRAHAM B., *West Richland, Washington*

- **HEINZ VINEGAR.** "Use Heinz Vinegar to divert a trail of ants."

  —DONNA B., *Altus, Oklahoma*

- **MCCORMICK** OR **SCHILLING BLACK PEPPER.** "Just sprinkle black pepper where you have seen ants or at a point of entry into your house."

  —CHARLIE M., *White Sulphur Springs, West Virginia*

- **MCCORMICK** OR **SCHILLING CHILI POWDER.** "Sprinkle chili powder around doorways, windows, and entrance ways to help stop ants. Ants can't stand it."

  —KEVIN S., *Dallas, Texas*

- **MCCORMICK** OR **SCHILLING CINNAMON.** "Cinnamon gets rid of ants, especially if ants get into pet food. It really works well."

  —DEBBIE H., *Riverside, California*

- **MORTON SALT.** "To get rid of ants without any ant traps, sprinkle the area with Morton Salt and they'll be gone."

  —SANDRA B., *Hillsdale, New Jersey*

Kill ants with...

- **ALBERS GRITS.** "Sprinkle dry grits on an ant hill. Each ant will carry away one grit, eat it, drink water, and explode."

  —RANDY M., *Rock Hill, South Carolina*

■ **ARM & HAMMER BAKING SODA.** "Ants getting into your kitchen but you don't want to use poison? Dust baking soda in cracks, corners, and crevices. The ants will slow down and eventually disappear because baking soda is a poison to them."

—MICHELE M., *Richmond Hill, Ontario*

■ **BARBASOL SHAVING CREAM.** "Ant sprays stink so we have begun to use shaving cream. For some reason the little critters don't like it, and it seems to make them disappear."

—SANDY A., *Arbuckle, California*

■ **CREAM OF WHEAT.** "Pouring Cream of Wheat on an ant hill stops the ants."

—JOANN C., *Mesa, Arizona*

■ **FORMULA 409.** "When I was in my twenties, I was too poor to buy bug spray when the ants invaded my house, so I used Formula 409 instead. It works great on the ants, and when you wipe it away, your ceiling, walls, and counters are clean, too."

—LINDA L., *Aloha, Oregon*

■ **LYSOL.** "Lysol kills ants faster than Raid."

—KATHY D., *Lancaster, California*

■ **MINUTE RICE.** "Sprinkle raw Minute Rice where ants are a problem. The ants take the rice to the nest, they eat it, and the rice swells in their stomachs killing the whole nest. No pesticides."

—ELLEN R., *Parachute, Colorado*

■ **SKIN-SO-SOFT.** "Pour Skin-So-Soft on ants to kill them instantly. It smells nice and it's nontoxic."

—KEVIN W., *Escondido, California*

■ **SPRAY 'N WASH.** "You can use Spray 'n Wash as a great ant killer. It works better than the real stuff."

—PETER C., *San Luis Obispo, California*

■ **20 MULE TEAM BORAX** AND **DOMINO SUGAR.** "Mix one cup 20 Mule Team Borax, two-thirds cup sugar, and one cup water. Dip cotton balls in the solution. Lay the cotton balls around the house. Once the ants consume the sweet mixture, they are quickly on their way to ant heaven."

—MOLLIE D., *Mammoth, West Virginia*

- **WINDEX.** "Windex is better than any bug spray you can buy at the store. I work for Sears Pest Control and that's what I tell my customers. Why waste your money on bug spray when you can just grab your Windex?"

—TERESA O., *Dallas, Georgia*

Prevent ants from getting into a pet food dish with...

- **VASELINE PETROLEUM JELLY.** "Rub a small dab of Vaseline Petroleum Jelly around the bottom rim of the pet food bowl to prevent ants from getting into the food."

—TOWNSEND P., *Duncanville, Alabama*

Bees, Wasps, Hornets, and Yellow Jackets
Kill bees, wasps, hornets, and yellow jackets with...

- **ALBERTO VO5 HAIR SPRAY.** "Bees bothering you, but you have no bug spray? Get out the hair spray and spray the bee. It'll fly for a second and then drop, totally immobilized."

—MIKE S., *Los Angeles, California*

- **FORMULA 409.** "Formula 409 kills wasps, hornets, and yellow jackets with one squirt. They drop to the ground instantly and die within seconds."

—JENNIFER V., *Austin, Texas*

- **MOUNTAIN DEW** AND **DAWN.** "Add two teaspoons of Dawn detergent to an open can of Mountain Dew, and place the can near bees. They can't resist the mixture, drink it, and die."

—DONNA E., *Monroe, Wisconsin*

- **PARSONS' AMMONIA.** "Sudsy ammonia is an excellent wasp and hornet spray. It's cheap, effective, and natural. I've used it with much success against very aggressive species of wasps and hornets for years. Try it in a common spray bottle or a pressurized draw system."

—JIM L., *Lufkin, Texas*

- **WD-40.** "If you find a wasp nest and don't have any wasp spray, try using WD-40. It kills them."
  —SHERRY F., *De Ridder, Louisiana*

- **WINDEX.** "We use Windex to kill bees and wasps. We have two small children, and in the summer when the windows are open, we get these awful bugs in our house. We certainly don't want them to sting our boys, but we don't want to fill the house with pesticide either. So we spray them with Windex."
  —PATTI S., *Windsor, Connecticut*

Repel yellow jackets with...

- **BOUNCE.** "Tie a sheet of Bounce on a belt loop or purse and it will repel those nasty yellow jackets."
  —DIANA K., *Bucyrus, Ohio*

Bird Mites

Kill bird mites with...

- **LISTERINE.** "Mix one part Listerine to one part water in a spray bottle. Spray your bird for mites, making sure not to get any in the bird's eyes. Spray the entire cage to disinfect it."
  —PAULETTE B., *Nashville, Tennessee*

Bird Feeders

Prevent ants from climbing into a hummingbird feeder with...

- **VASELINE PETROLEUM JELLY.** "Rub Vaseline on the chain or string from which you hang your hummingbird feeder to keep ants away."
  —EARLENE S., *Goodman, Missouri*

Birds

Prevent birds from nesting with...

- **PAM NO STICK COOKING SPRAY.** "To prevent barn or cliff swallows from building nests in nooks and crannies where you don't want them, remove any nest material from the area and spray the spot with Pam. If the birds attempt to rebuild a nest in the spot, the Pam causes the new nest material to just slide off."

—CAROL H., *Portage la Prairie, Manitoba*

Prevent birds from standing or landing on any surface with...

■ **JOHNSON'S BABY POWDER.** "If you have trouble with bird droppings, sprinkle Johnson's Baby Powder where the birds land. Birds don't like the way baby powder feels on their feet."

—JOHN L., *Lakeside, California*

Cockroaches

Kill cockroaches with...

■ **ALBERTO VO5 HAIR SPRAY.** "Use Alberto VO5 Hair Spray to petrify roaches in their tracks."

—JOANN C., *Mesa, Arizona*

■ **ARM & HAMMER BAKING SODA** AND **DOMINO SUGAR.** "Mix one-half cup Arm & Hammer Baking Soda with one tablespoon Domino Sugar, and sprinkle the mixture in tight corners, cracks, and crevices where roaches hide. The sugar will lure the cockroaches to walk through the powder and lick it off their legs. Since cockroaches cannot digest baking soda, their stomachs explode internally."

—AMY G., *Palm City, Florida*

■ **DAWN.** "I use a tablespoon of Dawn dishwashing liquid in a spray bottle filled with water to kill roaches. They just go legs up and die."

—CHARLES G., *Chicago, Illinois*

■ **DOW BATHROOM CLEANER.** "Dow Bathroom Cleaner is wonderful for killing roaches dead in their tracks. Just aim and shoot. It actually takes less time to work than Raid."

—STEVE H., *Summerville, South Carolina*

■ **LYSOL.** "I spray Lysol Antibacterial Kitchen Cleaner on roaches, and I have never seen a bug die so quickly. In my house of small children, I feel better about chasing down a bug with an antibacterial spray rather than Raid or other insecticides, which do not seem to work very fast anyway. Besides, a roach scampers away so fast, you never know if it died or escaped. With Lysol, I get instantaneous results. Just wipe the area after the roach has been discarded and the floor is disinfected as well."

—CATE W., *Cary, North Carolina*

■ **20 MULE TEAM BORAX** AND **DOMINO SUGAR.** "Mix equal parts 20 Mule Team Borax and sugar, then sprinkle the mixture in places where roaches crawl."

—LORI S., *Binghamton, New York*

■ **WD-40.** "Spray just a little WD-40 on a cockroach and it is history."

—DONALD M., *Marietta, Georgia*

Crickets

Catch crickets with...

■ **SCOTCH PACKAGING TAPE.** "Take a strip of Scotch Packaging Tape and place each end on the floor with the sticky side up. This will catch crickets in a basement or garage."

—MARY G., *Decatur, Indiana*

Deer

Repel deer with...

■ **BOUNCE.** "Hang a fresh sheet of Bounce near tomatoes or other nibbled plants. The fragrance (oleander, a natural repellent) keeps critters at bay."

—MARK T., *Los Angeles, California*

■ **IRISH SPRING SOAP** AND **L'EGGS SHEER ENERGY PANTY HOSE.** "Put a bar of Irish Spring Soap in the leg of an old pair of L'eggs and hang it in your garden to prevent deer from eating plants."

—CANDY H., *Auburn, Washington*

Dogs and Cats

Keep dogs and cats off your lawn with...

■ **TABASCO PEPPER SAUCE.** "Sprinkle Tabasco Pepper Sauce along the perimeter of the yard."

—Douglas J., *Ithaca, New York*

Fire Ants

Kill fire ants with...

■ **CLOROX BLEACH.** "I live in the south where fire ants abound. Instead of buying expensive fire ant poisons, I pour one cup of Clorox directly on the fire ant mound. Instead of moving elsewhere, the ants are stopped dead in their little tracks."

—Bonnie K., *Midland City, Alabama*

Fleas

Kill fleas in carpeting with...

■ **MORTON SALT.** "Use uniodized Morton Salt on carpets to get rid of fleas. Sprinkle on carpets, let sit for at least three hours, and vacuum."

—Jim L., *Ojai, California*

■ **PINE-SOL.** "If your pets get fleas and bring them into your house, fill a spray bottle with Pine-Sol, and spray it on your furniture and carpets. This not only repels fleas but it also removes pet odors from the couches."

—Kimberly H., *Harrison, Arizona*

■ **20 MULE TEAM BORAX.** "When our house was invaded by fleas, I tried 'bombing' the house with insect killer, spraying the carpets with insecticide, steam cleaning the carpets, and putting down flea powder. Finally, a friend suggested 20 Mule Team Borax. I lightly sprinkled the borax on the carpets and tile floor and let it sit for twenty-four hours. Then I vacuumed it up. There was not a flea to be found. After all the expensive insecticides and the fumes, the borax did the trick. I have suggested this tip to many of my friends, and they have tried it with 100-percent success. My house has been flea-free for seven years."

—Vicki S., *Chapin, South Carolina*

Kill fleas sucked into your vacuum cleaner bag with...

■ **HARTZ 2 IN 1 FLEA COLLARS.** "After cutting off the excess length of a flea collar for our dog, my mother put that piece in the bag of her vacuum cleaner. That way, if she vacuumed up any fleas, they would be killed inside the bag."

—MIKE W., *Rome, Georgia*

Flies

Kill flies with...

■ **ALBERTO VO5 HAIR SPRAY.** "Can't seem to hit those pesky flies with a swatter? Spray them with Alberto VO5 Hair Spray. Hair spray freezes their wings. It's better than splattering them on the wall with a swatter, plus hair spray smells better than insecticide."

—DEBBIE R., *Philadelphia, Pennsylvania*

Weird Fact

HOT STUFF

"Fans of the television series *Roswell* sent three thousand bottles of Tabasco Pepper Sauce to network executives at Warner Brothers to save the show from cancellation. The reason? The three main characters on *Roswell* put Tabasco sauce on everything they ate, including chocolate cake. The network gave *Roswell* a green light for another season."

—AURELIA C., *Sarasota, Florida*

Gophers and Moles

Kill moles with...

■ **EX-LAX.** "Put a small piece of chocolate Ex-Lax in an active run. Moles can't resist it, eat too much, and that's the end of the moles."

—CLINT R., *Raytown, Missouri*

■ **WRIGLEY'S JUICY FRUIT GUM.** "If you have moles tearing up your yard, put on a pair of rubber gloves, unwrap one stick of Wrigley's Juicy Fruit Gum, and slide it into a mole tunnel. Moles love Juicy Fruit Gum. They eat the gum but cannot digest it, so they die. Just remember to wear gloves to avoid leaving a human scent on the gum. I have no moles in my yard."

—MARY N., *Asheville, North Carolina*

Repel moles or gophers from your garden with...

■ **MAXWELL HOUSE COFFEE.** "Did you know that spreading Maxwell House Coffee grounds on your yard will get rid of ground moles? Believe it or not, ground moles immediately take to the hills."

—SHIRLEY B., *Bronson, Michigan*

■ **TIDY CAT.** "Pour used Tidy Cat into the mole or gopher tunnels. The pests will smell the scent of their natural enemy and quickly tunnel into someone else's yard."

—CARL T., *Portland, Oregon*

Houseplants

Repel insects from houseplants with...

■ **DAWN.** "Put a drop of Dawn dishwashing liquid in a spray bottle, fill the rest of the bottle with water, shake well, and mist your household plants. The soap keeps bugs off the plant leaves. Pour the leftover water into the soil, and the bugs will surely stay away when the leaves taste like soap."

—CHAYA B., *Baltimore, Maryland*

Insects

Repel insects with...

■ **DAWN.** "Bug problem? Draw a line of Dawn across a back door or window (or wherever insects are getting in), and crawling insects cannot get across. They will stick to the soap. Works great for potato bugs, ants, and silver fish."

—GINA S., *Niagara Falls, Ontario*

■ **SKIN-SO-SOFT.** "Put a tablespoon of Skin-So-Soft in a spray bottle and fill with water. Shake well, then spray on yourself and window screens for insect repellant."

—WARDE M., *Corona, California*

Kill insects with...

- **FORMULA 409.** "Formula 409 all-purpose cleaner kills insects quickly and cleanly without harsh odors. A couple of squirts usually does the trick (use more for large cockroaches)."

  —JENNIFER V., *Austin, Texas*

Lure insects away from a barbecue or picnic with...

- **HEINZ APPLE CIDER VINEGAR.** "If you pour Heinz Apple Cider Vinegar in a large bowl, you can use it to attract flying pests. Last summer, flies, mosquitoes, and moths decided to join our barbecue. I poured some apple cider vinegar into a bowl and set it near the food. At the end of the night, there were countless critters floating in the bowl."

  —MIGUEL D., *Chenoa, Illinois*

Prevent insects and spiders from entering your house through windows and doors with...

- **WD-40.** "Spray your door frames, window sills, frames, and screens with WD-40. I tried this as a last resort and it worked all summer. The WD-40 does smell a bit at first but dissipates quickly. Of course, don't spray doors and windows with WD-40 if you have babies or small children who might wipe their hands on it."

  —MELISSA M., *Oklahoma City, Oklahoma*

Mice

Repel mice with...

- **BOUNCE.** "Put Bounce sheets anywhere you want to deter mice. We're farmers, and we put them around our bags of seed and in our stored equipment. It works like a charm and makes everything smell nice in the bargain."

  —MARGO H., *Iona, Minnesota*

- **S.O.S STEEL WOOL PADS.** "Place S.O.S pads in holes in the wallboards to keep mice away."

  —ELAINE G., *Magee, Mississippi*

Kill mice and rats with...

- **COCA-COLA.** "Put Coca-Cola in a bowl and set it out where you have mice. The mice love Coke, drink it, and, unable to expel the gas, they die."

  —MARY A., *Pittsburgh, Pennsylvania*

- **HERSHEY'S CHOCOLATE SYRUP.** "Bait a mouse or rat trap with Hershey's Chocolate Syrup. We call it 'Death by Chocolate.'"

  —BILL W., *Pennsauken, New Jersey*

- **JIF PEANUT BUTTER.** "Bait a mouse or rat trap with Jif Peanut Butter. Mice actually prefer peanut butter to cheese."

  —BILL W., *Pennsauken, New Jersey*

Mosquitoes

Kill mosquitoes with...

- **JOY.** "Tired of mosquitoes? Put two or three drops of Lemon Joy in a dinner plate, fill with water, and place the dish on the patio. Mosquitoes will flock to it, fall in and die, or at worst get a few feet away and die."

  —TOM C., *Indianapolis, Indiana*

Slugs

Kill slugs with...

- **FORMULA 409.** "Formula 409 is a great killer for slugs in your garden. Turns them nuclear green as they shrivel and die."

  —SYDNEY B., *Amarillo, Texas*

- **MORTON SALT.** "Morton Salt dissolves slugs. Pour salt on top of the slug and watch it shrivel up in about five minutes until it's dried and dead."

  —HARRIET B., *Clearwater, Florida*

Snails

Kill snails with...

- **BUDWEISER.** "Fill a saucer with beer and set it in the garden. Snails like the taste of beer, crawl in, get drunk, and drown."

  —KEVIN S., *Dallas, Texas*

Repel snails with...

■ **MORTON SALT.** "Repel snails with salt without hurting the environment by simply sprinkling salt lightly around your garden."

—BRADLEY D., *Bell Canyon, California*

Spiders
Kill a spider with...

■ **ALBERTO VO5 HAIR SPRAY.** "If you are afraid of spiders, use hair spray to kill them. It freezes them in their tracks."

—RENA P., *Oklahoma City, Oklahoma*

■ **FORMULA 409.** "I spray spiders with Formula 409 to kill them so I don't have to squish them."

—ROXANE T., *Oak Forest, Illinois*

Squirrels
Repel squirrels from a bird feeder with...

■ **CRISCO ALL-VEGETABLE SHORTENING.** "Use Crisco to grease the pole of a bird feeder, then watch the squirrels try to climb up."

—CATIE M., *New York, New York*

■ **MCCORMICK** OR **SCHILLING CAYENNE PEPPER.** "Keep the squirrels out of your bird feeder by coating the bird seed with Cayenne Pepper. The birds can't taste the pepper but the squirrels can and don't like the taste."

—JEANE G., *Troy, New York*

■ **VASELINE PETROLEUM JELLY.** "Coat a bird feeder pole with Vaseline and watch the squirrels slip and slide but never make it up the pole. Rain won't wash the Vaseline off the pole."

—LIZ G., *Tampa, Florida*

Weevils
Keep weevils out of flour with...

■ **WRIGLEY'S SPEARMINT GUM.** "Placing a wrapped stick of Wrigley's Spearmint Gum in your flour canister will keep weevils out—without flavoring the flour. It can also be used in other food-stuffs that are susceptible to weevils. It lasts for a long time. I just replace the gum whenever I open a new bag of flour."

—Kay S., *Hastings, Nebraska*

Worms

Kill worms with...

- **MORTON SALT.** "After it rains my patio is covered with worms. I toss salt over all of them, watch them shrivel up and die. Then I send my husband out to sweep them up."

—Lyn F., *Garland, Texas*

Rough It

Campfires

Start a campfire with...

- **DORITOS.** "Doritos tortilla chips work as kindling. They burn long enough to start damp wood on fire."
  —HENRY B., *Edson, Alberta*

- **MORTON SALT.** "Sprinkle salt on a rock, place kindling around it, and rub the salt with a second rock to start a fire for outdoor camping."
  —PEGGY P., *Phoenix, Arizona*

- **VASELINE PETROLEUM JELLY.** "To start a campfire, apply Vaseline to a stick and light with a match."
  —RICHARD M., *Ada, Michigan*

Camping

Bathe yourself with...

- **HUGGIES BABY WIPES.** "When I was an infantryman in the U.S. Army, we were constantly out in the field for training. Being in the field for a week to six months at a time made for a miserable experience if you didn't maintain your personal hygiene. If you asked where to find a hot shower, you'd be laughed at, since there usually weren't any available. Some of us more savvy Joes packed Huggies Baby Wipes in a Ziploc bag in our rucksacks. We could use them to take a quick 'foxhole shower' without removing much of our camouflage clothing. And the used/dried wipes could be reused as emergency toilet paper, if the need arose. This might be a tip to pass along to campers."
  —WILLIAM A., *Dansville, New York*

Hang soap from the water pump when camping with...

- **L'EGGS SHEER ENERGY PANTY HOSE.** "Cut off the leg from a used pair of L'eggs Panty Hose, place a bar of soap inside the foot, tie a knot to secure the bar of soap, then tie the other end of the panty hose to the water pump."

  —DENISE N., *Mt. Prospect, New York*

Can Caddies

Remove can caddies with ease with...

- **PAM NO STICK COOKING SPRAY.** "I used to have a hard time getting cans out of can caddies. Now I spray Pam inside the caddy, wipe out any excess spray, then insert the can. After finishing my drink, I can easily slip the can out of the caddy."

  —JENNIFER A., *Whitakers, North Carolina*

Drinking Cups

Improvise drinking cups with a...

- **DANNON YOGURT CUP.** "Clean out empty Dannon Yogurt cups and they're useful as drinking cups."

  —JOHN P., *Albuquerque, New Mexico*

Fishing

Lure fish with...

- **ALKA-SELTZER.** "Experienced fishermen know how to attract fish on a slow day. When using hollow plastic tube jigs, simply break off a piece of an Alka-Seltzer tablet and insert it into the hollow tube jig. As the jig sinks in the water, the Alka-Seltzer tablet begins to produce a stream of bubbles, attracting fish."

  —DAVE G., *Scarborough, Ontario*

- **ALTOIDS.** "You can use spearmint-flavored Altoids as bait when you are fishing. The fish love it."

  —BRIAN R., *Olney, Maryland*

- **L'EGGS SHEER ENERGY PANTY HOSE.** "Cut strips of used panty hose to make fishing lures."

  —JENA W., *La Grange, Texas*

■ **PLAY-DOH.** "Roll pink and orange Play-Doh into a tiny ball, place on your hook, and watch the salmon and trout attack."

—JILL L., *Chesterton, Indiana*

■ **SKIN-SO-SOFT.** "Spray Skin-So-Soft onto the end of a fishing lure. It will attract fish to your hook."

—DIANE R., *Harlan, Iowa*

■ **WD-40.** "Salmon fishermen in Oregon and Washington spray WD-40 on trolling lures before trolling for salmon. Salmon have excellent 'smellers,' to detect the slightly different waters flowing into the ocean—so they can identify the specific stream they 'hatched' in and return there to spawn. Fisherman think the WD-40 disguises the human odor on lures, which are known to frighten off salmon and prevent biting. Every trolling boat out there seems to have a can of WD-40 aboard, and the fishermen do spray it on their lures before fishing."

—DAVID G., *Wapiti, Wyoming*

Bait a hook with...

■ **FORSTER CLOTHES PINS.** "Use a clothes pin to pick up leeches when you're fishing and need to bait your hook."

—SANDRA O., *Ely, Minnesota*

Store jigs with...

■ **ZIPLOC STORAGE BAGS.** "Coil up jigs and place each one in its own Ziploc bag before putting them in your tackle box. This prevents them from getting tangled up and making a mess out of your tackle box."

—STEVE S., *San Jose, California*

Lubricate a fishing reel with...

■ **PAM NO STICK COOKING SPRAY.** "Use Pam No Stick Cooking Spray as you would use silicone spray to make casting easier and quicker."

—TERRY H., *Phoenix, Arizona*

Clean corrosion from fishing rods with...

■ **SNO BOL.** "Sno Bol takes the corrosion off fishing reels, chrome fixtures, and almost anything that gets corroded."

—BARB H., *Orlando, Florida*

Prevent chaffing when fishing in salt water with...

■ **VASELINE PETROLEUM JELLY.** "Fishermen use Vaseline Petroleum Jelly to prevent chaffing from saltwater build-up in the crotch. Spread the jelly inside each thigh before going in salt water to run nets or fish."

—ROBERT T., *Jacksonville, North Carolina*

Weird Fact

A GENUINE LIFESAVER

"Soldiers in the military use Pam No Stick Cooking Spray to clean tank-gunnery firing devices. We sprayed Pam into the 'Hoffman Devices' prior to loading them. To clean the devices that had been sprayed with Pam only required water from a hose. No tank commander would be caught dead without his spray can of Pam when using Hoffman Devices. Hoffman Devices simulate the firing of the main gun on a tank."

—JERRY G., *South River, New Jersey*

Ice

Make large ice cubes for Thermos bottles with a...

■ **DANNON YOGURT CUP.** "Fill clean, empty Dannon Yogurt cups three-quarters full with water, and put them in the freezer to make ice cubes perfectly sized for a Thermos bottle."

—ABBY H., *Manhattan, Kansas*

Odors

Trick your sense of smell so you can withstand a foul odor with...

■ **VICKS VAPORUB.** "Put a dab of Vicks VapoRub under your nostrils when performing an odorous task."

—JAY N., *Port Townsend, Washington*

Pots and Pans

Prevent campfire soot from sticking to pots and pans with...

- **MURPHY'S OIL SOAP.** "Coat the outside of pots and pans with Murphy's Oil Soap before using the cookware over an outdoor fire. The black soot from the fire will wash right off."

  —ROSANNE M., *Kipawa, Quebec*

- **PALMOLIVE.** "Before cooking over an open fire, coat the bottom of your pots and pans with Palmolive dishwashing liquid. The black soot that forms on the bottom of the pots and pans wipes right off."

  —PAM L., *Peterborough, Ontario*

Showers

Make a camping shower with...

- **TROJAN NON-SCENTED CONDOMS.** "Fill a condom with water and hang it from a tree. Gently poke four or five holes in it. Instant shower. Caution: Do not use a condom for its intended purpose after poking holes in it."

  —CARLIE G., *Chula Vista, California*

Sink

Make a camping sink with a...

- **CLOROX BLEACH BOTTLE.** "When I take my Girl Scouts camping, we poke a small hole in the side of a clean, empty Clorox Bleach bottle (near the bottom) and then plug the hole with a golf tee. We fill the bottle with water to wash our hands."

  —KIM E., *Norwich, Connecticut*

Snorkling

Attract fish with...

- **EASY CHEESE.** "When snorkling, use aerosol Easy Cheese to attract fish. This is the best bait I have ever used to view the underwater world. Easy Cheese allowed me to see beautiful tropical fish all over the Caribbean."

  —SARAH K., *Burlington, Vermont*

Solar-Powered Water Heater
Heat water with...

■ **CLOROX, COCA-COLA,** AND **DOWNY.** "I save empty bleach bottles, two-liter soda bottles, even fabric softener bottles. I paint them black with tempera paint and fill them with water. I set them in full sun in the morning and by about dinner time, the water is hot enough to use for washing dishes, bathing our puppies, or soaking my husband's feet (with baking soda added). With enough containers, I've even heated my daughter's wading pool."

—CATHERINE H., *West, Mississippi*

Sew It

21

Buttons

Fortify buttons on shirts with...

- **ELMER'S GLUE-ALL.** "With your fingertip, rub a tiny drop of Elmer's Glue-All on the thread around each button. This prevents the thread from coming loose and stops the buttons from falling off. It's also a great way to stop a loose button from falling off while you are at work or far from home."
  —MARK B., *Akron, Ohio*

Sew buttons on coats with...

- **ORAL-B DENTAL FLOSS.** "Use dental floss to sew on buttons, especially on kids' clothes. They'll be more durable."
  —MARY KAY M., *Deming, New Mexico*

Dying

Dye wool with...

- **KOOL-AID.** "I have used Kool-Aid to dye wool from my sheep before spinning it. The acid in it helps cut through the lanolin on the wool and makes the dye take better."
  —MARILYN T., *Canterbury, Connecticut*

Darken stockings with...

- **LIPTON TEA.** "If you're getting a tan on your legs because your stockings are too light, soak the stockings overnight in a strong solution of Lipton Tea, rinse, and wear."
  —MARJORIE S., *Savannah, Georgia*

Embossing

Emboss with ease with...

- **MR. COFFEE FILTERS.** "When embossing, you can pour the powder onto a Mr. Coffee Filter and then back into the jar without leaving any residue on the filter. The filter can be used over and over again, leaving lots of money to buy more stamps."

  —LINDA O., *Jackson, Mississippi*

Embroidery

Stabilize embroidery with...

- **BOUNCE.** "Place a used sheet of Bounce on the back of t-shirts or sweat shirts (for stability) when you cross-stitch or embroider designs on them. It's less expensive and more convenient than purchasing interfacing."

  —MELANIE P., *Kittanning, Pennsylvania*

- **MR. COFFEE FILTERS.** "Mr. Coffee Filters are great to use as stabilizers under fabric when sewing on a machine."

  —DEBBIE M., *Winter Springs, Florida*

Hand Cleaner

Keep hands clean while working on craft projects with...

- **HUGGIES BABY WIPES.** "Keep a box of Huggies Baby Wipes close at hand when working on needle craft for periodically washing your hands. The wipes will keep oils off the fabric with a lot fewer trips to the sink to wash with soap and water."

  —KATHLEEN M., *Spring Valley, California*

Needles

Make needles glide through fabrics with...

- **BOUNCE.** "Run your sewing needle through a dryer sheet before you begin sewing and the needle will glide smoothly through your fabric."

  —BRENDA C., *Valparaiso, Indiana*

Quilting

Quilt with...

- **BOUNCE.** "Sew the right side of the fabric piece to a sheet of Bounce, leaving a place to turn the stitched piece. Turn the piece to the right side, and you have a pattern piece with raw edges already turned, ready to sew to your quilt block."

  —VICKY D., *Olalla, Washington*

Sewing Machines

Make tough materials glide through a sewing machine with...

- **VASELINE PETROLEUM JELLY** AND **REYNOLDS CUT-RITE WAX PAPER.** "When sewing material with sequins or anything that has been glued to the surface, the needle on the machine always sticks and the thread constantly breaks. But if you rub Vaseline on the presser foot every so often and place a sheet of wax paper under it, the fabric glides through."

  —CELINA J., *Harlem, Montana*

Sewing Patterns

Store sewing patterns with...

- **ZIPLOC STORAGE BAGS.** "Keep sewing patterns in Ziploc Storage Bags."

  —SHERRY U., *Glen Burnie, Maryland*

Wash It

22

Bacteria

Kill bacteria in the laundry with...

- **HEINZ WHITE VINEGAR.** "Add one-quarter cup of Heinz White Vinegar to your laundry (especially cloth diapers) during the rinse cycle to kill bacteria, eliminating the need for harsh chemicals."

    —SUSAN L., *Lowell, Massachusetts*

Bleach

Whiten clothes with...

- **HYDROGEN PEROXIDE.** "Add one cup of hydrogen peroxide to a load of whites and wash as normal."

    —MURRAY W., *Honolulu, Hawaii*

Bloodstains

Clean bloodstains from clothes with...

- **HEINZ VINEGAR.** "Did you know that Heinz Vinegar takes out bloodstains? Saturate the stain with vinegar, wait five minutes, then blot with a clean cloth."

    —MARY O., *Ellsworth, Maine*

- **HYDROGEN PEROXIDE.** "Pour peroxide directly on the stain and let it foam before washing. The peroxide breaks down the protein in the blood and then releases the stain."

    —AMY B., *Hannibal, Missouri*

- **IVORY SOAP.** "First rinse the garment with cold water, rub a bar of Ivory Soap over the area, let sit for a couple of minutes, then rub the area again. Repeat if necessary."

    —DEBRA C., *Torrance, California*

- **WINDEX.** "Windex removes blood almost immediately from most fabrics. Spray the garment, rinse, then spray again if necessary."

  —CATHERINE B., *Athens, Georgia*

Campfire Soot

Clean campfire soot from a windbreaker with...

- **MURPHY'S OIL SOAP.** "I have used Murphy's Oil Soap to remove soot from a campfire off my windbreaker with excellent results."

  —KATHERINE R., *Atkinson, Nebraska*

Colors

Prevent colors from bleeding with...

- **HEINZ WHITE VINEGAR.** "If you put one cup of vinegar in a sink of cool water, add colored clothing, and let sit for one hour, the colors won't bleed in the washing machine."

  —JANET G., *South Whitley, Indiana*

- **MORTON SALT.** "Add one-quarter cup salt to a load of colored clothes to prevent the colors from bleeding onto each other."

  —JUDITH A., *Salem, West Virginia*

Crayon

Remove crayon from clothes with...

- **DAWN.** "If you ever run a child's garment with a crayon in the pocket through the dryer, remove the affected clothing from the dryer, treat the stains with Dawn, then re-wash in hot water using Dawn as the detergent. Use less because it foams more, and run through the final rinse twice. Poof! The crayon is gone."

  —DEBBIE R., *Philadelphia, Pennsylvania*

Curtains

Prevent nylon curtains from clinging with...

- **BOUNCE.** "Rub your iron over a sheet of Bounce Fabric Softener when ironing nylon curtains to prevent them from clinging to themselves over the edge of the board."

  —NANCY S., *Grand Rapids, Michigan*

Stiffen and whiten curtains with...

■ **EPSOM SALT.** "When washing white curtains, add one cup Epsom Salt to the final rinse water. It will make the curtains a little stiffer and a lot whiter."

—MARY K., *Scranton, Pennsylvania*

Deodorant Stains

Clean deodorant stains from clothes with...

■ **HUGGIES BABY WIPES.** "I learned from a television show about how models prepare to do a runway show that models use Huggies Baby Wipes to clean deodorant stains from clothes."

—KELLI K., *Atlanta, Georgia*

Deodorize

Wash musty smells from towels and clothes with...

■ **HEINZ WHITE VINEGAR.** "Use one cupful of Heinz White Vinegar in your wash cycle to deodorize clothes."

—JANA C., *Crawfordsville, Indiana*

Detergent

Wash clothes with...

■ **JOHNSON'S BABY SHAMPOO.** "I wash my clothes with Johnson's Baby Shampoo. They get just as clean as if I had used Tide or Cheer, plus they smell great. Try one capful per load of clothes. It works great."

—GINA N. , *Carrollton, Texas*

Dirt Stains

Remove stains from white clothing with...

■ **SPIC AND SPAN.** "Spic and Span takes heavy soil or dirt out of clothes."

—AIMEE L., *Boise, Idaho*

Down Jackets

Fluff a down jacket with...

■ **WILSON TENNIS BALLS.** "Put a couple of tennis balls in your dryer to fluff the feathers in down-filled coats and jackets while drying."
—SHIRLEY C., *Southfield, Michigan*

Dry Cleaning

Pre-treat stains with...

■ **HELLMANN'S** OR **BEST REAL MAYONNAISE.** "Mayonnaise is great to pre-treat stains on clothes made of dry-clean-only fabrics."
—ALISON T., *Findlay, Ohio*

Excess Soap

Remove excess soap from clothes in the washing machine with...

■ **HEINZ WHITE VINEGAR.** "Add one cup Heinz White Vinegar to the rinse cycle to remove excess soap from the wash load. Great for towels and washcloths."
—P. J. S., *Fairbanks, Alaska*

Food Stains

Clean food stains from clothes with...

■ **HUGGIES BABY WIPES.** "Use Huggies Baby Wipes to clean a spill from clothes to prevent stains. I've used Baby Wipes to wipe up tomato sauce and chocolate stains, and when it dries, you can't tell there was ever a spill."
—SHELLY M., *Oceanside, New York*

■ **PINE-SOL.** "Pine-Sol works great on getting food stains out of clothes."
—MELODY F., *Kansas City, Kansas*

■ **SOFT SCRUB.** "Wet the garment, add Soft Scrub cleanser, and let sit until the stain is gone."
—RENEE C., *Manchester, New Hampshire*

- **WINDEX.** "I spilled marinara sauce on my favorite pair of tan pants. Windex took it right out. You just need to apply it immediately after you make the mess. I love Windex. I carry a bottle in my car for those kinds of emergencies."

  —LILA W., *San Diego, California*

Clean grape juice stains from clothing with...

- **RESOLVE CARPET CLEANER.** "I work in a day-care center, and grape juice gets spilled on clothes frequently. We use Resolve Carpet Cleaner and it works great."

  —REBECCA R., *Knoxville, Tennessee*

Formaldehyde

Neutralize formaldehyde when washing clothes with...

- **CARNATION NONFAT DRY MILK.** "Here's a helpful hint for people with sensitive skin: Adding one-quarter cup Carnation NonFat Dry Milk to your rinse water when washing clothes neutralizes the formaldehyde released each time a garment is laundered."

  —MARGE F., *Santa Barbara, California*

Grass Stains

Remove grass stains from clothes with...

- **DOMINO SUGAR.** "Make a paste of Domino Sugar and water, cover the grass stain with the mixture, let sit for one hour, then wash clean."

  —BRANDON N., *Peace River, Alberta*

- **KARO CORN SYRUP.** "Rub Karo Corn Syrup onto a grass stain and wash as normal. Grass stains will disappear completely."

  —JODI T., *Thunder Bay, Ontario*

- **MURPHY'S OIL SOAP.** "Rub Murphy's Oil Soap into grass stains on clothes, then wash the garment in your regular wash load."

  —CAROL C., *Danville, Virginia*

Grease and Oil Stains

Pre-treat grease and oil stains on clothes with...

- **ARM & HAMMER BAKING SODA.** "Sprinkle the grease stain with Arm & Hammer Baking Soda, and scrub gently with a wet scrub brush. The baking soda lifts the grease."
  —PAM B., *Lake Geneva, Wisconsin*

- **COCA-COLA.** "Pour a can of Coca-Cola into a regular-size load of laundry to help get grease out of work clothes, like blue jeans."
  —BRIAN K., *Coldwater, Michigan*

- **COMET.** "Wet the spot, sprinkle on Comet, and use a toothbrush lightly to form paste. Let set overnight, then rinse out with warm water.
  —KATE C., *Shavertown, Pennsylvania*

- **CRISCO ALL-VEGETABLE SHORTENING AND DAWN.** "First rub Crisco into the grease spot, then add Dawn dishwashing liquid. Rub the spot well before tossing the garment into the washer with your regular detergent."
  —JUDIE B., *Napa, California*

- **EASY-OFF OVEN CLEANER.** "I've used Easy-Off Oven Cleaner as a laundry treatment. It seems to remove any type of grease or oil stain from clothing. Just spray, wait a few seconds, and throw into the washing machine. Works great."
  —LINDA R., *Grangeville, Idaho*

- **FORMULA 409.** "Formula 409 is great in the laundry room. I use it to pre-treat my clothes. It's a great stain remover."
  —JANET S., *Shelbyville, Indiana*

- **GUNK BRAKE CLEANER.** "Use Gunk Brake Cleaner to remove grease from clothing. Spray the stain, then launder the garment as usual. It works great. I used it to get automotive grease off a tuxedo shirt."
  —DAVE W., *Albany, New York*

- **HEINZ VINEGAR.** "Someone in my house left ChapStick in the pocket of their jeans, and when it went through the wash, I ended up with wax and oil stains over everything. I rewashed with a cup of vinegar and detergent, and it all came out."
  —DANIELLE K., *Boxborough, Massachusetts*

■ **JOHNSON'S BABY POWDER.** "Before putting the garment in the regular wash, rub Johnson's Baby Powder into the stain, and launder in cold water. Baby powder absorbs the grease and oil, and the spot washes out along with the powder."

—LAUREN S., *Raleigh, North Carolina*

■ **LESTOIL.** "Rub Lestoil into spots that have been in clothing for awhile and launder as usual. It works better than most stain removers."

—DIANA H., *Eastlake, Ohio*

■ **PINE-SOL.** "Pine-Sol takes most grease stains out of clothes."

—AIMEE L., *Boise, Idaho*

■ **RUG DOCTOR.** "Put Rug Doctor carpet cleaner on laundry stains and let soak, then launder in the regular load."

—SUSAN M., *Edson, Alberta*

Gum

Clean chewing gum from clothes with...

■ **CUTEX NAIL POLISH REMOVER.** "Cutex Nail Polish Remover easily removes gum from clothes without leaving a stain or mark."

—LINDA D., *Consecon, Ontario*

Ink Stains

Remove ink from fabrics and other materials with...

■ **ALBERTO VO5 HAIR SPRAY.** "The acetone in Alberto VO5 Hair Spray removes indelible marker and ballpoint pen marks from clothing, leather, plastics, and metals."

—LADONNA B., *Harrison, Ohio*

■ **HUGGIES BABY WIPES.** "Baby Wipes remove most inks (not indelible) from fabric. I discovered this when my little girl wrote all over the cushion in our rocking chair when she was about eighteen months old."

—QUINN H., *Liberty Hill, Texas*

■ **PURELL.** "Saturate the ink stain with Purell and blot with a paper towel. Repeat. The stain will fade more each time until it disappears. Safe for dry-clean-only fabrics."

—PATTY K., *Houston, Texas*

■ **SOFT SCRUB.** "Stubborn ink stains come out of clothes by simply putting a dab of Soft Scrub cleanser on the spot for a few minutes and then laundering as usual."

—DEBBIE S., *Ft. Walton Beach, Florida*

Irons

Clean a steam iron with...

■ **COLGATE TOOTHPASTE.** "Squeeze toothpaste on a dry, soft cloth and scrub off the gunky build-up on the bottom of your steam iron (when the iron is cool). Then wipe clean with a damp cloth."

—LISA B., *Arlington, Texas*

Linen Tablecloths

Clean stains from a linen tablecloth with...

■ **CASCADE.** "Pour liquid Cascade dishwasher soap over the stains on a linen tablecloth, launder as usual, and the stain will come out."

—CINDY C., *Walton, New York*

Lint

Prevent lint from clinging to clothes with...

■ **HEINZ VINEGAR.** "Add one cup Heinz Vinegar to each wash load in lieu of fabric softener. Vinegar also removes the soap from the clothes, which helps people who have allergic reactions to detergent."

—DAVID H., *Oklahoma City, Oklahoma*

Capture lint from a washing machine drain with...

■ **L'EGGS SHEER ENERGY PANTY HOSE.** "Cut off the foot of an old pair of L'eggs Panty Hose and attach it to the end of the washer hose to catch all the lint as it comes out, preventing the drain and pipes from clogging." —DONNA C., *Dearborn Heights, Michigan*

Remove lint from clothes with...

■ **SCOTCH CLEAR PACKAGING TAPE.** "Use a long piece of packaging tape, wrapped sticky-side out around your hand, to remove lint from a garment." —GOLDA G., *Lakewood, New Jersey*

Lipstick

Remove lipstick from clothes with...

■ **ALBERTO VO5 HAIR SPRAY.** "Spray Alberto VO5 Hair Spray on the lipstick stain, let sit overnight, and then wash in regular cycle of the washing machine." —JANECA K., *Aurora, Colorado*

■ **COLGATE TOOTHPASTE.** "A dab of Colgate Toothpaste, rubbed into the stain, takes out lipstick stains from clothes." —CELESTA H., *Lubbock, Texas*

Makeup

Clean makeup from clothes with...

■ **HUGGIES BABY WIPES.** "My favorite use for baby wipes is to get makeup out of clothes. They work amazingly well without damaging the clothes." —KIM B., *Sherman Oaks, California*

Mold and Mildew

Clean mold and mildew from clothes with...

■ **COCA-COLA.** "Emptying a can of Coca-Cola into a washing machine filled with moldy clothes and soaking for thirty minutes in a regular cycle with detergent will remove the mildew from the fabric." —GENIA B., *Roland, Oklahoma*

Paint

Clean acrylic paint from clothing with...

■ **SMIRNOFF VODKA.** "Soak the stained area with Smirnoff Vodka for a few minutes, then blot with a dry cloth."

—JULIE F., *Hollister, Missouri*

Perspiration

Deodorize smelly clothes with...

■ **HEINZ WHITE VINEGAR.** "Remove perspiration smells from laundry by adding one cup of Heinz White Vinegar to your wash while the machine is filling. If the perspiration smells really strong, let the laundry soak for an hour before starting the rinse cycle."

—VERONICA O., *Del Rio, Texas*

Sheets and Pillow Cases

Freshen bed linens with...

■ **BOUNCE.** "After putting clean pillow cases on pillows, place a sheet of Bounce inside each side. It makes the pillow smell so good you'll just want to lie on it all day. I am going to go lie on my pillow now."

—SUSAN Y., *Carlsbad, California*

■ **FEBREZE.** "Before ironing pillow cases for guest beds, I spray the pillow case with Febreze. The result? Crisp, fresh-smelling linen that any guest would love to lay their head on."

—JUDIE S., *St. Joseph, Missouri*

Smoke

Deodorize cigarette smoke from clothing with...

■ **SMIRNOFF VODKA.** "This trick is commonly used in the theater, where costume rental companies frequently charge extra to clean rental costumes if they smell of cigarette smoke upon their return. Mix one part Smirnoff Vodka to three parts water in a trigger spray bottle, spray the clothing, and let dry. Spraying smoke-infused costumes with vodka neutralizes the smell."

—MICHAEL M., *Atlanta, Georgia*

Spray Starch

Starch clothes when ironing with...

■ **DOWNY.** "Instead of using spray starch when ironing, mix one tablespoon Downy and two cups of water in a spray bottle and spray clothes to get soft and fresh results."

—RUTH L., *Salinas, Puerto Rico*

Make a permanent crease in slacks with...

■ **HEINZ WHITE VINEGAR.** "In sewing class, I learned to use a spray bottle filled with Heinz White Vinegar to make permanent creases in slacks. Simply spray the slacks, fold where you'd like the crease to be, and iron."

—FRANCES M., *Whittier, California*

Stains

Clean stains with...

■ **CASCADE.** "I use Cascade dishwasher detergent to soak out *any* stain from my clothes. Mix one-half cup of Cascade in a sink of very hot water, making sure it is completely dissolved before adding laundry. Soak overnight to remove ink, blood, grease, grass, and mildew."

—DARLENE L., *Rockport, Texas*

■ **DAWN.** "Dawn dishwashing liquid gets stains out of clothes— even whites. I have always used Dawn instead of buying expensive stain removers. No matter how bad the stain, squirt a dab of dish-washing liquid on it. Take an old toothbrush and scrub the Dawn into the stain. When you are sure that the stain is totally saturated with dishwashing liquid, throw the garment in the wash with the rest of your clothes. The Dawn will wash out the stain."

—KIMBERLY H., *Harrison, Arizona*

■ **MURPHY'S OIL SOAP.** "Murphy's Oil Soap, full strength in a spray bottle, is the best stain remover for clothes. Spray on the spot, let sit for a bit, and wash normally."

—VALERIE C., *Quispamsis, New Brunswick*

Suds

Eliminate excess suds with...

▪ **DOWNY.** "If you accidentally pour too much Tide in your washer, causing too many suds, pour in one capful of Downy. It will eliminate most of the suds."

—CAROLYN B., *McMinnville, Tennessee*

Sweaters

Launder sweaters with...

▪ **JOHNSON'S BABY SHAMPOO.** "I put baby shampoo in the water when I launder my sweaters. My sweaters come out feeling soft and smelling clean."

—BEVERLEY S., *Lac du Bonnet, Manitoba*

Urine

Deodorize urine-stained sheets with...

▪ **HEINZ VINEGAR.** "Add a cup of Heinz Vinegar in the laundry water for bedding or clothing that's stained with urine. It takes out the urine smell."

—LISA D., *Hopkins, Michigan*

Whites

Whiten whites with...

▪ **CASCADE.** "Mix a quarter-cup Cascade in a bucket of water and soak yellowing white garments in the mixture to remove all the yellow, then launder as usual."

—SHARON R., *Valencia, Pennsylvania*

▪ **COFFEE-MATE.** "Use powdered coffee creamer to whiten your clothes (cotton shirts, underwear, socks) just by mixing it with hot water and letting the clothes soak in it."

—IRENE K., *Fidott, Illinois*

Wrinkles

Remove wrinkles from pants with...

■ **HEINZ WHITE VINEGAR.** "Fill a spray bottle with vinegar, spray pants, and hang to dry to remove any wrinkles."

—KELLIE W., *Lancaster, Kentucky*

Yellow Stains

Remove yellow stains from clothes with...

■ **BAR KEEPERS FRIEND.** "Have you tried Bar Keepers Friend for removing yellow dingy stains out of clothes? Soaking white clothes in Bar Keepers Friend overnight will bring them back to white again."

—LISA N., *Indianapolis, Indiana*

Wear It

23

Bellybutton

Hide a protruding bellybutton with a...

■ **BAND-AID BANDAGE.** "When you are pregnant and your belly button pops out, you can use a Band-Aid to keep it flat under your clothes."

—REBECCA S., *Wilmington, Delaware*

Bras

Prevent nipples from showing through clothing with...

■ **SCOTCH TAPE** OR **BAND-AID BANDAGES.** "If you don't want your nipples to show through a form-fitting shirt or dress, place a small strip of Scotch Tape or a Band-Aid over each nipple."

—TEANTAE T., *Columbia, Maryland*

Substitute for a braless bra with...

■ **SCOTCH PACKAGING TAPE.** "Instead of buying those expensive stick-on bras, use Scotch Packaging Tape. You get about seventy 'bras' per roll. It works really well."

—SARAH Y., *Carlsbad, California*

Control-Top Underwear

Make control-top underwear with...

■ **L'EGGS SHEER ENERGY PANTY HOSE.** "Cut the legs off a pair of ruined L'eggs Panty Hose and use as an inexpensive pair of control panel underwear."

—KRISTEN S., *Bay St. Louis, Mississippi*

Deodorize

Deodorize smelly shoes or sneakers with...

■ **BOUNCE.** "Place a sheet of Bounce inside shoes, let sit overnight, and by morning your shoes will smell fresh again."

—CHERYL K., *Huron, South Dakota*

■ **FEBREZE.** "Spray Febreze in stinky shoes and sneakers to get rid of the odor."

—WENDY I., *Honolulu, Hawaii*

■ **20 MULE TEAM BORAX.** "Consistently sprinkle 20 Mule Team Borax into shoes or sneakers and the smell will vanish. My husband and his family have used this tip for years. Using 20 Mule Team Borax in your shoes also helps clear up athlete's foot."

—MICHELLE F., *Middletown, Ohio*

Hats

Prevent perspiration stains on the inside of a hat headband with...

■ **STAYFREE MAXI PADS.** "Since Stayfree Maxi Pads are self adhesive and disposable, simply stick one inside your hat along the headband where your forehead rests. When the maxi pad gets sticky and gummy from sweat, replace it with a fresh one."

—LAURA P., *Vancouver, British Columbia*

Panty Hose

Prevent runs in panty hose with...

■ **ALBERTO VO5 HAIR SPRAY.** "Use hair spray on your nylons so you get fewer runs."

—LISA W., *Biloxi, Mississippi*

Stop a run in panty hose with...

■ **LIQUID PAPER.** "Coat the end of the run or edges of the hole liberally with Liquid Paper and let dry."

—CAROLEE M., *DeMotte, Indiana*

Patent Leather

Revive patent leather shoes with...

- **VASELINE PETROLEUM JELLY.** "Coat with Vaseline and buff. They'll shine like new."
  —Rebecca G., *Springfield, Indiana*

Scuff Marks

Clean scuff marks from shoes with...

- **ALBERTO VO5 HAIR SPRAY.** "Just spray a little Alberto VO5 Hair Spray on the scuff mark and rub with a towel or wash rag. It takes a little elbow grease, but it works. The scuff mark will disappear."
  —Tricia H., *Sweetwater, Texas*

- **COLGATE TOOTHPASTE.** "Just take a pea-sized drop of Colgate Toothpaste, rub it over the scuff marks with a bristle brush, and— *voila!*—the marks are gone."
  —Jennifer V., *Houston, Pennsylvania*

- **CUTEX NAIL POLISH REMOVER.** "A drop of nail polish remover on a cotton ball gets scuff marks off white shoes."
  —Melanie R., *Butler, Ohio*

- **FANTASTIK.** "Spray the area with Fantastik and wipe clean with a cloth."
  —Mary P., *Dunwoody, Georgia*

Real-Life Story

DON'T ASK, DON'T TELL

"During eight years in the United States Air Force and two in the U.S. Reserves, we used panty hose for a fast touch-up shine or to increase the shine on a freshly polished boot, shoe, or holster. We also used to wear panty hose under a uniform during exercises in a tick and/or leech infested area to prevent becoming their host."
—Lance R., *Chicago, Illinois*

Shoelaces

Repair frayed shoelaces with...

■ **MAYBELLINE CRYSTAL CLEAR NAIL POLISH.** "Dip the ends of frayed shoelaces in Maybelline Crystal Clear Nail Polish and let dry so the ends hold together and fit through the holes."
—VIRGINIA T., *Wilkes-Barre, Pennsylvania*

Shoes

Polish shoes with...

■ **LUBRIDERM.** "When traveling, if my shoes need to be shined, I use Lubriderm. It's clear, it's harmless, and it works."
—CHUCK K., *Hanover, Massachusetts*

■ **PLEDGE.** "To make your shine last longer and glimmer better on your shoes, spray with Pledge and buff dry. The Pledge also helps shoes repel water stains in winter."
—ROBERT J., *Grand Haven, Michigan*

■ **STAR OLIVE OIL.** "Polishing your shoes with Star Olive Oil rejuvenates leather shoes."
—JUDITH W., *New York, New York*

■ **VASELINE PETROLEUM JELLY.** "Applying Vaseline on your shoes, boots, or purse makes them shine while waterproofing them at the same time. Just apply a generous amount and rub in with a cloth."
—SUSAN Z., *Muskego, Wisconsin*

Shine shoes with...

■ **L'EGGS SHEER ENERGY PANTY HOSE.** "L'eggs Panty Hose are great for putting a shine on shoes."
—MARGO J., *Honolulu, Hawaii*

■ **O.B. TAMPONS.** "When I was in the Navy, we used tampons to polish our boots. They held up quite nicely and the o.b. brand was a popular favorite with no applicator to bother with."
—TAMARA B., *Akron, Ohio*

■ **STAYFREE MAXI PADS.** "When I was in boot camp in the Navy, we had to have spit-and-polish shoes. We would apply black shoe polish paste, then wipe the shoes with deodorant maxi pads. The liquid would melt the polish and let it dry to a shiny glaze. Passed inspection every time."

—RICH S., *Lancaster, Pennsylvania*

Shine suede shoes with...

■ **MAXWELL HOUSE COFFEE.** "Make a cup of Maxwell House Coffee and brush the black coffee onto black suede shoes to eliminate the worn grayish look and revive the black appearance like new."

—TRIXIE B., *Worcester, Massachusetts*

Clean rock salt from leather shoes with...

■ **HEINZ VINEGAR.** "Rock salt used for melting ice in winter gets on leather shoes and leaves white stains. To remove them, rub Heinz White Vinegar on the stain and wipe with a clean, wet cloth."

—GREG P., *Plymouth, Michigan*

Prevent shoes from squeaking with...

■ **WD-40.** "Spray WD-40 on a squeaky shoe at the spot where the sole and heel join. It stops the squeak."

—JEAN R., *Millsboro, Delaware*

Sneakers

Clean sneakers with...

■ **COLGATE TOOTHPASTE.** "I've used Colgate Toothpaste to clean the rubber part of my Converse All-Star sneakers. Just use toothpaste, water, and an old toothbrush, and they're back to being white."

—TOM S., *Poplar Bluff, Missouri*

■ **DOW BATHROOM CLEANER.** "Dow Bathroom Cleaner works well as sneaker cleaner. Just spray on, let sit two minutes, then rinse clean."

—JIM L., *Maplewood, Missouri*

Static Cling

Eliminate static electricity in socks, panty hose, and under-garments with...

- **BOUNCE.** "Rub a Bounce sheet on socks or petticoats (while being worn) to stop static problems."

—LISA P., *Sweetwater, Texas*

**For more offbeat uses for
brand-name products,
visit Joey Green
on the Internet at:
www.wackyuses.com**

Acknowledgments

My heartfelt thanks go out to the thousands of people who have visited my website and taken the time to send me an e-mail sharing their ingenious tips for the brand-name products we all know and love.

I am grateful to my editor, Ed Claflin, for championing my cause and making this book a labor of love; associate editor Barry Richardson for his editorial savvy; production manager Jackie Boggi-Roulette for her expertise and efficiency; and copyeditor Kay Harrison for her stunning endurance.

I am also deeply indebted to my agent, Jeremy Solomon, for making this my twentieth published book.

Above all, all my love to Debbie, Ashley, and Julia.

Trademark Information

"Absorbine Jr." is a registered trademark of W.F. Young, Inc.

"Accent Flavor Enhancer" is a registered trademark of the B&G Food Company.

"Adolph's" is a registered trademark of Lipton, Inc.

"Afrin" is a registered trademark of Schering-Plough HealthCare Products, Inc.

"Ajax" is a registered trademark of Colgate-Palmolive.

"Albers" is a registered trademark of Nestlé.

"Alberto VO5" is a registered trademark of Alberto-Culver USA, Inc.

"Alka-Seltzer" is a registered trademark of Miles, Inc.

"Aloe Vera" is a registered trademark of St. Ives Laboratories, Inc.

"Altoids" is a registered trademark of Callard & Borser-Suchard, Inc.

"Arm & Hammer" is a registered trademark of Church & Dwight Co, Inc.

"Armor All" is a registered trademark of the Armor All Products Corp.

"Aunt Jemima" is a registered trademark of the Quaker Oats Company.

"Bag Balm" is a registered trademark of Dairy Association Co, Inc.

"Ban" is a registered trademark of the Kao Corporation.

"Band-Aid" is a registered trademark of Johnson & Johnson.

"Bar Keepers Friend" is a registered trademark of SerVaas Laboratories.

"Barbasol" and "Beard Buster" are registered trademarks of Pfizer Inc.

"Bayer" is a registered trademark of Bayer Corporation.

"Birds Eye" is a registered trademark of Dean Foods Vegetable Company.

"Biz" is a registered trademark of Procter & Gamble.

"Blistex" is a registered trademark of Blistex, Inc.

"Blue Bonnet" is a registered trademark of ConAgra Brands, Inc.

"Bon Ami" is a registered trademark of Faultless Starch/Bon Ami Company.

"Bounce" is a registered trademark of Procter & Gamble.

"Bounty" is a registered trademark of Procter & Gamble.

"Budweiser" is a registered trademark of Anheuser-Busch, Inc.

"Canada Dry" is a registered trademark of Cadbury Beverages Inc.

"Car-Freshener" is a registered trademark of Car-Freshener and Julius Sämaay Ltd.

"Carnation" is a registered trademark of Nestlé.

"Cascade" is a registered trademark of Procter & Gamble.

"ChapStick" is a registered trademark of A. H. Robbins Company.

"Cheerios" is a registered trademark of General Mills, Inc.

"Chloraseptic" is a registered trademark of Procter & Gamble.

"Chore Boy" is a registered trademark of Reckitt & Colman Inc.

"Cinch" is a registered trademark of Procter & Gamble.

"Clairol" and "Herbal Essences" are registered trademarks of Clairol.

"Cling Free" is a registered trademark of Benckiser Consumer Products, Inc.

"Clorox" is a registered trademark of the Clorox Company.

"Close-Up" is a registered trademark of Chesebrough-Ponds USA, Co.

"Coca-Cola" and "Coke" are registered trademarks of the Coca-Cola Company.

"Coffee-Mate" is a registered trademark of Nestlé.

"Colgate" is a registered trademark of Colgate-Palmolive.

"Comet" is a registered trademark of Procter & Gamble.

"Conair" and "Pro Style" are registered trademarks of Conair Corporation.

"Coppertone" is a registered trademark of Schering-Plough HealthCare Products, Inc.

"Cortaid" is a registered trademark of the Upjohn Company.

"Cover Girl" and "NailSlicks" are registered trademarks of Noxell, Inc.

"Crayola" is a registered trademark of Binney & Smith Inc.

"Cream of Wheat" is a registered trademark of Nabisco.

"Creamette" is a registered trademark of Creamette Borden, Inc.

"Crest" is a registered trademark of Procter & Gamble.

"Crisco" is a registered trademark of Procter & Gamble.

"Cutex" is a registered trademark of MedTech.

"Cutty Sark" is a registered trademark of Berry Bros. & Rudd.

"Dannon" is a registered trademark of the Dannon Company.

"Dawn" is a registered trademark of Procter & Gamble.

"Desitin" is a registered trademark of Pfizer.

"Dickinson's" is a registered trademark of Dickinson Brands Inc.

"Dixie" is a registered trademark of James River Corporation.

"Domino" is a registered trademark of Domino Sugar Corporation.

"Doritos" is a registered trademark of Frito-Lay, Inc.

"Dow" is a registered trademark of The Dow Chemical Company.

"Downy" is a registered trademark of Procter & Gamble.

"Dr. Scholl's" is a registered trademark of Schering-Plough HealthCare Products, Inc.

"Easy Cheese" is a registered trademark of Nabisco.

"Easy-Off" is a registered trademark of Reckitt & Colman Inc.

"Efferdent" is a registered trademark of Warner-Lambert.

"Eggo" is a registered trademark of the Kellogg Company.

"Elmer's Glue-All" and Elmer the Bull are registered trademarks of Borden.

"Endust" is a registered trademark of Sara Lee Corporation.

"Era" is a registered trademark of Procter & Gamble.

"Ex-Lax" is a registered trademark of Novartis Consumer Health, Inc.

"Fantastik" is a registered trademark of S.C. Johnson & Son, Inc.

"Febreze" is a registered trademark of Procter & Gamble.

"Folger's" is a registered trademark of Procter & Gamble.

"Formula 409" is a registered trademark of the Clorox Company.

"Forster" is a registered trademark of Diamond Brands, Inc.

"French's" is a registered trademark of Reckitt & Colman Inc.

"Fritos" is a registered trademark of Frito-Lay, Inc.

"Gain" is a registered trademark of Procter & Gamble.

"Glad" is a registered trademark of First Brands Corporation.

"Glade" is a registered trademark of S.C. Johnson & Son, Inc.

"Gojo" is a registered trademark of Gojo Industries, Inc.

"Gold Medal" is a registered trademark of General Mills, Inc.

"Grandma's Molasses" is a registered trademark of Mott's USA.

"Gunk" is a registered trademark of Radiator Specialty Company.

"Hartz" and "2 in 1" are registered trademarks of Hartz Mountain Company.

"Heinz" is a registered trademark of H.J. Heinz Company.

"Hellmann's" and "Best" are registered trademarks of Bestfoods.

"Hershey's" is a registered trademark of Hershey Foods Corporation.

"Huggies" is a registered trademark of Kimberly-Clark Corporation.

"Irish Spring" is a registered trademark of Colgate-Palmolive.

"Ivory" is a registered trademark of Procter & Gamble.

"Jell-O" is a registered trademark of Kraft Foods.

"Jet-Dry" is a registered trademark of Benckiser Consumer Products, Inc.

"Jet-Puffed" is a registered trademark of First Brands International.

"Jif" is a registered trademark of Procter & Gamble.

"Johnson & Johnson" is a registered trademark of Johnson & Johnson.

"Joy" is a registered trademark of Procter & Gamble.

"Karo" is a registered trademark of CPC International Inc.

"Kikkoman" is a registered trademark of Kikkoman Foods, Inc.

"Kellogg's" and "Mini-Wheats" are registered trademarks of the Kellogg Company.

"Kingsford's" and the Kingsford logo are registered trademarks of CPC International Inc.

"Kiwi" is a registered trademark of Sara Lee Corporation.

"Kleenex" is a registered trademark of Kimberly-Clark Corporation.

"Knox" is a registered trademark of Nabisco.

"Kodak" is a registered trademark of Eastman Kodak Company.

"Kool-Aid" is a registered trademark of Kraft Foods.

"Krazy" is a registered trademark of Borden, Inc.

"Lady Speed Stick" is a registered trademark of the Mennen Co.

"Land O' Lakes" is a registered trademark of Land O Lakes, Inc.

"L'eggs" and "Sheer Energy" are registered trademarks of Sara Lee Corporation.

"Lestoil" is a registered trademark of the Clorox Company.

"Lifesavers" is a trademark of the Lifesavers Company.

"Lipton," "The 'Brisk' Tea," and "Flo-Thru" are registered trademarks of the Thomas J. Lipton Company.

"Liquid Paper" is a registered trademark of Liquid Paper Corporation.

"Listerine" is a registered trademark of Warner-Lambert.

"Lubriderm" is a registered trademark of Warner-Lambert.

"Lysol" is a registered trademark of Reckitt & Colman Inc.

"Maalox" is a registered trademark of Novartis Consumer Health, Inc.

"Marshmallow Fluff" is a registered trademark of Durkee Mower Inc.

"Massengill" is a registered trademark of SmithKlein Beecham.

"MasterCard" is a registered trademark of MasterCard International Incorporated.

"Maxwell House" and "Good to the Last Drop" are registered trademarks of Maxwell House Coffee Company.

"Maybelline" is a registered trademark of Maybelline.

"McCormick" and "Schilling" are registered trademarks of McCormick & Company, Incorporated.

"Mennen" and "Afta" are registered trademarks of the Mennen Co.

"Mentadent" is a registered trademark of Chesebrough-Pond's USA Co.

"Miller Lite" is a registered trademark of the Miller Brewing Company.

"Minute Rice" is a registered trademark of Kraft Foods.

"Miracle Whip" is a registered trademark of Kraft Foods.

"Morton" and the Morton Umbrella Girl are registered trademarks of Morton International, Inc.

"Mott's" is a registered trademark of Mott's USA.

"Mountain Dew" is a registered trademark of PepsiCo, Inc.

"Mr. Coffee" is a registered trademark of Mr. Coffee, Inc.

"Mr. Muscle" is a registered trademark of S.C. Johnson & Sons, Inc.

"Murine Tears" is a registered trademark of Ross Products Division.

"Murphy" is a registered trademark of Colgate-Palmolive Company.

"Mylanta" is a registered trademark of Johnson & Johnson Merck Consumer Pharmaceuticals Co.

"Nair" is a registered trademark of Carter-Wallace, Inc.

"Neosporin" is a registered trademark of Warner-Lambert.

"Nestea" and "Nestlé" are registered trademarks of Nestlé.

"Neutrogena" is a registered trademark of Neutrogena Corp.

"Niagara" is a registered trademark of CPC International, Inc.

"NoSalt" is a registered trademark of RCN Products, Inc.

"Noxzema" is a registered trademark of Procter & Gamble.

"o.b." is a registered trademark of McNeil-PPC, Inc.

"Ocean Spray" is a registered trademark of Ocean Spray Cranberries, Inc.

"Old English" is a registered trademark of Reckitt & Colman, Inc.

"Orajel" is a registered trademark of Del Laboratories, Inc.

"Oral-B" is a registered trademark of Oral-B Laboratories.

"Orville Redenbacher's Gourmet" and "Popping Corn" are registered trademarks of Hunt-Wesson, Inc.

"Oxo" is a registered trademark of the Thomas J. Lipton Company.

"Palmolive" is a registered trademark of Colgate-Palmolive Company.

"Pam" is a registered trademark of American Home Foods.

"Pampers" is a registered trademark of Procter & Gamble.

"Parsons'" is a registered trademark of Church & Dwight Co., Inc.

"Paul Mitchell" is a registered trademark of John Paul Mitchell Systems.

"Pepto-Bismol" is a registered trademark of Procter & Gamble.

"Phillip's" is a registered trademark of Bayer Corporation.

"Pine-Sol" is a registered trademark of the Clorox Company.

"Play-Doh" is a registered trademark of Hasbro, Inc.

"Playtex," "Living," and "Made Strong to Last Long" are registered trademarks of Playtex Products, Inc.

"Pledge" is a registered trademark of S.C. Johnson & Sons, Inc.

"Pond's" is a registered trademark of Chesebrough-Pond's USA, Co.

"Preparation H" is a registered trademark of Whitehall-Robbins.

"Prestone" is a registered trademark of Prestone Products Corp.

"Procter-Silex" and "Ulta-Ease" are registered trademarks of Procter-Silex.

"Purell" is a registered trademark of Gojo Industries, Inc.

"Q-Tips" is a registered trademark of Chesebrough-Pond's USA Co.

"Quaker Oats" is a registered trademark of the Quaker Oats Company.

"Rain-X" is a registered trademark of Unelko Corporation.

"ReaLemon" is a registered trademark of Borden.

"Red Devil" is a registered trademark of Reckitt & Colman Inc.

"Reddi-wip" is a registered trademark of Beatrice Cheese, Inc.

"Resolve" is a registered trademark of Reckitt & Colman Inc.

"Reynolds Wrap" is a registered trademark of Reynolds Metals.

"Rit" is a registered trademark of BestFoods.

"Rolaids" is a registered trademark of Warner-Lambert.

"Ronsonol" is a registered trademark of the Ronson Consumer Products Corp.

"Rug Doctor" is a registered trademark of Rug Doctor.

"Saran Wrap" is a registered trademark of DowBrands, Inc.

"Scope" is a registered trademark of Procter & Gamble.

"Scotch" and "3M" are registered trademarks of 3M.

"Scott's" and "Liquid Gold" are registered trademarks of Scott's Liquid Gold-Inc.

"Scrubbing Bubbles" is a registered trademark of S.C. Johnson & Sons, Inc.

"Secret" is a registered trademark of Procter & Gamble.

"Selsun Blue" is a registered trademark of Ross Products Division.

"7-Up" is a registered trademark of Dr Pepper/Seven-Up, Inc.

"Shout" is a registered trademark of S.C. Johnson & Sons, Inc.

"Silly Putty" is a registered trademark of Binney & Smith Inc.

"Simple Green" is a registered trademark of Sunshine Makers, Inc.

"Skin-So-Soft" is a registered trademark of Avon Products.

"Slinky" is a registered trademark of James Industries.

"Smirnoff" is a registered trademark of United Vintners & Distributors.

"Smucker's" is a registered trademark of the J.M. Smucker Co.

"Sno Bol" is a registered trademark of Church & Dwight, Co. Inc.

"Soft Scrub" is a registered trademark of the Clorox Company.

"Softsoap" is a registered trademark of Colgate-Palmolive.

"S.O.S" is a registered trademark of the Clorox Company.

"Spam" is a registered trademark of Hormel Foods Corporation.

"Spic and Span" is a registered trademark of Procter & Gamble.

"Spray 'n Wash" is a registered trademark of DowBrands L.P.

"Sprite" is a registered trademark of the Coca-Cola Company.

"Stanley" is a registered trademark of the Stanley Works.

"Star" is a registered trademark of Star Fine Foods.

"Static Guard" is a registered trademark of Alberto-Culver USA, Inc.

"Stayfree" is a registered trademark of McNeil-PPC, Inc.

"STP" is a registered trademark of First Brands Corporation.

"Stridex" is a registered trademark of Blistex, Inc.

"SueBee" is a registered trademark of Sioux Honey Association.

"Sunlight" is a registered trademark of Lever Brothers Co.

"Super-Soaker 2000" is a registered trademark of Larami Limited, a subsidiary of Hasbro, Inc.

"Sure Jell" is a registered trademark of Kraft Foods.

"Tabasco" is a registered trademark of McIlhenny Company.

"Tang" is a registered trademark of Kraft Foods.

"Thompson's" is a registered trademark of the Thompson's Company.

"Tide" is a registered trademark of Procter & Gamble.

"Tidy Cat" is a registered trademark of the Ralston Purina Company.

"Trojan" is a registered trademark of Carter-Wallace, Inc.

"Turtle Wax" is a registered trademark of Turtle Wax, Inc.

"20 Mule Team" and "Borax" are registered trademarks of United States Borax & Chemical Corporation.

"Uncle Ben's" and "Converted" are registered trademarks of Uncle Ben's, Inc.

"USA Today" is a registered trademark of Gannett News Service.

"Vaseline" is a registered trademark of the Chesebrough-Pond's USA.

"Vegemite" is a registered trademark of Kraft Foods, Inc.

"Velcro" is a registered trademark of Velcro Industries.

"Vicks" and "VapoRub" are registered trademarks of Procter & Gamble.

"Visine" is a registered trademark of Pfizer, Inc.

"Water Pik" is a registered trademark of Teledyne Water Pik, Inc.

"WD-40" is a registered trademark of the WD-40 Company.

"Wesson" is a registered trademark of Hunt-Wesson, Inc.

"Westley's" is a registered trademark of Blue-Coral Slick 50, Ltd.

"White Rain" is a registered trademark of White Rain Company.

"Wilson" is a registered trademark of Wilson Sporting Goods Co.

"Windex" is a registered trademark of S. C. Johnson & Sons, Inc.

"Wish-Bone" is a registered trademark of Lipton, Inc.

"Wonder" is a registered trademark of Interstate Brands Corporation.

"Woolite" is a registered trademark of Reckitt & Colman Inc.

"Wrigley's," "Juicy Fruit," and "Wrigley's Spearmint" are registered trademarks of Wm. Wrigley Jr. Company.

"Zest" is a registered trademark of Procter & Gamble.

"Ziploc" is a registered trademark of DowBrands.

Index

A

Absorbine Jr., 129
Accent Flavor Enhancer, 198
Adolph's Meat Tenderizer, 142, *159*
Afrin, 162-163
Ajax, 194
Albers Grits, 222
Alberto VO5 Conditioning
    Hairdressing, 210, 216,
Alberto VO5 Hair Spray, 29, 67,
    68,157, 160, 171, 200, 224,
    226, 229, 233, 250, 252, 258,
    259
Alka-Seltzer, 18, 91, 111, 157, 169,
    171, 236
Aloe Vera Gel, 125
Altoids, 189, 236
Arm & Hammer Baking Soda, 1, 4, 8,
    10, 19, 21, 30, 31, 33, 37-38,
    40, 43, 45, 55, 70, 72, 74, 91,
    94, 99, 114, 115, 120, 142,
    144, 145, 149, 157, 159, 199,
    200-201, 206, 223, 226, 249
Armor All, 42, 43, 84, 110, 212
Aunt Jemima Original Syrup, 119, 145

B

Bag Balm, 151
Ban Deodorant, 142, 157
Band-Aid Bandages, 79, 162, 178, 257
Bar Keepers Friend, 256
Barbasol Shaving Cream, 7, 13, 25,
    47, 85, 106-107, 125, 176,
    212, 223
Bayer Aspirin, 132

Best Real Mayonnaise, 5, 36, 82, 136,
    155, 161, 200, 213, 217, 218,
    247
Birds Eye Sweet Green Peas, 156
Biz, 38
Blistex, 169
Blue Bonnet margarine, 5
Bon Ami, 71, 111
Bounce, 10, 12, 17, 20, 21, 25, 26,
    27, 33-34, 39, 44, 66, 71,
    73-74, 80, 89, 97, 109, 110,
    126, 130, 154, 179, 182, 190,
    193, 198, 200, 202, 206, 209,
    211, 225, 227, 231, 242, 243,
    245, 253, 258, 262
Bounty Paper towels, 52, 59, 171
Budweiser Beer, 2, 62, 121, 132-133,
    232

C

Canada Dry Club Soda, 13, 16, 46,
    70, 108
Canada Dry Ginger Ale, 59
Car-Freshener Pine Trees, 10
Carnation Condensed Milk, 2, 59, 97,
    145, 176
Carnation Nonfat Dry Milk, 1, 52,
    121, 248
Cascade, 11, 17, 21, 24, 40, 44, 45,
    46, 67, 91, 104, 107, 108,
    109, 112, 181, 183, 216, 251,
    254, 255
ChapStick, 89, 98, 150, 151, 162, 163
Cheerios, 199
Chloraseptic Spray, 128, 168
Chore Boy Scouting Pads, 172

Cinch, 106
Clairol Hair Coloring, 192
Clairol Herbal Essences Conditioner, 128
Clairol Herbal Essences Shampoo, 2, 104
Cling-Free, 183
Clorox Bleach, 25, 36, 37, 55, 82, 92, 114, 133, 136, 137, 138, 159, 172, 178, 180, 195, 212, 228, 239, 240
Close-Up Classic Red-Gel Toothpaste, 21, 128, 129
Coca-Cola, 2, 9, 18, 19, 21, 41, 48, 49, 50, 57, 61, 62, 65, 70, 75, 76, 81, 82, 85, 90, 93, 97, 98, 104, 123, 125, 157, 159, 165, 180, 183, 184, 190, 191, 193, 208, 217, 232, 240, 249, 252
Coffee-Mate, 31, 255
Colgate Toothpaste, 16, 24, 28, 31, 34, 38, 40, 43, 79, 89, 97, 99, 102, 105, 107, 116, 131, 140, 146, 155, 157, 208, 211, 214, 251, 252, 259, 261
Comet, 8, 78, 249
Conair Pro Style *1600*, 24, 48
Coppertone, 3
Cortaid, 140
Cover Girl Nailslicks, 189
Crayola Crayons, 132, 174, 187, 213
Crayola Chalk, 174, 222
Cream of Wheat, 223
Creamette Spaghetti, 51
Crest Toothpaste, 28, 36, 108, 120, 140, 146, 215
Crisco All-Vegetable Shortening, 30, 121, 123, 124, 129, 151, 153, 162, 173, 177, 233, 249

Cutex Nail Polish Remover, 73, 102, 122, 126, 217, 219, 220, 250, 259
Cutty Sark Scotch Whiskey, 165

D

Dannon Yogurt, 86, 124-125, 134, 136, 152, 170, 176, 199, 236, 238
Dawn dish liquid, 8, 46, 47, 71, 91, 135, 173, 193, 224, 226, 230, 245, 249, 254
Desitin, 146, 167
Dickinson's Witch Hazel, 171
Dixie Cups, 120, 173-174
Domino Sugar, 4, 5, 6, 125, 143, 145, 156, 181, 223-224, 226, 227, 248
Doritos, 235
Dow Bathroom Cleaner, 11, 16, 20, 31, 44, 77, 106, 192, 226, 261
Downy Fabric Softener, 3,6, 10, 15, 21, 81, 83, 109, 127, 175, 182, 184, 195, 196, 198, 201, 211, 240, 254, 255
Dr. Scholl's Moleskin, 116

E

Easy Cheese, 203, 239
Easy-Off Oven Cleaner, 11, 13, 24, 28, 29, 35, 41, 76, 77, 78, 84, 104, 109, 249
Efferdent, vii, 17, 18, 21, 32, 36, 39, 42, 43, 44, 108, 112, 118, 131, 202
Eggo Waffles, 57
Elmer's Glue-All, 68, 95, 113, 116, 130, 147, 166, 169, 172-173, 241
Endust, 80, 88

Epsom salt, 114, 133, 174, 246
Era, 66
Ex Lax, 229

F

Fantastik, 259
Febreze, 7, 198, 205, 253, 258
Folger's Instant Coffee, 119, 185
Formula *409*, 223, 224, 231, 232,
    233, 249
Forster Clothes Pins, 188, 237
French's Mustard, vii, 146
Fritos Cheese Dip, 197

G

Gain, 182
Glad Flexible Straws, 60-61, 64, 180,
    197
Glad Trash Bags, 11, 120-121, 173,
    188, 198
Glade Air Freshener, 34
Gojo Hand Cleaner, 29
Gold Medal Flour, 115, 145, 181,
    193, 197
Grandma's Molasses, 50
Gunk Brake Cleaner, 14, 249

H

Hartz 2 in 1 Flea Collars, 229
Heinz Ketchup, 5,12, 23, 38,49,119
Heinz Vinegar, 3, 4, 8, 11-12,14, 19, 22,
    23, 26, 40, 42, 46, 51,52, 54,
    55-56, 59, 86, 91-92, 93, 94,
    104, 106, 107, 109, 110, 113,
    114, 118, 129, 133, 138, 141,
    142, 144, 147, 149, 150, 151,
    154, 155, 160, 163-164, 165,
    166, 167-168, 182, 183, 192,
    195, 206, 211, 212, 213, 222,
    231, 244, 245, 246, 247, 249,
    251, 253, 254, 255, 256, 261

Hellmann's Mayonnaise, vii, 3, 5, 36,
    82, 136, 148, 154, 200, 213,
    217, 218, 247
Hershey's Chocolate Syrup, 232
Huggies Baby Wipes, 7, 12, 14, 20,
    23, 24, 27, 28, 33, 35, 36, 42,
    43, 45, 77, 85, 105, 112, 122,
    123, 179, 194, 196, 198, 204,
    205, 210, 214, 217, 235, 242,
    246, 247, 250-251, 252
Huggies Diapers, 67, 134
Huggies Pull-Ups, 135
Hydrogen peroxide, 108, 113, 131,
    132, 165, 170, 244

I

Irish Spring Soap, 227
Ivory Dish Liquid, 6
Ivory Soap, 158, 162, 244

J

Jell-O, vii, 22, 48, 91-92, 118, 119,
    154, 163, 179
Jet-Dry Sparkle, 110
Jet-Puffed Marshmallows, 58, 126
Jif Peanut Butter, 4, 7, 19, 29, 31, 33,
    57, 63, 74, 84, 105, 135, 156,
    168, 203, 216, 217, 218, 219,
    221, 232
Johnson's Baby Oil, 1, 4, 77, 81, 109,
    110, 122, 123-124, 129, 160,
    191, 203, 220, 221
Johnson's Baby Powder, 13, 77, 93,
    124, 207, 209, 226, 250
Johnson's Baby Shampoo, 124, 196,
    201, 246, 255
Joy, 114, 232

K

Karo Corn Syrup, 150, 173, 248
Kellogg's Corn Flakes, 117

Kellogg's Frosted Mini Wheats, 133
Kikkoman Soy Sauce, 146
Kingsford's Corn Starch, 8, 46, 115, 151
Kiwi Scuff and Stain Remover, 185
Kiwi Shoe Polish, 194, 213
Kleenex Tissues, 72
Knox Gelatin, 125, 134, 137, 172
Kodak Film canister, 189
Kool-Aid, 5, 12, 34, 62, 71, 112, 120, 177, 192, 241
Kraft Real Mayonnaise, 161
Krazy Glue, 81, 87, 118, 148, 159-160, 164, 174

L

L'Eggs Sheer Energy Panty Hose, 1, 22, 51, 64, 69, 76, 79, 95, 126, 137, 149, 164, 178, 227, 236, 252, 257, 259, 260
Lady Speed Stick, 116
Land O'Lakes Butter, 215, 220
Lemon Joy, 114, 232
Lestoil, 13, 250
Lifesavers, 163
Lipton Tea, 3, 40, 59, 130, 142, 144, 148, 153, 162, 164, 167, 183, 241
Liquid Paper, 78, 88, 90, 126, 258
Liquid Tide, 66 (*see also* Tide)
Listerine, 20, 86, 106, 110, 111, 112, 135, 143, 151, 158, 168, 169, 170, 184, 202, 205, 216, 225
Lubriderm, 260
Lysol, 30, 45, 205, 223, 226-227

M

Maalox, 170
Marshmallow Fluff, 122
Massengill Disposable Medicated Douche, 205

MasterCard, 25, 208
Maxwell House Coffee, 2, 6, 10, 22, 26, 41, 49, 53, 54, 56, 58, 63, 69, 75, 90, 111, 139, 181, 188, 230, 261
Maybelline Crystal Clear Nail Polish, 78, 88, 89, 93, 95, 98, 99-100, 115, 141, 150, 159, 204, 260
McCormick or Schilling Black Pepper, 79, 222
McCormick or Schilling Cayenne Powder, 233
McCormick or Schilling Chili Powder, 222
McCormick or Schilling Cinnamon, 222
McCormick or Schilling Cream of Tartar, 22, 38, 46, 85
McCormick or Schilling Food Coloring, 68, 69, 99, 101, 120, 177
McCormick or Schilling Meat Tenderizer, 143
McCormick or Schilling Vanilla Extract, 37, 39, 146-147, 191
Mennen Afta, 167
Mennen Speed Stick, 10
Mentadent Toothpaste, 32
Miller Lite Beer, 53
Minute Rice, 63, 223
Miracle Whip, 3, 37, 50, 68, 72, 128, 136, 159, 163, 185, 220
Moleskin, 116
Morton Salt, 4, 5, 15, 16, 19, 22, 27, 38, 40, 92, 110, 134, 137, 164, 167, 222, 228, 232, 233, 234, 235, 245
Mott's Applesauce, 34
Mountain Dew, 224

Mr. Coffee Filters, 20, 34, 47, 50, 52, 58, 60, 68, 69, 89, 99-100, 118, 123, 135, 175, 197, 242
Mr. Muscle, 184
Murine Tears, 66
Murphy's Oil Soap, 40, 83, 196, 239, 245, 248, 254
Mylanta, 150, 152

N

Nair, 92
Neosporin, 140, 153
Nestea, 167, 194
Nestlé Hot Chocolate Mix, 51
Neutrogena, 164
Niagara Spray Starch, 121
NoSalt, 176
Noxzema, 147, 148

O

O.B. Tampons, 260
Ocean Spray Cranberry Juice Cocktail, 5
Old English Furniture Polish, 214
Orajel, 115, 145, 147, 155, 158, 166
Oral-B Dental Floss, 172-173, 241
Orville Redenbacher's Gourmet Popping Corn, 188
Oxo Liquid Beef Concentrate, 214

P

Palmolive Dishwashing Liquid, 152, 200, 239
Pam No-Stick Cooking Spray, 6, 29, 32, 51, 54, 61, 64, 71, 73, 74, 75, 90, 91, 93, 96, 98, 100, 101, 135, 138, 152, 185, 201-202, 203, 212, 221, 225-226, 236, 237, 238
Pampers, 14, 143-144, 202, 206

Parson's Ammonia, 11, 32, 35, 158, 205, 224
Paul Mitchell Tea Tree Oil Shampoo, 160
Pepto-Bismol, 116
Phillip's Milk of Magnesia, 116-117, 140, 149, 152, 158, 177
Pine-Sol, 228, 247, 250
Play-Doh, 80, 237
Playtex Living Gloves, 58
Pledge, 20, 28, 47, 79, 98, 109, 110, 210, 212, 260
Pond's Cold Cream, 30
Preparation H, 140, 142, 143, 145, 147, 149, 150, 153, 158, 160, 164, 166, 167, 170, 220
Prestone Windshield Rain Relief, 111
Procter-Silex Ultra-Ease Iron, 57, 210
Purell Hand Sanitizer, 7, 20, 28, 32, 37, 82-83, 150, 179, 218, 251

Q

Q-Tips Cotton Swabs, 176, 192
Quaker Oats, 117, 149, 154, 164, 177, 181

R

Rain-X, 47, 111
ReaLemon, 4, 17, 19, 29, 36, 38, 53, 64, 110, 118, 156, 205
Red Devil Lye, 194
Reddi-wip, 3, 64, 117, 124, 129
Resolve Carpet Cleaner, 195, 248
Reynolds Wrap, 17, 23, 37-38, 51, 58, 60, 102, 175, 243
Rit Dye, 194
Rolaids, 158-159
Ronsonol Lighter Fuel, 219
Rug Doctor, 250

S

Saran Wrap, 161
Scope Cool Peppermint Mouthwash, 203
Scotch Tape, 257
Scotch Packaging Tape, 61, 132, 166, 180, 187, 219, 227, 252, 257
Scott's Liquid Gold, 219
Secret, 159
Selsun Blue Shampoo, 150
7-Up, 56, 59, 132
Shout, 14, 40, 81
Silly Putty, 33, 78, 208, 209
Simple Green, 32
Skin-So-Soft, 79, 81, 84, 104, 122, 185, 191, 199, 203, 211, 216, 218, 219, 221, 223, 230, 237
Slinky, 181, 187, 203, 204
Smirnoff Vodka, 9, 14, 17, 28, 30, 32, 47, 56, 86, 113, 127, 155, 156, 253
Smucker's Concord Grape Jelly, 147
Sno Bol, 105, 108, 237
S.O.S. Soap Pads, 24, 231
Soft Scrub, 247, 251
Softsoap Antibacterial Hand Gel, 23, 38, 42, 144
Spam, 179
Spic and Span, 246
Spray 'N Wash, 110, 138, 223
Sprite, 59, 132
Stanley Knife, 99
Star Olive Oil, 3, 5, 118, 125, 136, 145, 160, 199, 204, 260
Static Guard, 130
Stayfree Maxi Pads, 86, 123, 127, 185, 258, 261
STP Carburetor Cleaner, 14, 83
Stridex Medicated Pads, 20
SueBee Honey, 117, 140-141, 143, 147, 155

Sunlight dishwashing liquid, 9, 147
Super-Soaker 2000, 92
Sure-Jell, 144

T

Tabasco Pepper Sauce, 19, 23, 228, 229
Tang, 26, 63, 112, 120
Thompson's Deck Wash, 44
Tide, 14, 25, 35, 66, 75, 84, 119, 150
Tidy Cat, 75, 117, 230
Trojan Non-scented Condoms, 63, 204, 239
Turtle Wax, 89, 105, 107, 108, 111
20 Mule Team Borax, 100, 138, 223-224, 227, 228, 258

U

Uncle Ben's Converted Brand Rice, 165, 176
USA Today, 37, 47

V

Vaseline Petroleum Jelly, 31, 71, 76, 96, 97, 100, 119, 125, 126, 127, 128, 130, 144, 148, 151, 168, 170, 186, 191, 201, 211, 217, 224, 225, 233, 235, 238, 243, 259, 260
Vegemite, 72, 131
Velcro, 87, 178
Vicks Vaporub, 148, 154, 159, 169, 238
Visine, 141

W

Water Pik, 196
WD-40, 5, 11, 15, 24, 39, 48, 75, 80, 81, 85, 87, 94, 95, 141, 143, 186, 197, 208, 213, 214, 218, 220, 225, 227, 231, 237, 261

Wesson Corn Oil, 6, 16, 54, 87, 100, 186, 202, 211, 214, 218
Westley's Whitewall Tire Cleaner, 186
White Rain Hair Conditioner, 83
Wilson Tennis Balls, 41, 70, 72, 82, 88, 99, 101, 102, 103, 105, 175, 182, 207, 247
Windex, 15, 38, 143, 220, 224, 225, 245, 248
Wish-bone Italian Dressing, 60
Wish-bone Ranch Dressing, 64
Wonder Bread, 13, 15, 27, 35, 39, 50, 172-173

Woolite, 9
Wrigley's Juicy Fruit Gum, 229-230, 233-234
Wrigley's Spearmint Gum, 79, 86, 96, 178

Z

Zest, 103
Ziploc Storage Bags, 50, 54, 55, 56, 60, 62, 65, 67, 94, 156, 173, 187,188, 189, 193, 237, 243

About the Author

Joey Green—author of *Polish Your Furniture with Panty Hose, Paint Your House with Powdered Milk, Wash Your Hair with Whipped Cream,* and *Clean Your Clothes with Cheez Wiz*—got Jay Leno to shave with Jif peanut butter on *The Tonight Show,* Rosie O'Donnell to mousse her hair with Jell-O on *The Rosie O'Donnell Show,* and had Katie Couric drop her diamond engagement ring in a glass of Efferdent on *Today.* He has been seen polishing furniture with Spam on NBC's *Dateline,* cleaning a toilet with Coca-Cola in *The New York Times,* and washing his hair with Reddi-wip in *People.*

Green, a former contributing editor to *National Lampoon* and a former advertising copywriter at J. Walter Thompson, is the author of twenty books, including *The Zen of Oz: Ten Spiritual Lessons from Over the Rainbow, Selling Out: If Famous Authors Wrote Advertising,* and *The Road to Success is Paved with Failure.* A native of Miami, Florida, and a graduate of Cornell University, he wrote television commercials for Burger King and Walt Disney World, and won a Clio Award for a print ad he created for Eastman Kodak. He backpacked around the world for two years on his honeymoon, and lives in Los Angeles with his wife, Debbie, and their two daughters, Ashley and Julia.